More Memories

Also by the author

Memories

More Memories

RALPH EMERY

with TOM CARTER

G. P. PUTNAM'S SONS
New York

G. P. Putnam's Sons
Publishers Since 1838
200 Madison Avenue
New York, NY 10016

Copyright © 1993 by Ralph Emery with Tom Carter

Library of Congress Cataloging-in-Publication Data

Emery, Ralph.
  More memories / by Ralph Emery with Tom Carter.
    p. cm.
  Continues: Memories.
  Includes index.
  ISBN 0-399-13890-0 (acid-free paper)
    1. Emery, Ralph. 2. Entertainers—United States—Biography.
3. Country music—United States—Biography. I. Carter, Tom,
1947–. II. Emery, Ralph. Memories. III. Title.
PN2287.E523A3 1993
781.642'092—dc20   93-24009 CIP
[B]

Designed by Rhea Braunstein

Printed in the United States of America

1   2   3   4   5   6   7   8   9   10

This book is printed on acid-free paper.

*To my boys
Steve, Mike, and Kit*

Acknowledgments

Despite the fact that this book is made up of my memories, I found it necessary to call on many people to enhance those memories that were a bit vague. In some cases my memories led me down a path where I found new information. Sometimes I got very lucky.

First of all I want to thank E. W. "Bud" Wendell, CEO and President of Gaylord Communications, for his help with the Roy Acuff and Fan Fair stories.

I would like to thank the ladies in my office, Terry Schaefer, Angie Wallace and Julia Cole, who spent many hours transcribing the tape-recorded notes for this book.

I would also like to thank Joyce Jackson, who was Jim Reeves' secretary and gave me a keen insight into "Gentleman Jim." Also I would like to thank Mary Reeves for her participation as I attempted to reconstruct what happened to Jim in the summer of 1964.

A tip of my hat to Darrell McCall for relating much information about the life of a musician on the road.

Thanks to Red Stewart and Pee Wee King for telling me the story of the "Tennessee Waltz" backstage at the Missouri State Fair.

In developing the story about Garth Brooks, I relied on radio interviews with Garth as well as information received from Jimmy Bowen, the CEO of Liberty Records (Garth's label), and Lynn Shults of *Billboard* magazine who discovered Garth at the Bluebird Cafe. A special thank-you to Paul Corbin of The Nashville Network for telling me the story of the "infamous" Garth Brooks video tape relating to "The Thunder Rolls" that was never aired.

In developing the story about husbands of famous female singers I am indebted to Ken Dudney, George Richey, Mooney Lynn, and Charlie Dick for their cooperation.

My thanks to Bill Ivey, the Executive Director of The Country Music Foundation, for his tip about how Pierre Cossette saved the Grammy Awards Show. And thanks to Pierre for his cooperation.

While I am at it, I would also like to thank Alan Stoker and Chris Skinker at the Country Music Foundation Library for always responding to my many requests.

One story that I became obsessed with was the plane crash that killed Patsy Cline, Hawkshaw Hawkins, Cowboy Copas, and pilot Randy Hughes, who was Patsy's manager. I got the idea for this story from Brian Burnes of the *Kansas City Star,* who called me in February of 1993 to ask why I was not on the benefit show in Kansas City on March 3, 1963, as I was in the program with my name right under Patsy Cline's. I told him "I had the flu" and "couldn't make it." He was writing a piece on the thirtieth anniversary of the crash. Brian subsequently put me in touch with Mrs. Ann Wilson, the widow of the disc jockey for whom the benefit was given. I would like to thank her for relating to me her conversation with Patsy Cline backstage at Patsy's last performance. I would also like to thank Mildred Keith, a country music fan, for the pictures of Patsy Cline, Cowboy Copas and Hawkshaw Hawkins taken at Kansas City on March 3, 1963, and for other information she gave me relating to Patsy Cline backstage that day, and finally for helping me find the real reason that Roy Acuff did not go to Kansas City.

For this story I called on Billy Walker, who helped arrange the show at Kansas City, and Charlie Dick, who told me that he would have been on that fateful airplane ride had the show not been a freebie. He gave up his seat so that "Cope" and "Hawk" could cut their expenses.

My thanks also to Bill Colbert, Jr., of Colemill Flying Service, who helped me find Bill Whitmore, the now retired FAA investigator who covered the Patsy Cline plane crash. Thanks to Mr. and Mrs. Bill Whitmore for their hospitality. I sat on their screened-in back porch on a rainy Saturday and listened to Bill recount the details of this terrible crash. Bill also shocked me by showing me the actual clock from the aforementioned plane. The hands stopped at the time of impact. Bill then gave it to me to place into the Country Music Hall of Fame and Museum. He had the clock for thirty years and was most happy to place it where others could see it. It got to be eerie talking to Bill as he informed me that he and his wife had taken the Jim Reeves plane to East Tennessee the week before Jim Reeves crashed in it. He and Mrs. Whitmore brought the plane home on Sunday and Jim Reeves took it to Arkansas the following Thursday.

In developing the story of Roy Acuff I called on Anne Boatman of The Nashville Network, who was very patient. Also "Bashful Brother Oswald," Roy Neal Acuff and his wife, Susan, Debbie Logue, executive secretary to Hal Durham at the Grand Ole Opry, and Otto Kittsinger, one of our researchers at "Nashville Now," whose contributions were invaluable.

Another story that required a lot of input was the story of the Grammy show that made its only appearance in Nashville in 1973. For their assistance I wish to thank Bill Turner, my producer at "Nashville Now," Bill Ivey again, Joe Adair of WSMV-TV, who operated the center camera that night, Pierre Cossette, the show's producer, and John "Plugger" Lunn of our "Nashville Now" staff, who also worked that Grammy show.

In developing the story of the Oak Ridge Boys, I want to thank Steve Sanders, Joe Bonsall, Duane Allen, Richard Sterban, Bill Golden and the man who has managed the group twice, Don Light.

For information about the development of Fan Fair, I tip my hat to two old friends and former bosses, Irving Waugh and Elmer Alley.

A thanks to Bill Ormes for the story of "Big Foot" Jones, a man we both liked at WAGG in Franklin, Tennessee.

Thanks to Arthur Smith for coming by my office on a very busy day and telling me the story of "Duelin' Banjos."

For the Roger Miller story, my gratitude to Mary Miller for her input.

I would also like to thank Frank Sutherland of the *Nashville Tennessean,* our morning newspaper, for permission to use the picture of Roger Miller at the now famous plane crash site in Camden, Tennessee. Frank, I would also like to thank you for your support of my first book.

A thank-you to my manager Bill Carter for his help with the Reba McEntire story. He managed Reba for a number of years, including the year that she was Entertainer of the Year for the first time.

I would like to thank Ryan Hargrove of WTPR in Paris, Tennessee, for an overview of that station's history.

I also want to thank Jim Hagans for the many wonderful photographs he made available to me for use in this book.

Thanks to Conrad Jones, Tom Bryant, and Mike Bohan who have recorded and edited twenty-two years of syndicated radio shows from which many of these stories are taken.

A special thanks to my wife, Joy, who participated along with Tom Carter in making the final edits for the text of this book.

A book like this would be impossible without the support of people like David Hall and Tom Griscom at The Nashville Network.

I would like to thank Mel Berger, my book agent at William Morris, for developing the idea for the second book. Until he suggested it, I hadn't thought of the possibility.

My thanks to George Coleman, my editor at Putnam, for helping me to see that the glass was "half full."

And finally, a big thank-you to the "stars" of Country Music plus the countless musicians, writers, producers, and directors with whom I have had the pleasure of working for over forty years.

Foreword

Acouple of years ago I wrote a book that hit the *New York Times* best-seller list for twenty-five weeks. Booksellers and publishers were scratching their heads, saying "Ralph who?" and trying to figure out where this surprise hit had come from. For fourteen days in December of 1991 the book, *Memories,* could not be found on North American book shelves because it had sold out. It eventually became the second best-selling nonfiction work in the United States at that time; its sales were surpassed only by Katharine Hepburn's autobiography.

This book then became a *New York Times* paperback bestseller, and I was asked to do a sequel, the book you're now holding. Now, I'm citing all of the above not to brag, mind you. Those who bought the first book didn't need to ask, "Ralph who?" and for that I'll be eternally grateful. No, the point of all this is to exemplify the irony of my first book's creation.

I wrote it to get rid of a guy.

This guy, who soon became my collaborator and friend, first approached my car one night as I was leaving "Nashville Now," the talk show I host on The Nashville Network. He said he had written a book with Ronnie Milsap, who had been a guest on my program that same evening. This guy said he wanted to help me write my life story.

"Sure," I said and brushed past him to drive home. I had to get up at 4:40 A.M. the next morning for a local television show I was doing and didn't have time to put up with a freelance writer who needed a project. Besides, I had taken a stab at writing my autobiography once before and had met with a writer to whet his appetite a bit.

I think the writer was uninterested. He never showed up again.

But this other guy did show up again, shortly after the first encounter. Later, he told me he hid near my car because that's where I became his captive audience as I fumbled to get my car keys and hang my stage clothes inside.

The guy caught me in that predicament perhaps six times, each time spewing out a thirty-second pitch as to why I should write an autobiography and do it with him.

"Okay," I said, "but I don't think there would be much interest in my story. If you're so confident there is, why don't you see if you can get the interest of a publisher and then maybe we'll talk."

Again, I shut my car door and showed the guy my tail lights as I drove into the night.

Ten days later he was back saying Macmillan wanted to do my book.

"Let's talk," I said, surprised, and we made an appointment for the first time in a place away from my parking space.

It'll come as no surprise to you that entertainers are approached regularly by people with sometimes strange or lofty ideas for their careers. You can't imagine the get-rich-quick schemes and pie-in-the-sky proposals I've been pitched. I work about fifty hours a week, and often on weekends doing personal appearances, so I really didn't want to think about yet another proposition. But he did say a publisher was interested . . .

Slowly, I began to recall my early life and, as I did, I felt a special satisfaction that comes when one human being is totally honest with another. I told him things I'd never told anyone, and this is some guy I'd met after dark in a parking lot. As the tape recorder rolled, I struggled against fears of self-revelation. I was rewarded with a sense of self-cleansing.

People in show business are in the business of showmanship. We manufacture an image, a mood. To give a show means to act one way when you might feel another. I've been a creature of that craft for forty-two years.

Writing a book, however, is everything, that show business is not. Instead of putting on layers of paint, you strip them off. Instead of presenting an attitude, you reveal emotions.

Working with a collaborator can be at times like confessing to an analyst. And analysis can be traumatic. But it can be healing.

Caught up in the momentum, I joyfully pressed on.

I suppose most subjects of autobiographies become very intimate with their collaborators. I did. I had to adjust to the presence of someone who was always asking questions, which was really a turn of the tables for me, an interviewer. I made the adjustment more rapidly than I thought I would.

I had been urged for years by numerous Nashville entertainers to write a book. I had interviewed virtually everybody in the business, and they thought my memories were worth putting to paper. I wasn't very interested. I figured the people I had known knew themselves better than I did, and they could go write their own books. Besides, each time I go to the bookstore I'm amazed at how many books are being published and simultaneously annoyed that I can't read enough of them, since I love reading. I didn't think the world needed yet another book.

Being wrong was wonderful.

In December of 1992 I had gone to Colorado with my wife, Joy, for our annual ski trip. My executive assistant, Terry Schaefer, called to tell me that the book I had resisted so fiercely had eased its way up the *Times* list to number three. Earlier I'd told Joy that what I would like most of all for Christmas was a bestseller. I got my wish, and my celebration was underway.

The most touching part of this book experience dealt with my return visit to McEwen, Tennessee, where I spent my childhood. I walked the ground where I had played as a lad. I stood in the graveyard where my grandparents had been laid to rest. I heard as an adult the sounds I had heard as a child. This time I listened.

My broadcast apprenticeship began in McEwen, where I was born and grew up through childhood. In the small, agricultural community, I played pretend radio with my best friend, Woody Holland. We were both fifteen.

I moved, when I was seven, from McEwen to Nashville to join my mother, who was working there and had remarried. And I'd go back and visit McEwen mostly in the summers.

I was the "announcer" and Woody the "star" of our make-believe show. We used an ancient wire recorder, and played back our broadcasting fantasies for our ears only.

Such pretending might be laughed at by today's teenagers, but for Woody and me it was a link to a world outside tiny, dusty McEwen.

I was happy in McEwen and often count my blessings today at having spent so much time in such a wholesome and non-threatening environment.

The most complicated setting in our simple town was the train station, the community social center. In the evening, scores of people ambled to the station just to see each other and who was getting on and off the train, even though many new arrivals were strangers. I sat spellbound for hours watching travelers with the fascination that international airports hold for some folks today.

I'd sometimes listen to the hum of bumblebees hovering above the glistening steel ribbons of railroad track. Eventually the insects' sounds would be overpowered by the building noise of an approaching locomotive. Soon, the din was so loud I could scream at the top of my lungs and not be heard. Then the teeming engine would rumble past the wood-frame station, where the ground shook from charging tons of black, churning steel.

Every day, the McEwen station master stuck the town's mail pouch on a hook adjacent to the track. An engineer would extend a pole from the speeding locomotive toward the pouch and snag it flawlessly at sixty miles per hour.

I watched that coal-and-water-powered version of the pony express a thousand times promptly at noon and never once saw the speeding engineer miss his target.

Some of my fondest childhood recollections have to do with my dog Tony, whom I named after the heavyweight boxer Tony Galento, another casualty of the champion, Joe Louis. Tony and

I romped over the rolling grasslands for hour upon leisurely hour. He never wore a leash and always came home at sundown. His neatest trick, however, was to run under the trains passing through McEwen while they were in motion. He'd dart under one set of thick, steel wheels and bolt onto the other side of the tracks before the next set of wheels cut him in half. The slow-spinning iron never even shaved the tail of my daredevil dog.

Such recollections afford me a protective peace that is a dip into serenity. I seemed to belong in McEwen, my pastoral playground, where everybody showed me attention and acceptance at almost any time.

Some recollections, however, bring memories of utter embarrassment. I still remember my first foray into show business. I laid an egg. Jim Ralston, my across-the-street neighbor and high-school buddy, and I were part of a giant halftime festivity during a Thanksgiving Day football game between Nashville high schools. We were to ride a tandem bicycle across the playing field while the East High marching band played "Bicycle Built for Two." Obviously, we were the center of attention from fans on both sidelines.

Jim and I worked for weeks building our two-wheel float. It let us down seconds after our pedaling debut, collapsing before hundreds of guffawing fans.

My efforts had ended in disaster, and I raced to get the tangled metal and spokes off the field. The irony of this situation is perhaps the impact that it made on both our lives. I became a television host, comfortable performing before millions. Jim became an engineer for NASA as part of the team that designed the space shuttle.

These childhood memories and those childhood friends will always occupy a special place in my heart. After I wrote my first book, *Memories,* I learned again who my dear friends are, and that was still another blessed by-product of writing my life story. Johnny Cash, Barbara Mandrell, Randy Travis, and Jimmy Dean all did commercials for my book—for free.

That first book taught me a lot about the dedication of some of my fans, many of whom I met initially at my few book signings. One man flew to Nashville from Jackson Hole, Wyoming, because he had heard me mention on "Nashville Now" that I was doing a book signing there. He stood in line, got my autograph, and turned right around and flew back to Jackson Hole. I felt warm when people who had nothing in common but their interest in my book met in line. Many waited so long that they became friends by the time they reached the autograph table. They exchanged names and telephone numbers, along with promises to stay in touch. Such seemingly insignificant incidents made me realize how wonderful even the smallest incidents in life could be.

One woman told me she had stood in line for two hours to get my autograph. "And I only stood in line an hour to get Elvis'," she said.

Talk about a compliment! I had to laugh in appreciation.

My greatest regret about my earlier memoir involves my ex-wife, the singer Skeeter Davis. She was unhappy with the picture I painted of our relationship. Frankly, I didn't even want to mention her in the book, but was persuaded to do so by Tom Carter, who said my autobiography would lack credibility if I failed to discuss a four-year marriage. So I discussed it truthfully.

The chapter about Skeeter was not pleasant for me to recall, write, or obviously, for her to read, but still I feel it had to be done if I were going to be honest.

I asked Barbara Mandrell to read the manuscript of my first book, *Memories*, early on before anyone else, for I knew she would be totally honest in her evaluation. She was and pointed out two mistakes I had made. I then asked her what she got from the chapter about Skeeter Davis. Barbara said, "I got that you loved her very much." I said, "That's right," and later when the book came out I think Skeeter missed this point as I have heard nothing but angry feedback from her.

Writing a book, simply put, is the hardest job I ever *loved*. One doesn't always know how far to go in telling stories about friends. Some might feel that the friendships are ours but their stories are their own. How much does an author tell about those he knows and loves? Where does my obligation for honesty stop and their right to privacy begin? There is a line, and perhaps there are times I crossed it, and perhaps I'll cross it again in this one. My motivation, however, is always honesty, and never malice. I love my friends too much to do that.

In that vein, not one of the scores of celebrities, with the exception of Skeeter, registered displeasure with the treatment of their lives.

The only other person who even remotely indicated unhappiness was my mother, whose displeasures surfaced at a Christmas dinner. From out of nowhere she said she didn't like what I wrote in a certain chapter.

I had completed that chapter more than a year earlier and couldn't recall what she had in mind.

"I didn't like what you said about me," my mom said.

She didn't belabor it, and it was never mentioned again.

Speaking of my family, for those of you who read the first book, here's an update: Kit was recently honorably discharged from the United States Air Force and is now enrolled at Belmont University in Nashville. Mike Emery graduates this year from Middle Tennessee State University with a degree in environmental science. Steve Emery continues his successful dental practice as an endodontist and has recently moved into a new office designed by my wife, Joy, who utilized her recently acquired bachelor's degree in interior design from O'More College in Franklin, Tennessee.

That is the long and short of the status of my immediate family. I have other, non-related, members whom I've never met and never will. They feel like family because they know so much about me now—probably more than they ever wanted to know!

After all, who, other than family, would take such an interest? A man with such an expansive circle of figurative family is blessed indeed. I humbly felt that because I cared, and learned how much I was cared about, that I should write a second book.

And so I did. I sincerely hope you enjoy it.

ONE

On my first day in professional radio I met a man who looked as if it was his last day of life.

I walked into a tiny cafe in Paris, Tennessee, a city of about 5,000 persons in 1951, and scanned the room for the general manager of WTPR, a 250-watt dusk-til-dawn station. I stayed at the Ben Franklin Hotel the night before, where I paid $2 for lodging and a wake-up knock. Several guests in several rooms had to share one bath, but I didn't care.

Recently graduated from John Richbourg's Nashville radio school, I had landed a real job behind a real microphone. I couldn't have been more excited if I were going to work for WNBC.

In Paris, Richbourg told me to ask for his old friend, Virgil Lindner, WTPR's general manager, who would become my mentor.

"Imagine being hand-led through my first day by the guy who runs the place," I thought to myself. "I knew that radio was the right thing for me to do!"

I had gone to the station earlier, asked for Lindner, and was told that he was at the corner eatery. But when I entered the diner, my eyes fell on a shrinking man with coffee stains all over his shirt. He sat slumped, chain-smoking and staring vacantly over a half-filled cup of coffee. I was sure I was in the right place, so I decided to ask the disheveled customer if he knew Mr. Lindner. I hoped Lindner wouldn't come in and watch me talking to the stranger. I wanted my first impression to be positive.

I timidly approached the withdrawn and soiled man and started to speak, but he cut me short.

"You must be Ralph Emery," he said. "I'm Virgil Lindner."

I was going to start work for a gross weekly salary of $45. I surmised that the general manager worked for much more. Why, I wondered, would the highest-paid executive at a radio station look like such a bum?

In all the weeks at broadcasting school, no one had suggested that I was entering a notoriously low-paying craft. I had been so obsessed with learning my skills that I had never thought about long-term financial compensation.

Lindner was a man who had risen to the top of his professional world. His appearance indicated he was locked at the bottom of the economic ladder. It was my first confrontation with financial distress that would grip my life for years to come, hanging on long after I was named "disc jockey of the year" several times for my All-Night Show from 1957 until 1972 on WSM.

It's astonishing to me now that I would have actually begun my career without ever checking into its compensatory potential. In my youthful zealousness and unhappiness, however, all I had thought about was calling attention to myself by becoming a broadcaster.

The sight of Lindner that first morning left me speechless, a condition that should never happen to a broadcaster. I was making just the kind of first impression I didn't want to make.

When our discussion moved to my own salary I discovered I would take home $39.50 weekly. I took a sleeping room for $5 a week, and commuted to Nashville on weekends. My social life consisted of evenings in the lobby of the Greystone Hotel, the nicest of Paris' two hotels, where I watched the electronic snow on a new contraption called television. Then it was early to bed so that I might sign on the station at sunrise.

Living alone and talking to myself over a microphone was not exactly the therapy needed for someone suffering from feelings of isolation and loneliness. But it was my auspicious career beginning.

And it was a giant step forward from the streets of Nashville and the impersonal treatment at East High School. My circumstances were dire but better than they had ever been. At eighteen, I knew I wasn't holding the world by the tail, but at least I was learning how to grab it.

I went back to WTPR on my twenty-fifth anniversary in broadcasting. By then, my All-Night Show had completed its run, I was successfully embroiled in syndicated television, and I was only seven years away from the premiere of "Nashville Now," my current television talk show that is the highest-rated program on The Nashville Network, the nation's sixth largest cable television channel with 56 million subscribing households. A lot of folks were surprised at my return to the WTPR microphone for the quarter-century celebration.

I was delighted.

It's been said one doesn't know he's poor until he meets someone who's rich. I similarly didn't know how bleak my living conditions were, and how demanding my job was, in 1951. More important, I also didn't realize then how valuable the training was on that AM farm-to-market outlet. I couldn't buy the valuable lessons I received from a 250-watt radio station.

In Richbourg's school, for example, I had honed my skills primarily as an announcer. I had not been taught about radio promotions, and how invaluable they are to a station's financial lifeline. Neither had I been taught that nothing is more valuable to promotions than the radio personalities with whom listeners are familiar.

At WTPR I learned quickly.

Armed only with a microphone and a staff car with no brakes, my shyness was thrust into metropolitan Paris, Tennessee, where I was told to knock unannounced on its good citizens' doors. I'd ask them if I might look inside their refrigerators. If I found an RC Cola (a station sponsor), I would give them a case of the soft drinks. If I didn't find an RC, I would air their disappointment to other Paris listeners via my remote broadcast.

Gaining entry to people's homes in rural America was a lot easier forty-two years ago than it would be today. Imagine going to someone's door today and asking to peer into the intimacy of his dietary habits judged by the contents of his refrigerator.

In Paris, I'd sometimes go all day and not find one bottle of RC Cola. So I learned firsthand that valuable axiom of live broadcasting. I learned to fake it.

When I couldn't find the soda pop that was indirectly paying my salary, I'd conspire with cooperative listeners.

"Look," I'd say, "I'll give you an entire case of pop if you'll go on the radio and say I found some bottles in your icebox, and that you drink the stuff all the time because you think it's wonderful."

Even in the more innocent America of 1951, I had no trouble getting co-conspirators. I had people endorsing RC Cola who had never had a swallow of the stuff!

From that promotional gimmick I also learned a lot about life. I discovered that many lives were worse than mine.

I often went into homes where crying children were hanging on to a beleaguered woman, her unemployed husband slouching in a thread-bare sofa. I'd open their refrigerator and find it empty. I felt uncomfortable offering a case of soft drinks to someone who didn't have bread or milk.

But those people had their pride. Not once was I denied admission to a house, and not once was I told that I couldn't peer inside their refrigerators, even though they knew I'd find nothing inside. I was a guest in their homes, albeit uninvited. They couldn't have given me a morsel, but they gave me hospitality. Such was the lifetime conditioning of the God-fearing and grass-roots folks of Paris, Tennessee.

I have known broadcasters who were prima donnas. They thought their velvet tonsils were the ticket to an independence that would save them from doing anything other than talking. They wouldn't have lasted at WTPR in 1951.

I had never studied the technical end of radio, such as being an engineer, in broadcasting school. Yet I quickly learned that I would have to learn engineering and learn it thoroughly enough to run the station by myself. Mastering the task should have been worth three hours of graduate credit toward a degree in physical education.

I ran my legs off.

On Sunday mornings, I programmed country music until I received my first fan letter. The author said that programming country music on Sunday morning was like eating green beans for breakfast. Her point was well taken, so I asked management to let me introduce a Southern Gospel format. My request was granted.

Along with the religious music went live broadcasts from two Paris churches. I was the engineer for each remote program in sanctuaries located several blocks from the radio station.

I would play an Air Force or Navy recruiting disc, a fifteen-minute previously recorded program containing music and recruiting appeals. As that show aired, I drove the station jalopy as if it were a drag racer to a Sunday School and set up the equipment and sped back to the station in time for the end of the military show. I'd then call the Sunday School, tell whoever answered that the microphone was set up in the vestibule, and ask him to say "test, test" into it. When the military show signed off, I'd introduce the pastor of the Sunday School, who would read a Bible lesson aloud for thirty minutes.

During that half hour, I'd leap back into the car and race to a second church. I'd set up a microphone and repeat the engineering required for the remote broadcast. I'd speed back to the station, sign off the Sunday School teacher, then go live to the second church for a live worship service.

I don't know what would have happened if that old car had ever broken down as I raced around Paris on Sunday mornings. Yes I do. The military disc would have played to its end, then its needle would have gone "clunk, clunk, clunk" over the air as it revolved on the turntable.

But I made every appointment always just in time.

I learned a lot at that station about the mechanics of radio, including how to take telephone lines, designated for broadcasting, off a utility pole and hook up an amplifier for a play-by-play, remote sports broadcast.

The most popular National League baseball team in the South in 1951 was the St. Louis Cardinals. Farmers came in from their fields during afternoon games to listen to Harry Carey, "The Voice of the Cardinals," as he announced the play with Stan Musial, Enos Slaughter, and others from the team that had earlier produced Paul and Dizzy Dean and the famous "Gashouse Gang" infield.

You could hear Cardinals baseball over WTPR. I once thought the programs were electronically stolen from the Cardinals' network, but have since learned they were not. WTPR aired them legally by tuning in to a radio station in Kentucky that carried Cardinals baseball. WTPR bought the games and broadcast the Kentucky signal through our board and over the air. Had WTPR not paid, it would have been bootleg baseball.

Carey would recite the scores at the end of each inning. That was our cue to flip a switch to cut off the feed from Kentucky. While the announcer in Kentucky was reading his commercial, we'd read a commercial from a local sponsor. I had to be aware of how long the commercial in Kentucky ran, so I kept that audio in my headset, which meant that I was reading one commercial into the Paris microphone while listening to another a hundred miles away.

If the distant commercial finished before mine, I would have to accelerate my speech to get back to baseball before the end of the station break. If I finished first, and the faraway commercial was still playing in my ear, I'd fall into an ad-lib about the St. Louis Cardinals.

It was seat-of-your-pants radio.

Harry Carey today is the voice of the Chicago Cubs. He's a star on cable television and owns a successful Chicago restaurant. Whenever I hear his voice, I unavoidably think about talking over him from a tiny sound booth in Paris, Tennessee.

TWO

Daylight had not yet broken when I entered Franklin's WAGG and walked the dark halls to the studio where I signed the station on the air. I was a wake-up voice for the city.

This Sunday morning, however, I had company.

The head of an unconscious man rested listlessly in the open window of an idling taxi. I walked up to the cab apprehensively and asked the driver if I could be of service.

"He ran me around Nashville all night," the cab driver complained. "He demanded to come to this address and asked me to let my meter run until the place opened. Then he passed out."

The driver and I helped the passenger, whom I now recognized, out of his fare and to his feet. He mumbled under his breath. I cursed out loud.

I wrestled him into the building and through the maze of corridors, flipping light switches with one hand and struggling to hold him with the other. We stumbled into the control room, where I propped him up in a chair.

I walked around a table and eased behind the microphone.

"Good morning, everybody, this is Ralph Emery," I said, and hit the button that would spin the turntable and send music into the sleepy, predawn quiet of Franklin, Tennessee.

Nothing happened.

I hit the button again frantically and braced against the terrifying panic common to live broadcasting when things don't work.

"Why won't this music play?" I screamed silently.

Then I noticed the head that had fallen on my turntable. Its weight prevented the record player from spinning.

I leaned over the table, bent at the waist, which allowed me only the strength of my arms, and furiously struggled to get the hulk off my machinery. I had to wrestle him delicately, however, because I didn't want him to make a commotion if he woke up. With his weight moved, the turntable lurched into motion with the slurred whine of a car ignition grinding in cold weather. The noise went over the air.

So I went through the rest of the show without trying to move him again. I pulled part of my shift that day with only one turntable, which meant that I could never segue from song to song, and was forced to provide banter, no matter how unnecessary, between selections.

The troublesome drunk was Ellis Franklin Jones, Jr., better known as "Big Foot" Jones, a flesh-and-blood fixture of WAGG. He was a case in point of my learning how to tolerate not my underlings—but my superiors.

The drunk was vice president and chief engineer of the station. On the one hand, he could have fired me. On the other hand, I didn't want his slurring and cursing leaking into my microphone.

So I called Bill Ormes, the station owner, to come get Big Foot.

Big Foot's favorite trick was to get loaded, then go visit his old cronies at WLAC in Nashville. He often used their telephone to place national and international calls.

His voice was no stranger to the White House switchboard, and he once called Franco of Spain and actually got through! WLAC's management regularly gave him a monthly accounting of his long-distance activity, and he'd reimburse the station without question. I'd bet the telephone calls took a significant bite out of his salary, but Big Foot didn't seem to care because he had other income from a chicken hatchery.

His favorite expression was "rat's ass." He once sent a telegram to me written in military phonetic code. All it said was "Rodent's Rectum." I knew instantly who had sent the message.

◼

When I was a broadcasting student, I expected unconventional behavior to come from broadcasting's performers, not from its front offices. Yet, throughout my career, I've been impressed with the eccentricities of some of the men and women who headed broadcast facilities with multimillion-dollar annual cash flows. And I've never ceased to be amazed at some of their obviously bad decisions.

I was disillusioned when WSM decided to automate my show, alleviating the human appeal of the most popular talk/music format on its airwaves. Why would the front office want to fix something that was working so well? I wondered. How did it intend for the show's host to do live interviews with fans and celebrities when his talk had been previously recorded?

I didn't pose those obvious questions, but instead cooperated with management's game plan. I recorded my introductions of records and the out-play announcements. All of that was synchronized with the songs and put on the air. An inaudible tone on the tape after my introduction would start the record.

Live broadcasting had been the programming backbone of WSM for decades. Its automated alternative lasted one night.

It seems the songs were programmed into the show out of order, so that listeners heard my recorded introduction of Eddy Arnold followed by a song by Cowboy Copas. That confusion was beamed for about seven hours over thirty-eight states.

The formatted folly prompted a lot of mail and probably a lot of phone calls. No one knew. There was no human being in the studio to receive them.

I remember when the president of WSM wanted to program classical music for three hours preceding my All-Night Show, which, of course, was formatted with hard-core country music. The transition from the high-brow program into my show was awkward. The former show might end with a concerto. Mine would kick off with a bluegrass breakdown. But the president was an intelligent and sophisticated man who leaned toward culture. I frequently thought he endured the most popular type of programming at WSM merely for its mass acceptance.

Years after his retirement, I ran into him in Nashville a few hours after having done my morning television show on which I had introduced a novelty segment.

"Hey, Ralph," he yelled across a parking lot. "I watched your show this morning and I loved the 'Outhouse Races.' "

"That's pretty funny," I thought to myself. "If you had been running things, there is no way you would have let me put something like that on the air. You would have thought it was too lowbrow."

The biggest mistake I ever saw from management in my career was a decision to cut "Nashville Now" from ninety to sixty minutes on April 1, 1992. At the time, the show was the most popular on The Nashville Network. I likened it to General Motors deciding to discontinue production of Chevrolets, its most popular-selling automobile.

I was privy to the approximate 5,000 letters my show was generating weekly. I was privy to the favorable feedback I was getting regularly from my studio audiences whose members traveled from fifty states and Canada to watch the program. I was privy to the appreciation from celebrities who felt the show bolstered their careers.

I was not privy to the decision to cut its length. I heard about that from Bill Turner, who overheard it at a meeting. Upon huddling with Bill Carter, my attorney and manager, and David Hall, TNN general manager, I found out it was true.

I was never given a sound explanation, and I suppose the case could be made that none was due me. After all, my salary wasn't cut.

But Nashville was alive with rumors that I was about to be taken off the air. I knew my job was secure. I had a contract. I nonetheless had to rethink a format I knew like the back of my hand. I had to pace the show differently. But I never registered a word of complaint to management about its sweeping programming alteration.

Turner decided to cut the music of "Nashville Now" from eight to six songs. We temporarily deleted the audience participation part. That made for a loss of its "homey" feel, so that segment was revived.

There were many glitches that had to be overcome when a program with a staff of about forty was cut in length by thirty-three percent. About the time we got the new length running smoothly, management changed its mind again.

"Nashville Now" went back to its ninety-minute format on June 30, 1992. Due to voluminous protests from outraged fans, the format that had worked for nine years was reinstated after a three-month interruption.

My early days in radio exposed me to life's front lines in a way I would not have had otherwise. I met people in the trenches that were a far cry from the pampered and detached celebrities who would inhabit my world in years to come.

I can still see the face of a black mortician I came to know while working at WNAH, my second employer. The Nashville station paid me five dollars more a week than I had earned in Paris, from where I departed after only four months.

My new station relied heavily on religious programming for its cash flow and sold time to preachers who then solicited donations from listeners. That little station is still on the air and still peddling time blocks to preachers.

The old mortician worked at a funeral home owned by a preacher who gave Saturday afternoon sermons. I had to visit the parlor each week to turn on his amplifiers so he could preach and plead for funds to be sent to the funeral home.

There was nothing notable about the mortician, except that he always smelled of flowers and was a layman philosopher. His spirits were always high and his thoughts always pensive, despite being in a business that was always dying.

He told me that most folks died in the spring or the fall because that's when the tree sap would rise and fall. I doubted the scientific soundness of his theory but was always taken with the fervor with which he expounded whatever he believed.

I learned to format gospel music. That meant familiarizing myself with the quartets that monopolized the commercial, sacred singing of 1950s Southern radio. These songs were "feel good" music. It was impossible to hear them and not be uplifted, if not for their message, then for the sheer entertainment value of the singers.

The all-white quartets used exaggerated stage movements that were as camp as anything that ever came out of vaudeville. I used to sit for hours in Nashville's Ryman Auditorium, home of the Grand Ole Opry until 1974, and watch the Wally Fowler All-Night Sings comprised of minstrels who wailed about the glory of the heavenly life to come. They would clap to their own rhythm, or drop to their knees. They bellowed with hands raised, eyes closed, and spirits set free. Each group was remarkably similar in that its only instrumentation was a pianist whose fingers ran the keyboard with precise but predictable techniques that were interchangeable from quartet to quartet.

White, Southern gospel piano definitely has its own sound.

The thing I loved most about the electrifying quartets was that their members looked like they sounded. The bass singer's voice was always thick and full, and so, usually, was his torso. The tenor's voice was high and thin, and he was usually skinny. The lead and baritone singers, whose parts weren't always as distinctive, usually looked non-descript.

The piano players were almost always heavy set, sported pencil mustaches, and played with their entire arms. They assaulted the keys with flailing movements pronounced enough to be seen from the top balcony.

These groups put a lot of corny comedy into their programs. Contemporary television's "Hee-Haw" is sophisticated by comparison. The primitive humor appealed to the hard-working men and women of the agricultural South who left their fields only to go to church, or the "All-Night Gospel Sings" held weekly in Nashville, Atlanta, Memphis, or a dozen other towns on the circuit.

In almost every quartet, the comedian was usually the bass singer. He'd make faces behind another singer, and the audience would roar its approval. He'd pretend to be fainting from depleted breath as he sang lower and lower. He'd loosen his necktie flamboyantly as if that would help him go lower, and the crowd would yell even louder.

The tenor in these groups would stand on his tiptoes to exemplify his efforts to reach outrageously high notes, and the people screamed. He would gesture to the crowd to cheer him on to still higher notes, whereupon the bass singer would sneak up behind him, lift him by his waist, and the tenor would screech into a piercing octave. By then, the crowd's screaming and applauding was thunderous.

The fans knew exactly what they were going to see, and that's how they wanted it. Between songs, the patter lasted long enough to let the singers catch their breath, and was usually filled with cracks about a quartet member's ugliness, the fatness of his wife, or how loudly he snored on the bus while traveling from show to show.

The fans thought that stuff was really funny.

The singers all wore the uniform—the swept-back hairstyle—that was as much a part of Southern gospel quartets as four-four time. Their coiffures were combed and sprayed and chiseled into place with a rigidity that could have withstood thirty-mile-per-hour winds, which sometimes happened in outdoor programs.

The Southern gospel quartets had style, even if each's was the style of the others.

I sat spellbound for hours before the hypnotic recitals of the Statesmen, the Blackwood Brothers, the Florida Boys, Happy Edwards and the Harmoneers, the LeFevors with Little Troy Lumpkin, and many others.

The Ryman Auditorium, founded in 1892 as a gospel tabernacle, had no air conditioning and was about as hot as the hell about which the singers sometimes preached. The only ventilation came from hand-held fans donated by a funeral home. The fanning stirred the aromas of perspiration, inexpensive aftershave, perfume, and popcorn.

The All-Night Sing usually ended about 3 A.M., when the quartet members would return to the stage's edge to sell record albums and eight-by-ten glossy photographs of themselves. Men and women, children asleep on their shoulders, stood in line for as long as it took to buy souvenirs of their evening of the best heavenly music they would ever hear on earth.

It was predictable to the point of ceremony. The fans knew the first names of the singers, their wives, and their children. They supported those groups, many of whom rose to national prominence on obscure or self-owned record labels, with a devotion that surpassed anything in secular music. The quartets were not just the fans' entertainers, but their ministers as well.

I would have never known the electrifying world of Southern gospel quartets if I hadn't played their music on radio.

I would return to the Ryman Auditorium a few years later to become a staff announcer on the world-famous Grand Ole Opry and again be thrust into a social melting pot that I would not have encountered were it not for my wonderful world of radio.

At WNAH I confronted for the first time Nashvillians who despised what eventually would become one of the city's principal industries—country music.

These people thought the music was lullabies for the stupid. Some radio station owners shared the opinion in the early 1950s of several members of the Belle Meade Country Club, Nashville's most prestigious, that the fledgling country music industry was an embarrassment to the city.

Minnie Pearl, who can mix with the socially elite as easily as she mixes with the working class, told me how members of Nashville's old money used to make fun of the city's singers with their names painted on their cars.

Country stars put their names on their Cadillacs in which they and their bands drove from show to show. Eventually, they traveled in customized tour buses, and painted their names on those too.

Minnie told me about an editorial in a Nashville newspaper in the late 1930s, lamenting that country music was bad for the city and as an industry should be run out of town.

The industry upon which 1940s and 1950s Nashville founders

frowned grossed three billion dollars last year. I wonder how beneficial that was to the city's tax base.

In 1952 I met my very first celebrity of the hundreds who would cross my path in the coming years. It wasn't a gospel star, because none of those singers ever came by the radio stations to court the disc jockeys the way country stars did and still do.

I had just finished my afternoon, pop-music shift in the WNAH studios, inside Nashville's landmark James Robertson Hotel. I was walking through the hotel parking garage and spotted Red Foley.

I was star struck and then some. I couldn't take my eyes from the crooner, whose face that morning was about as red as his hair. Little did I know that someday Foley and I would appear together in shows, and that he would seek me out as a radio interviewer to promote his career.

Many mornings I walked into a restaurant at 5:30 A.M. on Church Street to peer at another man. His name was "Smiling" Eddie Hill and he was the overnight disc jockey on WSM, the city's legendary, 50,000-watt, clear-channel radio station. I stared in awe at the man whose voice was carried from sea to sea. He had a very intense admirer in me. He arrived each morning in a white Cadillac and sipped coffee after signing off his show.

I didn't own a car. I was as far away from automobile ownership as I was from becoming President.

I would have been embarrassed for Hill if he had known that I was in the restaurant and in radio. My own popularity was so minimal compared to his. He was the dean of country radio. I was an all but overlooked gospel disc jockey.

A magazine had reported that Hill was paid $50,000 annually. That was a fat salary in 1952. He never knew how much I idolized him, his car, and career. He never knew there was someone present who was mesmerized by his merely drinking coffee and chewing doughnuts. He didn't know, and neither did I, that in five years I would have his job.

THREE

Learning is the most wonderful thing about advancing your career. Make a mistake and attribute it to inexperience. If you're young, you enjoy an alternate excuse called youth.

I needed all the excuses I could muster for some egregious errors in my career's infancy.

That became apparent when I was twenty and soaring with confidence after having become the first Nashville disc jockey to interview Webb Pierce, the hottest country singer of the day. He was sent to me by Fred Rose, co-founder of Acuff Rose, then the largest music publishing house in Nashville, who also would send to my microphone in 1953 a balladeer from Arizona.

The guy had been a television show host whose guest was Little Jimmy Dickens. Dickens was incredibly impressed with the singer and returned to Nashville to brag about him to Rose.

Sheerly on the strength of Dickens' recommendation, Rose flew from Nashville to Phoenix to sign Marty Robbins to a publishing deal. It's incredible to me now that a major publishing house president would travel 4,000 round-trip miles to launch an international career for a songwriter-vocalist he had never seen or heard. But Dickens had been a mammoth star of the 1940s, and was still pretty stout in the 1950s. Rose had an incredible trust of Dickens' ear for talent.

I had Marty as a studio guest shortly after his first record was released. It was one of innumerable visits during a friendship that would last thirty years until his death in 1982.

Reporters have asked me a lot about the first time the legendary Marty graced my microphone. I wish I had a tape recording of the event. My recollections are sketchy and superficial and include little more than the fact that his hair was incredibly curly, and he was not outgoing. He was so shy, in fact, that he refused to look at the audience while performing at the Grand Ole Opry shortly after his Nashville arrival. Eventually, he would become ebullient to the point of flamboyance.

I had not reached the age of legal majority but nonetheless had the day's major country stars walking to and from my microphone regularly. It didn't take long for my hat size to expand. So I made my first significant broadcasting mistake and repeated it.

I now realize the outrageousness of my self-confidence. I knew very little about the country music I was programming that would eventually make mine a household name. My youthful priorities allowed more concern for how my voice sounded than for what it said. I was honing my style and paying little attention to my substance.

Those were the days when my Franklin, Tennessee, station had no *Billboard* magazine popularity survey, which would soon become the long and short of radio play lists.

My only contact with listeners, and their only feedback to me, was through the mail. In the summer of 1953 I began to receive a mountain of mail requesting "Dear John."

"Dear John" had been an enormous hit for Hank Williams, who had been dead only five months. Requests for his already popular songs mounted in the wake of his demise, so I wasn't surprised at the interest in "Dear John."

Williams' record company, MGM, had released a song before his death entitled "I'll Never Get Out of This World Alive." It bolted to number one ten days after his death and that year outsold all his other records.

I, however, was single-handedly keeping "Dear John," one of

Williams' earlier hits, alive because that's what I thought my listeners kept seeking in mailed requests.

If I had done that in 1993, someone would have called me the first hour to say I was playing the wrong song. But in a more polite United States involved in a police action 10,000 miles away in Korea, none of my Franklin listeners took the time or interest to do it.

The song that my listeners by hundreds wanted to hear was "Dear John," the newly released duet by Ferlin Husky and Jean Shepard, about a woman who dumps her boyfriend while he is serving in the armed services. Wartime listeners identified with the situation. The phrase "Dear John letter," perhaps coined earlier, was popularized by that song. After a while, I eventually realized my mistake.

I made another error that summer. I was victimized by my trust in those who took the time to write to me. I'd read their names over the air if that's what they wanted. I spent much of the summer reading a daily request from a particularly loyal woman listener. She always asked for the same love song and dedicated it to her man. Many listeners began to associate the couple with the tune. I never met the man, or the adoring woman who requested songs for him.

One day I got a letter that was more like a petition. It was signed by numerous women from Kingston Springs, Tennessee. They wanted to know why I continued to take requests for that nice young man from that old "thang."

The man was married to another woman. In the South of the early 1950s, adultery was still very taboo and scandalous. Sex even between married people was not acknowledged. This was the period when the comparatively new television medium was showing situation comedies about married couples who were always seen sleeping in separate beds. I was unknowingly broadcasting romantic updates about a couple involved in illicit love. I couldn't have hit on a more sensitive subject. Listeners in Kingston Springs, where virtually everyone knew everyone, were deeply offended.

The fine ladies of Kingston Springs knew he was being pursued by a home wrecker. I don't know if he ever left his wife for the "thang," but if he did, I'm guilty of unintentionally aiding and abetting their romance.

I never ceased to be astonished at how personal the mail was. Listeners would tell me about their marriages, errant children, financial woes, and almost anything they felt like saying. Many asked for money, although that was more prevalent later when I went on television.

There were three incidents that race to mind.

One involved an illiterate woman who lived in a shack with three children, no running water, no electricity, and a wood stove for heat. At Christmastime, my wife, Joy, my eldest son, Steve, and I were overcome with emotion in the face of the destitution. I played Santa Claus and we surprised the family on Christmas Eve with toys and other gifts. It was very rewarding.

Our fulfillment increased when Joy began to question the woman about her welfare payments.

"What do you mean, welfare?" she replied.

The woman had no concept of the social benefits to which she was legally entitled. Joy took her to Nashville's federal welfare office and got the woman on the recipients' list. Federal aid was set up for the children, and the Emerys were blessed with the opportunity to help this woman and her youngsters get a semblance of a life.

Another woman wrote during Christmastime that her twelve-year-old daughter wanted a "Pink Panther" bicycle for Christmas. The mother could barely afford the postage for the request, much less the bicycle. I bought her the bicycle, my Sunday School class donated clothes, and we all helped that woman and her daughter get on their feet.

There were times, however, when I was the target of fraud. People who didn't need money would write to ask for it. I would have to investigate to be sure I wasn't being taken. The requests, some of them bogus, continue to this day. Because of the enormous amount of mail received at The Nashville Network, I can no longer address the pleas.

The late Ernest Tubb, known for his generosity, often responded to letters requesting help. He bought furniture, groceries, clothes, paid overdue utility bills, satisfied past-due debts, and even gave cash to one family that was only pretending to be in need. They flat-out duped him.

I thought of that years later when Ernest died broke and in debt in a Nashville hospital.

But my giving, and that of many inside the Nashville entertainment business, has often been because we appreciated those who were listening to our work, thereby giving us a career. To paraphrase Buck Owens, it took people like them to make people like us. My gratitude clouded my judgment. I gave freely until I realized I wasn't always giving with good sense.

I had gotten married six months into my radio career, but that didn't stop another kind of correspondence from the listening audience. A few women wrote with suggestions, or open propositions, for marriage or affection, not always in that order.

A woman named Ruth followed me through three radio stations right up until the time I became more accessible due to my call-in format on the All-Night Show at WSM in 1957. She harassed me for ten years. She infrequently came to the station unannounced. She called almost nightly, sometimes hourly. Sometimes I would have long-distance listeners on hold, a celebrity guest waiting to do a live interview, and Ruth on the telephone line. I told her I was married, and asked her not to call, but to no avail. I eventually resorted to insulting her, became verbally abusive, and frequently hung up on her. Nothing helped.

The woman was a copy of the obsessive listener played by Jessica Walter in the Clint Eastwood movie *Play Misty for Me,* although she never did anything criminal. But, like the Clint Eastwood disc jockey, I simply couldn't shake her.

Then one day it ended as quickly as it began. She had been calling for more years than the age of my eldest son, only to disappear. I never heard from her again, and she became another one of the innumerable faceless statistics who have passed through my public life.

■

I often become sentimental when recalling my early days in radio, then an entirely different medium, pregnant with wholesome will. Radio personalities had personal contact with listeners to the occasional point of real involvement. I read baking recipes over the air, obituaries, and on rare occasions relayed personal messages from one loved one to another. Although I was an entertainer, I became a surrogate family member to many of my listeners. I knew scores by their first names. They approached me in restaurants, told me who they were, and I suddenly had a face to go with the name of a regular listening correspondent.

I had just put on a religious program one Sunday morning at WAGG when there was a knock on the studio door. The station was inside a concrete building near a tower in the middle of a field. A nearby farmer who had been listening had come by to tell me that his mare was about to foal. Having listened to me on the radio, he thought I was the type of guy who would enjoy seeing that. So while the tape-recorded preacher talked about life after this world, I watched a life enter the world, right there in the middle of a wind-swept pasture on a sunny Sunday in Tennessee. Then I walked with renewed peace back to the studio and resumed my faceless chatter to the working men and women of Franklin. I told them what I had seen, and some called with suggestions about what to eventually feed the new colt.

That kind of human touch, to and from listeners, is absent from the automated programming that dominates radio today. The homespun priorities of forty-three years ago would be corny in today's supercharged society, but still, it's a loss.

But I believe one of the reasons my All-Night Show was such an overwhelming success was because management let me be me. I could talk to listeners, put them on the air, and generally say what I was thinking. My listeners felt like they had a personal relationship with me. Each, I think, felt like I was talking directly to him or her.

One night, I recall, I played the end of a Hank Thompson song six times just because I liked the music. With each playing, I would point out instrumentation that I found particularly appealing and tell listeners what to listen for. Roy Clark heard me and said he thought I had the heart of a musician. Perhaps. But the point is I was exercising a very human approach to what used to be a very human and intimate medium.

Perhaps our high-stress nation could use more of the soothing effect of the human voice and less of the blaring electronic wizardry that consumes modern radio programming. Music stations today program numerous, non-stop songs, followed by an announcer who tells them what was played at the top of the order twenty to thirty minutes ago. Then it's back to more recorded music.

I would not be on North American television today were it not for my days in radio. I owe more to radio than to anything else regarding my career success.

But if I were starting my career anew with radio as we know it, I'd rather sell aluminum siding. In short, I would not want any part of the medium to which I once devoted my life, unless I could be me.

FOUR

The host of the All-Night Show who preceded me, "Smiling" Eddie Hill, used to joke about his job, "What I say may not be important, but it sure goes a fur piece."

The program was heard in almost every part of North America at one time or another, depending on atmospheric conditions, and became country music's best ambassador, especially in the 1960s before this kind of music received significant television coverage. I became host of the radio show in 1957.

Country entertainers were traveling millions of miles to thousands of auditoriums, bringing their art to people by day and by evening. WSM radio took over from there, staying on the air from 10:05 P.M. until 5 A.M.

An early-morning weather forecaster in Washington, D.C., knew that many of the climate systems affecting his city moved upward from the south along the eastern seaboard. He gave himself an advantage in predicting the weather for the nation's capital by first listening to conditions reported on the All-Night Show.

Willard Scott went on to become weather man on NBC's "Today Show."

A long-haul truck driver was a regular All-Night Show listener and caller in the 1960s, and went on to become a major songwriter and recording star before his untimely death in the early 1970s. His name was Jim Croce.

■

The old Sewart Air force Base was in Smyrna, just outside of Nashville. Pilots flew protective missions twenty-four hours a day over top-secret locations. Many called the Sewart base from their cockpits and asked to be patched through to my telephone. I, in turn, would put their voices on the air so that listeners from Maine to California could hear a bomber pilot in action as he might be flying over their state.

I took pains to strike up a relaxing rapport with the pilots, asking their names, where they were from, when they would be discharged from the military, and the like. They'd get comfortable talking about their favorite country stars, and then I'd try to trick them. "Well, where are you calling from tonight?"

"You know I can't tell you that," they'd always retort. I never did get a SAC flier to tell me his whereabouts.

One night in particular SAC pilots called the Nashville base from all over the western world. While they wouldn't give me their locations, they did tell me the names of their home air bases. The Sewart dispatcher asked if he could put them through to me one by one, and I consented. It was a military marathon from beyond the blue. Grounded listeners loved it.

No small part of WSM's overnight audience was in America's big cities where night shifts abounded. Many of the laborers had migrated north from the comparatively non-industrialized South to take jobs on assembly lines, running drill presses, working in foundries, and the like.

It wasn't surprising, therefore, when country stars began to work regularly in the upper Midwest and Northeast, going into metropolitan centers such as Philadelphia, Boston, Chicago, Milwaukee, and New York City.

A giant country show was performed in New York City's Madison Square Garden in 1964 for four performances. While I emceed those concerts, I kept thinking about the building's rich history. I could hear again the Joe Louis fights that enthralled me when I was a kid in McEwen.

Working men and women poured into the sprawling arena from all the city's boroughs. The show became a milestone in country music's advance, because Madison Square Garden was then the biggest indoor venue ever for a country music show.

Nashvillians took pride in the fact that their music was being performed in four shows at the cultural center of America. The shows were as much an event as concerts. The first was covered as such in preliminary reports and subsequent reviews in the *New York Times* and other presses, including national periodicals and network television.

Three stages were erected to accommodate the non-stop music, and cast members knew they were not just making music, they were making history. Everyone in the show was nervous.

Performers included Buck Owens, Ernest Tubb, Bill Monroe, Webb Pierce, Bill Anderson, Stonewall Jackson, Skeeter Davis, Porter Wagoner and others, including Leon McAuliffe, whose band played background for singers who didn't have their own group.

I was the master of ceremonies and had the pressure-filled task of coordinating the gala's flow. Each singer was allowed only two songs and encores were forbidden.

Most of the stars drove approximately 2,000 miles round-trip from Nashville, paid their band members, paid per diem, paid for hotel rooms, paid for bus diesel fuel, and much more, just to sing two songs in New York City.

The reason for the brief repertories lay in rigid rules governing the stage hands' and other production unions. The program had to end no later than 11:30 P.M. Going overtime by one second, promoter Vic Lewis was told, would cost him a minimum of $5,000. The sum, almost three decades ago, was a small fortune.

Lewis devised a performance schedule that every entertainer was ordered to obey. It showed the precise minute when each act would go on, and the minute each would go off. It allowed x-number of seconds for my transitions, then on to the first note in the next song. It was show business by the numbers.

Nashville entertainers, accustomed to leisurely chatting with an audience, were not used to the regimentation.

Lewis hadn't run off enough copies of his iron-clad schedule, perhaps trying to cut costs. I was given one of the few lists.

The entertainers continually had to send their band members to me to ask what time they were scheduled to go on stage.

I opened the show from center stage. I was then placed in the orchestra pit of that mammoth hall and was unable to understand clearly the lyrics in the vast space above me. I was checking my watch, trying to think of my next lines, and organizing uneasy entertainers, who wanted to know when it was time to start tuning their guitars. I was really stressed out.

Webb Pierce was not the hottest star on the show, but his popularity had been among the most pronounced. No one on the program had had bigger hits.

He emerged on stage to deafening applause, resplendent in a western Nudie suit, named after the designer. A half-dozen spotlights reflected from the maze of mirrors and sequins adorning his outfit. Webb was a one-man flashing sign.

He saw the program as an opportunity to expand significantly his record-buying audience, as did most of the performers. He, like most of the cast, was annoyed because he was allowed only two songs.

He became outraged when I took him off after only one.

Because of the distractions, I thought mistakenly that Webb had already sung two songs. He was stepping up to the microphone and just about to open his mouth when my voice filled the arena.

"Ladies and gentlemen, let's hear it for the 'Wandering Boy,' Webb Pierce! Thank you, Webb, for those great songs here at Madison Square Garden."

The applause rose, Webb blinked, and as I was contemplating the introduction to the next act I kept hearing, "Ralph! Ralph." I looked directly upward into Webb's angry and disbelieving eyes. He had traveled this far and undergone as much humiliation as anyone else in the show only to have his performance time cut in half.

The spotlight shone on his fury.

"Why did you take me off?" he hissed from the lip of the stage.

Everyone in the house knew the mistake was mine. Pulling Webb off stage prematurely was the equivalent of a comedy emcee demanding an early removal of Jack Benny.

"Ladies and gentlemen, I took Webb off the stage too soon," I said. "He was supposed to sing two songs like everybody else. So would you please give a warm Madison Square Garden welcome again to one of country music's great singers, Webb Pierce."

People were amused when I conceded my error.

I had blown it before a capacity crowd large enough to require the installation of portable seating on the arena floor. I could hear giggles from some condescending New Yorkers, and sensed the anger of one of the industry's biggest stars as he grimaced, setting up for his final number.

"Well," Webb said to the audience, "people make mistakes. I guess that's why they put erasers on pencils."

His remark was as gracious as he intended it to be, and he went into his next song.

My mistake had been time consuming, wasting precious seconds apologizing to the crowd, and reintroducing Webb.

The pressure was really on now, and the promoter kept coming by about every three minutes to tell me to hurry the show up.

"We're going to go overtime, damn it," he kept shouting above the music and applause. "You're going to cost me a mint! Get this show in high gear!"

The tension compounded to indescribable proportions when George Jones finished his second song and went into a third.

The promoter sprinted to my side seething, his mouth agape, and sweating as if he had just mopped the entire building by hand.

"What the hell is he doing?" he thundered at me and pointed at Jones. "He's not supposed to sing a third song! How are we going to get him off stage?"

Jones wore the impish smile that was the telltale sign of his mischievous mood. I had seen that look on him many times. He knew exactly what he was doing and was taking sadistic delight in throwing the entire show out of whack.

By now, the promoter was close to a heart attack, worrying about the forthcoming overtime charges. I was very stressed, to say the least, and kept asking myself what we were going to do. How were we going to get Jones off the stage?

Jones, meanwhile, was in fine voice.

He was now into his fifth song. He had gone overtime by 150 percent and still he kept singing.

Bill Monroe, the father of bluegrass music, noticed the promoter's and my distress from the wings.

This scholarly and graying gentlemen eased to my side and put his hand on my shoulder. I couldn't hear him above the riotous clapping of the crowd, enthralled because it was finally getting to hear an extended set.

"How are we going to get him off?" Lewis said.

Bill Monroe overheard him and said, "I'll get him off. You want me to get him off?"

"What?" I shouted back.

"I'm telling you I can get him off the stage," Bill said. "Do you want me to do it?"

I had no idea what he was talking about, but I also had no time left.

"Do whatever you can," I said.

Bill summoned a member of his band. The two walked on stage before that capacity crowd and sneaked behind the most critically acclaimed singer in the history of country music. Each grabbed Jones by an arm at precisely the same time.

Jones, still singing, was literally carried off the stage. His voice faded into the arena's awesome obscurity and his band members looked curiously at each other, and stopped playing one by one. The music ground to a faltered halt.

Jones resisted, but only as a comic gesture. He knew exactly what he had done, and he probably wondered just how he was going to be forced to exit. He had the mischievous grin of a school kid who expected to get caught.

George Jones would not have tolerated being removed like that from Madison Square Garden by anyone except for a handful of people such as his idols, Bill Monroe, Ernest Tubb, and Roy Acuff. Monroe knew that, and that's probably why he volunteered to go get Jones, rather than ask a stage hand to try to approach him diplomatically.

The crowd roared, thinking that Jones' unorthodox exit was a part of his act. He was finally off stage and there were only seven minutes left before the show's scheduled ending.

Buck Owens, then the most popular country singer in the world, took the stage by storm. Some of the members of his band were playing their instruments before others had even plugged in to their amplifiers. The clock was ticking.

Buck raced through his first song at a tempo that was faster than normal, and by the time the applause subsided, he was well into his second selection.

The promoter was standing behind me yelling, "Faster, faster." I feared his voice would leak into my microphone and into the arena.

Buck sang his final syllable, and I shouted, "That's it, everybody. Thanks for coming. Country Music Comes to Madison Square Garden is now history!"

The show was officially over. The time clock said 11:29:40. We had beaten our deadline by twenty seconds to save thousands of dollars!

Headlines screamed the triumphant invasion of the Big Apple by the minstrels from the South. The show was a resounding success.

"The country music jamboree was as ambitious, colorful, star-laden, uneven, beautiful and banal as a circus," wrote Robert Shelton in the May 18, 1964, *New York Times*. He went on to compare my emcee work to that of a ringmaster, and said I was "fluent" and "low-pressure."

"Other performers too numerous to mention contributed what

they could in the quick-step parade to the microphone," Shelton wrote. "There was a bit of noise, a lot of nostalgia, but enough good music making for this circus to be one that country music fans would long remember."

We had, we thought, taken a bite out of the Big Apple!

Six years later, the country star Bill Anderson sat before my overnight microphone and told the following story. He said he suspected he and his band members looked conspicuously out of place with their western boots and pompadours in the lobby of New York City's Waldorf-Astoria Hotel.

The group had gone to New York to become the second country act in history ever to appear on NBC's "Today Show." (The first was Flatt and Scruggs.) The billing was another milestone in the spread of country music to an expanding national audience.

"If you guys go over well on the show," Anderson was told by a "Today Show" producer, "we'll start using country acts once a month."

Word spread quickly among the staff of men wearing polyester in the largely velvet and satin hotel. Bill said the hotel operator mockingly called him "honey child" whenever he dialed her. She referred, in condescending tones, to the other southerners who were Waldorf guests, not knowing they were members of Bill's entourage occupying six rooms.

Bill and his players had to be at the NBC studios by 5 A.M. He instructed each musician to leave a wake-up call with the hotel operator for 3:30 A.M.

"You know, honey child, I don't think I could live down south," she said when Bill called her.

"Why is that?" Bill asked.

"Well, you're the fourth southerner to call me tonight who wants to be awakened at 3:30 in the morning," she said. "You people just get up too early for me."

The woman had never heard of Bill Anderson, but within days, he would appear on the "Mike Douglas Show," another major television forum of the day. Bill, at the time, was host to his own syndicated television show and had recorded two number-one songs that had crossed over to popular music surveys.

At that time I had been on the All-Night Show for thirteen years, spreading the gospel of country music from sea to sea. Just three years after Bill Anderson's "Today Show" debut, the recording industry would bestow its most prestigious awards, the Grammys, during nationally telecast ceremonies from Nashville. Yet stories like Bill Anderson's at the Waldorf, despite country music's victorious evening at Madison Square Garden, made me realize that I still had a lot of work cut out for me.

Country stars were more popular than they ever had been. But, as late as 1970, I realized that the majority of Americans still hadn't heard of the majority of the country music stars.

FIVE

Although the evolvement of the popularity of country music was gradual, it was nonetheless definite. I know, because as host of the All-Night Show, I was an eye witness.

In 1972 Fan Fair was born, and twenty years later is one of the world's most popular tourist attractions. It is Nashville's answer to New Orleans' Mardis Gras, but without the sin.

Twenty-four thousand people attended in July of 1993 and as many were turned away from the week-long festivity. Tentative plans are underway to move Fan Fair from the Nashville Fairgrounds to a place that will accommodate twice as many fans. All three television networks covered the 1993 show, and it was featured on "Entertainment Tonight" as well as the morning talk fests, including the "Today Show" and "Good Morning America." The release of mass media credentials was halted after 600 press passes were issued.

Fan Fair is the brainchild of Irving Waugh, retired chief executive officer of Opryland USA Inc., which houses the Grand Ole Opry, The Nashville Network, the Opryland theme park, and other attractions. The entities are owned today by Gaylord Communications. The sprawling Opryland Park was only six months away from its opening when Waugh became apprehensive.

"We were going to open on Memorial Day, in 1972, and as we moved into that last six or eight months of construction I became concerned about the investment and the chance that I thought we were taking, although I had pushed the company into it," Waugh told me. "Nashville at that time was the smallest market in the nation to attempt a theme park."

Waugh said he was looking for an idea that would focus attention on the Opryland complex and came up with an event that would simultaneously draw celebrities, fans, and the media.

He consulted with Elmer Alley, a Nashville television veteran, who gave me my first break in the medium. Alley wanted to stage something called "Folk Fair of America." Waugh thought the title carried connotations of folk music or jazz, not country, and changed it.

"My only real contribution to Fan Fair was to name it," Alley said in March 1993.

Alley, incidentally, became executive producer on "Hee-Haw," one of television's longest-running syndicated shows. He theorized that the show lost its ratings about three years ago when its format was "modernized." In the wake of fans' complaints, the show was put into rerun with airings of the original format and cast. The show was called "Hee-Haw Silver." But fans were reluctant to watch, and sponsors were reluctant to buy. Alley said he did not expect the show to return to the air in 1994 in either its new or rerun editions.

He said part of the problem lay in the fact that people who buy programming for television stations are young when compared to the cast and regular viewers of "Hee-Haw." The young programmers, he said, won't buy old programs. Alley said that senior citizens, who comprise the majority of "Hee-Haw" audiences, are perceived by Madison Avenue to be set in their ways. Young advertisers feel as though they are wasting their time advertising on shows viewed mostly by senior citizens.

"If a man has driven a Chevy for twenty years, he'll always buy a Chevy, no matter what else is advertised," Alley said.

Radio station WSM asked the Country Music Association to co-produce the first Fan Fair, Waugh recalled, contingent upon WSM's absorbing any potential losses.

Bud Wendell, the general manager of the Grand Ole Opry at the time, was put in charge of producing the first Fan Fair. It was held April 12th–15th, 1972, but later was moved to June to lure vacationers. The Opryland Park was opened after the first Fan Fair on May 27, 1972.

Waugh asked me if I would utilize my close friendship with Marty Robbins and ask him to appear at the first Fan Fair. I hate to take advantage of relationships, but I admired Waugh, and he sweetened the deal by saying that if I would get Marty to do the show, he would name the big television studio at Nashville's Channel 4 after me.

I did secure Marty and Waugh didn't name the studio after me. I reminded him of that recently. Waugh said, "I was given to exaggeration in those days."

The phenomenal growth of country music was not without growing pains. Performers, accustomed to working the Grand Ole Opry or touring with package shows, had trouble adapting to the new and more sophisticated outlets for their music. Country singers weren't always as compatible and adaptable as they are today.

I'll never forget the first time the Grammy Awards show was staged in Nashville in 1973 and broadcast in prime-time over CBS. The show was produced by Pierre Cossette.

The show had traditionally been broadcast from New York City or Los Angeles over ABC. ABC said it would not air the program, however, when Cossette announced he would produce it in Nashville.

"It will become too much of a country show," Cossette told me he was told by ABC officials. "You won't get the major artists to go to Nashville, so we just don't want it."

In 1973, very few major recording stars recorded country music.

Cossette was turned down by NBC, so that left CBS as the only remaining major television network in the days before the proliferation of cable channels.

Cossette went to New York City to see his old friend Bob Wood, then a decision-maker regarding CBS programming. "For a week, I was pleading with him to take the Grammys," Cossette said.

In the meantime, Cossette, without a buyer for his show, committed his personal funds to produce the program. After five days of begging the last man who could put his program on network television, a failed and dejected Cossette dined in New York's prestigious 21 Club for his final meal before returning to Los Angeles.

He ran into Lori Wood, Bob Wood's wife.

"Oh, Pierre, what are you doing in town?" Cossette said she asked him.

He told her and added that he was leaving for California that night, when she insisted that he spend the weekend with Wood and her.

Cossette said he knew Wood would not have approved of the invitation.

"Oh, great, I'll spend the week end with you, but don't tell Bob I'm coming," Cossette told Mrs. Wood.

Cossette used the entire week end as an opportunity to hound Wood to broadcast the Grammy Awards on CBS. Wood wouldn't relent, and on Monday morning, Cossette was still without a medium for the most esteemed program relating to the recording industry.

Cossette was walking down a hall in the Wood home at dawn when he noticed the door was ajar to Wood's and his wife's bedroom.

"I said, 'Jesus, I've got an idea,' " Cossette told me. "I'm still in my pajamas and I went back and I got my briefcase and I went into their bedroom and I climbed in bed between the two of them.

"I said, 'Bob, if you don't buy the Grammys show, I'm going to do to your wife what ABC did to me.' "

"Get out of my bedroom!" Cossette said Wood yelled. "I'll buy the fucking show, but get out of here!"

"And that's how it was sold," Cossette said.

The program has aired annually on CBS ever since.

Nashville was buzzing about the prestige the show would bring to the Athens of the South.

I wanted to attend as much as I had ever wanted anything in show business, and I did, but not until I rose from a hospital bed. I was suffering a recurring back problem. I was given a furlough and returned to the hospital after the show. I wore my hospital bracelet to the broadcast.

My wife, Joy, brought my tuxedo to the hospital. I lay in bed until it was time to go to the program, dressed, let her drive, and when we arrived I then wobbled into the theater, and saw first-hand a Grammy show in Nashville.

Production people from Nashville were used instead of people from Hollywood and New York, and that lessened the production overhead considerably. The main consideration for moving the show to Nashville, however, was to nurture the Southern branch of NARAS. Wesley Rose, part-owner of Acuff-Rose, then the largest music publishing company in Nashville, was president of NARAS. That had a lot to do with the Grammys' being held in Nashville, and the show was hosted by Andy Williams.

Local workers were asked to do things they hadn't done before, such as create artificial smoke during a mood number. There hadn't been much call before for synthetic smoke inside the old Tennessee Theater, a movie house.

The smoke was needed for a big number, starring rhythm and blues singer Curtis Mayfield, to set the tone for the evening. Nowadays smoke is used routinely in Nashville productions and is created by blowing air over vegetable oil and water. During that show, however, bug spray was used to create a smoky effect, according to many persons affiliated with the show's production. Cossette said he was not aware that insect repellent was utilized, but added he didn't know exactly how the smoke was manufactured. The extent of the backstage technical expertise came when workers cranked up smoke machines loaded with liquid bug spray intended to simulate smoke.

They let the spray accumulate before targeting it onto the stage and into the lungs of Curtis Mayfield. He began to cough and the spray leaked into the audience in the first few rows, where more coughing ensued. The bug spray had worked during rehearsal when back doors were open, allowing ventilation.

"Nobody could see him and he couldn't see the audience," Cossette said. "It was the god damndest thing you ever saw."

Mayfield struggled on and kept trying to sing, but soon hand-kerchiefs started flying in the audience like butterflies, and the bug spray billowed over national television. It was a production disaster that quickly became apparent to the millions watching the show.

Bill Turner, director of "Nashville Now," saw the show on television and recalled that "smoke" was so dense during a number by Johnny Cash that the singer was virtually invisible.

Someone thought to open the theater's back doors, and electric fans were pointed in that direction. The cloud of spray was discharged into an alley much faster than it had accumulated. Mayfield choked through a few more words, and the show continued.

The Grammy Awards never returned to Nashville.

Another indicator of country music's expanding popularity was the interest of motion picture producers, who began easing into Nashville in the late 1960s and were flocking to the city ten years later. Many feature films set in Music City U.S.A. were Hollywood productions by Academy Award–winning producers, directors, and actors. Others were locally produced. Almost none was produced without glitches as the makers of country music stepped from behind microphones and into the foreign world of celluloid.

Burt Reynolds, in his critically acclaimed touring show, "An Evening with Burt Reynolds," performs a two-hour monologue about his life, including his role in placing Nashville singers in Hollywood movies. Reynolds used Jerry Reed, Don Williams, Dolly Parton, Mel Tillis and others in movies produced in the late 1970s, when he was the number-one box office attraction in the world. During a 1992 video taping of his talk show, "Conversations," Dolly said he had done more to promote film making in Nashville than anyone else and indicated the entire country music community was indebted to him.

Reynolds first used Tillis as an actor in *W. W. and the Dixie Dance Kings.* Everybody knows Mel Tillis stutters. Everybody, that is, except the man who directed the film.

Tillis delivered his first line and, of course, botched it because of his stammer, Reynolds said. The cast and crew were giggling when the director yelled "cut." They were not laughing at Tillis. They instead chortled because his hesitation made the line funny.

The director was not amused. He pointed out, according to Reynolds, that Tillis' line did not call for him to stutter. He apparently thought Tillis was improvising, and let him have it in front of everyone on the set for taking liberties with the script.

Reynolds exploded. He has always been protective of country singers and confronted the director, physically accosting him.

The director apologized to Tillis for his ignorance and tactlessness, Reynolds said. In the meantime, a hypersensitive Tillis had retired to his trailer, where he began swallowing liquid consolation. A lot of country stars have been known to drink when their feelings were hurt.

The director called Tillis back to the set and told him his natural stutter was funny and since it was Tillis' trademark it would stay in the movie.

The director ordered Tillis to repeat his line, yelled "action," and the cameras rolled.

Tillis didn't stutter. He spoke his lines flawlessly, Reynolds said.

Many people with speech impediments do not have them when they're intoxicated. Tillis is one of them.

The director was clamoring for the comedy value of Tillis' stammer, but it wouldn't come.

The scene was re-shot the next morning when Tillis was sober. He delivered his lines perfectly, stuttering over almost every word.

I too was an uncertain actor in Nashville's early film making. I made my fourth forgettable film in 1966 soon after a fifteen-month leave from the WSM All-Night Show. I had appeared in two pictures with Marty Robbins in 1965.

The film was financed by a consortium of operators of drive-in theaters where the movie would play. Not all of the early Nashville films were as sophisticated as Burt Reynolds' movies.

My fourth film was initially called *Tobacco Road,* but had nothing to do with the best-selling novel by Erskine Caldwell. Perhaps its producers had never heard of the book, but they certainly did after copyright problems began to surface. The title was changed to *The Girl from Tobacco Row.* The film was legendary cowboy actor Tex Ritter's last.

Let's just say that neither I nor any of my co-stars were the targets of belabored consideration for Oscar Awards.

It was a crime movie, and I played a thug named Blinkie, because my character blinked whenever he saw sunlight. To avoid eye fluttering, Blinkie almost always wore sunglasses.

A pivotal scene in the movie was a shoot-out between Blinkie, other bad guys, and lawmen. The script was supposed to build toward a crescendo in the manner of the final gunfight in Gary Cooper's *High Noon.* The tension, however, more closely resembled that of an episode from "I Love Lucy."

The director had blocked out, in his mind, how the action would unfold for the big scene. At last the day for the gunfight filming arrived. Nashville fiddle player Gordon Terry, five other actors, and I were taken to a farm north of Nashville for the spellbinding gun play.

The cameras were set up, makeup was applied, and our direction as to who would fall where and when was given. All systems were go for the culmination of weeks of filming with gunfire.

But no one remembered to bring any guns.

Time is money in the movie industry. All of the people who were being paid at various union scales saw the performances of their crafts paralyzed. We might as well have been trying to film a thunderstorm without water.

"Well," I said, "I have a little .38 revolver that I carry in my car."

The gun was nothing more than a Saturday night special, but it saved the day.

It often takes hours to film a ten-minute scene, and that scene was no exception. Production stretched even longer, however, because five different actors had to be filmed shooting at each other using the same gun.

I'd take a shot at someone from one camera angle. The director would yell "cut," and I'd take the same shot from another angle. When all the angles were exhausted, the gun was taken from my hand and given to another actor, who would take numerous shots at me, again filmed from different angles, using my gun. Then someone ran the gun back to me so that I could return the fire that had been returned to me, again using the only gun on the set.

No one remembered to bring blank bullets either. The actors pointed the weapon, pulled the trigger, and tried to fake a recoil. The sound of gunfire was dubbed into the film later. There were no funds to rent, much less buy, a production lot. So the filming went on in the homes or on the lawns of the producer or his friends.

I remember standing in the producer's backyard on Nashville's Battlefield Drive, where I was supposed to hurl a Styrofoam rock at another actor and kill him. There was no money for a fake rock, so a real one was used. Actually, it was less like a rock and more like a concrete block.

Virtually nothing is ever captured on film in one take, I discovered, so I was directed to heft the rock above my head and propel it downward repeatedly. I feared I'd get a hernia and drop to my knees in agonizing pain before the rolling cameras.

My anxiety wasn't as great, however, as that of actor Snake Richards, at whom I repeatedly lobbed the rock. He was not a stuntman, as the budget had no allocation for one.

So the actor had to roll out of the path of a crippling rock a split second before it hit him. That, perhaps, was one of the most honest life-threatening scenes ever filmed.

"Don't throw that rock until I'm ready," he pleaded between takes.

In another film three years earlier, *Country Music on Broadway*, I played an emcee. I didn't have to study a lot for the part. The picture, produced by Audrey Williams, was intended to be a launching pad for the career of her son, Hank, Jr.

There was an old man in the movie played by Old Joe Clark, a country comedian from Kentucky. The plot was very thin, and was really little more than an excuse to let a bunch of singers sing. Throughout the story, the old man kept approaching me asking me to put him on the show.

My character wouldn't do it, and was somewhat mean to the old-timer.

The old actor was from a rural Kentucky town whose inhabitants saw the movie but didn't realize it was only "acting." I received a mountain of mail from people reprimanding me for my mistreatment of the old man.

Another peculiar thing about the movie was that a scene with Hank Williams, lifted from the "Kate Smith Show," was used. The negative for that scene, in the film laboratory, was mistakenly reversed. The error made Williams appear to be a left-handed guitar player, which he was not. The same film was used almost thirty years later in Hank Williams, Jr.'s "Tear in My Beer" video. The mistake was never corrected, even though Audrey Williams saw a screening of the film before its release.

Filming had gone on for days and the cast was weary. Many had to leave for live concerts and therefore wanted production to come to a halt. Production was interrupted, however, because the director, wishing to appease Audrey Williams, wanted to be sure she had a soft seat on which to sit during the final song, "I Saw the Light."

Audrey was to be perched atop a barrel in the center of the singers. The director feared the barrel would be too hard for her butt. The cast and crew looked furiously for a cushion while the production clock was ticking.

"Aw, Momma, sit down!" Hank, Jr., finally thundered. Her son was the only person who could have been so direct, and the set fell silent. Anxious cast members waited to see how the highstrung and temperamental woman would react.

Hank's order was all it took. The dilemma was solved as Audrey was quietly seated, the final song was filmed, and production was wrapped.

Another dangerous situation evolved during motion-picture filming with Nashville singer-guitarist Jerry Reed, who was overcome with carbon monoxide during the filming of *Survivors,* with Walter Matthau and Robin Williams.

Reed was sitting in a motor home that served as his dressing room. An exhaust leak sifted into the coach, where Reed became severely ill and disoriented. Williams happened to walk into the vehicle and noticed Reed's color. He suggested that Reed might need some fresh air.

Reed, unaware that he had been poisoned, said he thought Williams was right. He gathered his coat, stepped out of the motor home, and fainted dead away onto the ground.

"God as my witness," Reed told me, "I thought this was it. I never laid on the ground as helpless in my life, and I couldn't breathe."

A doctor was summoned, who happened to be working in the picture as an extra. He quickly administered resuscitation.

Reed subsequently credited Williams with saving his life and said the incident marked his closest brush with death.

"If God ever did anything, He snapped me to total attention laying on that ground," Reed said. "I found out later there is a point of no return where you're receiving carbon monoxide. I was just about there."

With the beginning of my television career that blossomed in the late 1970s, I stopped appearing in motion pictures because I had no time for films.

The last, and the only significant film in which I appeared, was in 1981 with Linda Hamilton, Earl Holloman, and Loni Anderson.

It was called *Country Gold* and played on CBS.

It too highlighted a bevy of Nashville stars, including Minnie Pearl, Mel Tillis, Tom T. Hall, O. B. McClinton, and Jerry Reed.

I once again didn't have to rehearse my part. I was cast as a disc jockey.

I remember three things about the film.

The first is that a scene had to be re-shot because Tillis continued to call me Ralph instead of Vernon, my character's name. The second is that Loni Anderson finished shooting in Nashville, went to Atlanta to appear in a picture with Burt Reynolds, and eventually married him.

The third is that she befriended me and was helpful between takes. I remember thinking how her kindness violated the snobbish stereotype that some Nashvillians have of Hollywood personalities.

I asked her if her real name was Loni, and she said yes, but that her father had fought in the Pacific theater of operations during World War II and had considered giving her a Polynesian name, LeiLoni.

"Lei ultimately wouldn't do," she told me. "He decided that all the boys would be making jokes and saying things like, 'Let's Lay Loni and similar stuff.' "

I had heard many stories behind the formation of names, but had never heard one behind a name's elimination. My show-business knowledge, I decided, continued to expand. And some of it would never be anything other than trivial fun.

SIX

A wonderful aspect of working in Nashville as late as the mid-1960s was that the popularity of our music was expanding just as the closeness of the musicians was growing.

Nashville had not yet lost its family spirit. Everybody on Nashville's Music Row knew every other musician there. We knew each other's children and their middle names. We knew who, in our musical family, was having financial problems, whose marriages were in trouble, who was drinking more than he should, who had been born again (again), and who was on drugs.

Country music makers then were still practitioners of unconditional love. We saw each other for what we were and loved what we saw.

But then the climate changed, from an intimate business to an impersonal, international industry.

I once went with Joe Talbot, who has held many executive positions within the Country Music Association, to a soiree for Ms. Olivia Newton John in the 1970s. She was a big pop star then, and her arrival in Nashville signified the recognition and expansion of the country music industry. Joe and I stood uncomfortably in the crowd, aware that there were many in the room whom we didn't know, unlike parties in the past when the business was smaller and more intimate.

"You know, Ralph," Joe said, "we worked long and hard to make our business big. And now that it is, it isn't fun anymore."

I knew exactly what he meant.

Today, some original members of the Grand Ole Opry who were once the Belles of Music Row cannot get into many of its offices.

Today's country stars juggle top song slots with each other on the popularity surveys and often never even meet, except for passing glances at awards shows. Even when they record duets, they often put their separate parts on tape in each other's absence.

In the middle 1960s, when a small cluster of people recorded all the songs on the country top-40, the performers recorded, traveled, ate, slept, worried, belched, confided, and rejoiced together. The country music family was still a band of people pulling for a common cause. Rock 'n' roll's popularity had surpassed country music's. As music went, country stars were in the minority, and minorities bond in a way majorities do not.

Many Nashville veterans, including some of the legends, say they regret some of the changes the country music industry has undergone. They also feel that the changes were unavoidable in the face of growth.

The deaths of Patsy Cline, Hawkshaw Hawkins, Cowboy Copas, Randy Hughes, Jack Anglin, Dean Manuel and Jim Reeves, all of them in two plane crashes and a car wreck in a sixteen-month period, drew our music family together like nothing else could.

The nation grieved. Nashville was paralyzed. The country music community was a collective teardrop.

Singer Jan Howard wrote in her autobiography that she heard me talking on the radio about Patsy Cline's plane shortly after it went down, with Copas, Hawkins, and Patsy's manager, Hughes, all on board.

Jan is confusing Patsy's crash with reports about Reeves' crash that happened about sixteen months later. The fact is, Jan herself awakened me at home to tell me Cline's plane was missing. I wasn't on the air on March 5, 1963, when Cline's plane disappeared because I had the flu.

"This is the saddest day of my life," said WSM announcer T. Tommy Cutrer, on the morning of March 6, 1963. He went on to say that the missing aircraft and its passengers had not been located. Searchers had tromped through woods all night around Camden in the western part of the state where several persons had reported hearing a crash.

"Craft Lost on Flight to City" read the headline in the March 7, 1963, *Nashville Tennessean*. The story took precedence over another front page report about organized labor's first challenge to French President Charles de Gaulle. Hundreds of thousands of French workers had walked off their jobs in a show of support for a coal miners' strike that crippled the country, but a missing Nashville aircraft got the major news play.

The doomed plane was returning to Nashville from Kansas City, Kansas, where the entertainers had done a benefit show for the family of Cactus Jack Call, a disc jockey killed in an automobile wreck on January 25, 1963. After laying over in Kansas City for one day due to inclement weather, the plane stopped for fuel in Dyersburg, Tennessee, shortly before 5 P.M. Hughes, the pilot, called his wife from Dyersburg to say he would be home soon. He asked her to go to Cornelia Fort Airpark, a private airport, and tell the manager to turn on the lights. The plane was airborne at 6:07 P.M. Its passengers would be dead in twenty minutes.

A cold front, ushered by a southwesterly wind, had just passed through Dyersburg, according to the National Weather Service, then the United States Weather Bureau. The yellow and green Commanche 250 went virtually unnoticed as it idled to the tiny airport's fuel bay. None of the airport personnel apparently gave more than a passing glance to four disembarking passengers, all of whom were national or international celebrities dressed as civilians.

Pilot Hughes was briefed by airport weather source Leroy Neal about the inadvisability of flying into the backside of a cold front. Hughes was told about limited visibility and area thunderstorms.

Hughes also consulted that day with then airport manager William E. Braese. Braese explained to Hughes that he would be flying part of his trip out of radio contact due to low altitude forced by conditions. Hughes, therefore, would have to rely on his flight instruments.

Hughes was not instrument-rated.

He reportedly told Braese that once airborne, he would determine the ferocity of weather and return to the ground if necessary.

The quartet's return to Nashville, where each passenger made his home, was already frustrated by a one-day weather delay in Kansas City. Perhaps the passengers' eagerness to get home prompted them to fly despite adverse conditions at Dyersburg. The plane received twenty-seven gallons of fuel and was airborne.

At approximately 9 P.M., the Nashville office of the Weather Bureau issued an advisory that Commanche N7000P had not arrived at its destination. A telephone check was made to all airports along the route. The plane was nowhere to be found. It was certain, however, that the plane was down. Fuel-exhaustion time had elapsed.

Sam Webb was a logger who lived about two miles northwest of Camden. He had stepped onto his porch to observe the foreboding sky. Webb saw light rainfall and felt forceful gusts. He recalled suddenly hearing an airplane over his house. He said the deafening volume told him the plane's altitude was unusually low.

Strangely, he remembered that his wife and ten-year-old daughter were watching "Laramie" on television.

"Mommy, that plane is going to light!" the child exclaimed.

"The plane circled twice," said Webb, "and then seemed to go straight into the ground. The impact had the sound of a shotgun fired point-blank into the ground. It was sort of a dull thud."

The Huntingdon, Tennessee, office of the highway patrol was notified of the suspected crash. A search party congregated within an hour. The effort was fruitless, as nightfall had fallen solidly on the rural and isolated woods.

More searchers joined the effort at dawn. At approximately 6:15 A.M., the wreckage was spotted from a fire tower. Searchers converged on the site to discover twisted metal and human dismemberment. Identification of body parts was impossible, except for a part of the skull of Patsy Cline, adorned with a woman's long hair. There were no survivors.

Bill Whitmore, former operations inspector for the Federal Aviation Administration, investigated the crash, and recovered the plane's clock, which had stopped at 6:20 P.M. (The clock is pictured in the photo insert in this book.) Whitmore's official conclusion was that the pilot had experienced vertigo, as evidenced by the fact that the plane's throttle was wide open. Whitmore said the aircraft had a cruising speed of 170 miles per hour. Since it was hurling downward under the force of gravity, he estimated it was traveling at approximately 300 miles per hour upon impact.

Only one tree at the crash site was broken, indicating the plane came in at an almost perfectly vertical angle. The force of the crash resulted in a crater that was four feet wide and six feet long, dug by a plane that was torn apart. The hole had been filled by overnight rainfall and had to be pumped to recover parts of the aircraft and bodies.

The damaged tree was about one foot in diameter. Whitmore said the plane's propeller had sheared its trunk into two pieces.

News of the crash and its dead celebrities spread fast. Curiosity and souvenir seekers gathered within the hour, Whitmore said.

While many appeared to be in a grieved trance, and others wept openly, their looting would make it difficult for Whitmore to do his job. One person was seen removing a shoe containing a human foot. Other details are too gruesome to report here.

The *Nashville Tennessean,* a day after the crash, described the carnage and wrote, in part:

"Raymer Stockdale of Stockdale and Milan Funeral Home in Camden, Tennessee, said identification of the men could be made only by their billfolds—which miraculously weren't torn away.

Bits and scraps of the plane were scattered all over the area. One section said Commanche 250.

A piece of metal high in a tree said 'Jack Pad.' One tire was far off to the left, another far to the right, the third straight down the hollow.

The hole where the single-engine plane first hit the steep hillside was filled with water, lending support to many statements that rain accompanied the stout gusts of wind at the time of the crash.

A white belt with 'Hawkshaw Hawkins' in gold letters lay beside a black-and-white cowboy boot. Another black-and-white cowboy boot lay 18 feet up the woods, two feet from the black-and-silver broken neck of a guitar saying 'Hawkshaw.'

A black sock fluttered seven feet above in a tree branch.

A soft slipper, gold and muddy, just like the one Patsy Cline was seen wearing at Dyersburg, pointed to the impact site.

A silver expansion watch band, broken, rested near the Flyers' Bible. Clothes flapped in the breeze.

Scattered pieces of a green-backed jigsaw puzzle littered the sloping area—simple to solve compared to the massive puzzle of jagged metal and torn flesh.

'Keep America Beautiful' proclaimed a green plastic litter bag with a picture of a small airplane.

Red hand-printing on a pocket-sized piece of note paper sang out part of a tragic song—'Boo Hoo Hoo Hoo.' "

Curiously, no flight plan was ever filed with the Federal Aviation Administration. Authorities were therefore uncertain as to what route Hughes was taking to Nashville, which is why it took so long to find the crash sight.

Singer Billy Walker was an Opry favorite whose recording of "Funny How Time Slips Away" was the first of approximately fifty versions of the song. He was then a major star beloved by

Nashville. He was supposed to be a passenger on the downed aircraft. But his then wife's father was ill in Texas, and Walker needed to return quickly to Nashville to be with his children so that she might go to her father.

When Hawkins became aware of Walker's problem, he gave Walker his commercial airline ticket for the flight back to Nashville and agreed to take Walker's seat on the private plane.

"Here, kid, you take my place on the plane," Walker told me Hawkins told him. Hawkins' kindness cost him his life.

Walker said his house was telephoned by former *Nashville Tennessean* columnist Red O'Donnell hours after the aircraft was reported missing. The columnist spoke with Walker's daughter. O'Donnell read to her an obituary he had written about Walker. It had been moved over the news wires. Walker told me that O'Donnell wanted to check the story for accuracy. The notice contained a major mistake.

It reported the death of a man who was alive.

"I started getting calls from people all over the country," Walker told me in October 1992.

I too could have been on that fallen aircraft. I was scheduled to appear on the same benefit show in Kansas City but became ill and could not go. I would have probably returned to Nashville on a commercial flight with Walker. Yet, if someone had offered his seat on the Piper to me, I might have accepted. Roy Acuff was billed on the program but decided at the last minute not to go, as per the wishes of his wife, Mildred. She was afraid for him to go to Kansas City because of the bad weather. How prophetic.

"Those children [the other stars on the show] will make enough money [for the widow] without you," Mildred reportedly told Acuff. Had he gone, he too might have flown back to Nashville on the doomed aircraft.

Such thoughts are moot and serve no purpose in retrospect, except to remind me of the fragility of mortality.

Hawkins, a West Virginia native, had been with the Opry for eight years at the time of his death. He was married to Jean Shepard, who performs on the Opry to this day. His hits included "I Love You a Thousand Ways," "Slow Poke," and "Soldier's Joy."

Three days before Hawkins' death, "Lonesome 77203" became his first number-one record. After a lifetime in country music, he spent the last seventy-two hours of his life at the top of his craft.

Patsy Cline was thirty, and the biggest star in the entourage. She was in the prime of her life and career when she died. In three years she had scored monumental hits with "I Fall to Pieces," "Crazy," "She's Got You," and "Sweet Dreams." She had been voted "Outstanding Female Vocalist" in a consensus of various country music publications. The award was the industry's most prestigious, as the Country Music Association was not to give out its coveted awards until 1967. Patsy Cline was the first woman to dethrone Kitty Wells in the popularity polls.

Sweet Dreams, a motion picture starring Jessica Lange about the life of Patsy Cline, portrayed Patsy as complaining about having to go to Kansas City to do the benefit. Charlie Dick, the late singer's husband, said in 1993 that it wasn't the benefit that spawned her reluctance, but the travel itself. She said she was road weary, but that fatigue was not enough to stop her from wanting to help a needy family.

Mrs. Ann Wilson, Call's widow who has since remarried, told me in March 1993 that she resented the portrayal of Patsy as someone who didn't want to help. She said the film biography was a direct contradiction to the attitude of the woman she met backstage in Kansas City on March 3, 1963.

"She [Patsy] was compassionate and caring," Mrs. Wilson told me. "She seemed very glad she had done the benefit show, contrary to the way she was made to look in *Sweet Dreams.*"

Mrs. Wilson said that Patsy referred to her own automobile crash on June 14, 1961, after which she lamented about scars that remained on her forehead, and their cosmetic liability to her show business career. She had lain in a Nashville hospital in critical condition for weeks.

"She told me she didn't know why God had spared her life in the car wreck," Mrs. Wilson said. "I told her it was probably so she could do wonderful things like she was doing that afternoon at the benefit."

"When she was recovering from the auto accident she came to the studio on crutches," said Owen Bradley, Patsy's record producer. "Her ribs were still so sore she couldn't hit the high notes. She came back a week later and did the entire session over again."

The song she recorded on that session was "Crazy," Patsy's second-biggest record.

Mrs. Wilson gave me an original program from the benefit show. I hadn't known until then that I had received billing for the show.

In April 1993, I was contacted by Ms. Mildred Keith, a Patsy Cline fan who visited the singer before the show. Ms. Keith's hobby was photographing country music stars who played Kansas City. She gave me one of the last photographs ever taken of Patsy Cline. Ms. Keith snapped it seconds before Patsy walked on stage. Ms. Keith said she approached Patsy's dressing room, which she was sharing with Dottie West.

Ms. Joyce Jackson, secretary to the late Jim Reeves, once told me that Dottie tried to get Patsy to return to Nashville with her in her car.

"Hey," Joyce quoted Patsy as saying, "I came out here on that bird and that's how I'm going home."

When Ms. Keith approached Dottie and Patsy's dressing room in Kansas City, she could hear from the hall that Patsy was upset. She said that Dottie kept reassuring her, telling her things would be all right.

"I don't think she [Patsy] was crying about the death of Jack Call," Ms. Keith told me in 1993. "I think there was something else going on."

The Cline photograph taken by Ms. Keith shows the subject holding a tissue, which Ms. Keith said Patsy was using to blot tears. That picture, as well as a shot of Hawkshaw Hawkins, appear elsewhere in this book.

Had the four victims walked away from the crash, Hughes would have been the target of a lot of criticism due to his admonitions by the Dyersburg airport manager not to fly.

An awesome outpouring of concern was extended to Mrs. Kathy Hughes, because her husband was Randy Hughes and her father was Cowboy Copas.

Nashville bled demonstrable grief for days.

Stories about the crash, the search, and the funerals were picked up by the national media. Both metropolitan Nashville newspapers were besieged with queries from out-of-town publications, and Nashville's television stations were filing two reports daily to parent networks.

"There are going to be lots of memories when we go back to auditoriums where we have been with them," said Minnie Pearl at the time. "We have had so many laughs together."

The Nashville office of Western Union was clogged with telegrams from across the nation as well as from Europe, Africa, and Australia.

Tennessee Governor Frank G. Clement said the entertainment world "suffers a great professional loss and Tennessee suffers a great personal loss. They were typical of the serious-minded, hard-working professional people dedicated to country music artistry."

The *Nashville Tennessean* published a list of eulogies from luminaries to the fallen greats. About sixteen hours after the bodies were discovered, I went on the air at WSM.

I had had Cowboy Copas on my Friday night show. He had brought his new record along but didn't have time to stay. I played the song and mentioned that "Cope" would return on Monday night. I did my next show looking at an empty seat, the seat where he would have been.

I had interacted with all of their ghosts countless times. Alone in the semi-dark studio, playing hymns and their records, the weight of my grief was suffocating. I asked my listeners not to call me with song requests. All the while, I felt I had to say something conciliatory to my listeners. My shift that night was the hardest seven hours I ever worked.

I sat there listening to Hawkins' resonant records and thought about his delight in auto racing. He and my best friend in the business, Marty Robbins, used to race midgets, and I smiled as I recalled the tall and lanky Hawkins trying to fit his angular frame into the tiny confines of the pint-sized cans of metal and rubber. Marty went to Hawk's funeral, the only one I ever saw him attend. We talked afterwards about the last time I had seen them compete on an oval track inside a fairgrounds building. Exhaust accumulation made breathing virtually impossible.

I have thought about Patsy Cline a thousand times since her death. Nashville has produced few female stars of her magnitude, and it has never produced a comparable legend.

I have recoiled at my own observations of inaccuracies in *Sweet Dreams*. The movie, for example, indicated Ms. Cline's plane crashed into a mountain when, in fact, there are no mountains in western Tennessee.

I rejoiced in the summer of 1991 when MCA Records released a collection of Patsy Cline hits, recorded a quarter century earlier, that sold 3.5 million copies. On April 10, 1993, the record was number-one on *Billboard*'s Top Catalog Albums Chart. It had been released 99 weeks earlier.

The woman, even in death, has unsurpassed longevity.

I remember vividly the spirit of sadness that gripped the capacity crowd at her memorial service. Her casket was closed. Relatives and friends of others in the fatal crash were on hand, and the service was a ceremony of mutual consolation. Almost everyone there had lost someone in the fallen plane.

Mourners were standing on the funeral home lawn, about to enter the service, when rumors swept through the gathering about Jack Anglin. Jack, along with Kitty Wells' husband, Johnny Wright, comprised a successful 1950s Nashville duo, Johnny and Jack. The rumor turned to fact.

Jack had been killed in a car wreck while en route to Patsy's funeral. "Wreck Claims Fifth Opry Member," the front-page headline read in the March 8, 1963, *Nashville Tennessean*. The newspaper carried a photograph of Anglin's crumpled car along with the caption, "Anglin was the fifth Opry personality killed in three days."

The following Saturday night, the entire Opry cast assembled en masse, and a capacity crowd rose to its feet inside the

Ryman Auditorium. The Opry manager, Ott Devine, delivered a tribute.

"They would want us to keep smiling," he said. "Let's continue in the tradition of the Grand Ole Opry."

The Jordanaires were joined on stage by every member of the Opry and the ensemble sang "How Great Thou Art." The rendition met with thunderous applause, then deafening silence.

Roy Acuff and his Smokey Mountain Boys virtually ran onto the stage and broke into a rousing fiddle number. The Opry, now missing some who had helped build it, was back underway. It has been on schedule ever since.

Country stars, with good intentions, have traditionally recorded songs about the unexpected deaths of their peers. I think of all the tribute ballads devoted to Hank Williams and Jimmie Rodgers. Word went out from the Opry, however, that no one record such a number about anyone who died in 1963. Disc jockeys were also asked not to play these kinds of records. The Opry wanted to avoid any hint of commercialism attached to the deaths.

"How much more can we take?" was the underlying question among the mourners at Patsy's memorial service. We spent the rest of that week burying our dead. We spent a year in mourning, then answered that question the following summer.

On July 31, 1964, I was working the All-Night Show, and sketchy reports kept coming in from fans and officials about a missing plane whose pilot was thought to be Jim Reeves. The first reports, however, only said that a plane was down and the pilot was a famous entertainer.

The ambiguous dispatches were daggers in my heart. I didn't know what to think, or who might have been in the crash. The reporting was intended to spare grief until the identification had been confirmed. But it was cruel nonetheless to the loved ones of all the country entertainers who were flying.

I heard from Jim Ed Brown and his sisters, Bonnie and Maxine, who made up the immensely successful "Browns," a trio on RCA Records. They suspected that the missing pilot was Jim

Reeves, although I had no other information to substantiate that. Soon, their inclinations would be proven correct.

Eventually, there was a confirmed report and I read it on the air, and the switchboard lit up. Once again, the most loyal fans in the world were hysterical about one of their missing.

I got a call from a friend of Mary Reeves, now Jim's widow.

"Stop saying that Jim Reeves is missing," she snapped.

"I'm sorry that Mary is upset," I replied. "We have been getting these reports and I thought they were important."

"I don't care about your job," she said. "You're upsetting Mary."

That call hurt. I was fond of Mary Reeves. But I was an anchor man in an on-going news story that had shocked the nation. So I relayed the information to radio listeners as I received it. (On April 5, 1993, I asked Mary Reeves if she could remember what she was doing when she was told Reeves' plane was missing. She said she could but declined to tell me, as discussing it twenty-nine years after the fact was still painful.)

The next two days were wrenching. Jim Reeves' plane was missing, but nowhere to be found. He, and his passenger, Dean Manuel, Reeves' pianist, had simply fallen out of the sky, disappearing from a radar screen at 4:55 P.M. somewhere over Nashville's Radnor Lake, west of Franklin Road.

A Nashville air traffic controller told the Civil Aeronautics Board that he had asked Reeves, via radio, if he was clear of the turbulence on his approach to the Nashville Airport.

Reeves said, "Negat——"

At that instant, the airplane disappeared from the radar scope. No one but Dean Manuel ever heard the live voice of Jim Reeves again.

Days later, Marty Robbins told me that he had been washing his hair during a turbulent thunderstorm. The act was one of his idiosyncrasies. He said rain water made his hair soft.

"I was standing in that downpour with lather on my head and I heard an airplane up above," he said. "What silly son of a bitch is flying in this weather?"

A C.A.B. report would put Reeves' time of death at about

the same time Marty heard the plane fly over his Brentwood home.

Marty, Eddy Arnold, myself and numerous others participated in the strenuous search. One-hundred-degree temperatures aren't uncommon in Nashville in August, and we were scaling the steep, snake-infested hills around Brentwood, Tennessee, looking for what we dreaded to find. In that heat, the bodies would be decomposing fast.

For forty-four non-stop hours we hunted for Reeves and Manuel by sunlight and with flashlights. The glare from helicopter searchlights illuminated the sweat-streaked and exhausted faces of the late-night searchers. I wrestled through underbrush until sundown, then hurried home for a shower and a race to the station to man telephones during the All-Night Show.

There is a waning tradition in the South of sitting up all night with mourners in the wake of a death. I found that to be true even when death is only suspected. Many Opry stars sat silently in my studio during those high-stress nights while Reeves' plane was missing. They didn't talk much, not even when music was played, and there was no danger of voices going over the air.

Doing the show became a quandary for me. On the one hand, I was feeling very somber, and wanted to be respectful of the missing and their families. On the other hand, I had a responsibility to entertain.

The Tennessee Army National Guard and the Davidson County Civil Defense Rescue Team were brought into the search on the third day. Searchers were moved to the east side of Radnor Lake, and the dense and tangled foliage was combed grid by grid. From my car I was monitoring the movement of hundreds of other volunteer searchers via radio. But I was privy only to the public coverage that was non-stop. Then the music was interrupted and a bulletin was flashed. The tangled metal that had been Reeves' plane was found. In the twisted maze were unidentifiable body parts. The only identifiable extremity was a finger bearing a giant diamond ring. Reeves' ring. This ring can be seen today at the Jim Reeves Museum in Nashville.

His plane had flown full speed into a treetop, and experts guessed Reeves had a bout of vertigo. He had been thrown from the aircraft and the whirling propeller had sliced him apart. Body fragments clung high in the tree next to the mangled fuselage. The wreckage was found by Bob Newton, a county rescue team member. Twenty square miles were combed by 2,000 searchers, 100 of whom were on horseback.

Scorched metal indicated a fire in the cockpit. The plane probably was struck by lightning.

Ms. Jackson told me in 1993 that Reeves had a phobic fear of flying. She said he had taken flying lessons, and had become a pilot, in an attempt to overcome that fear.

I didn't attend Reeves' funeral because the Tennessee National Guard flew his body to Carthage, Texas, his home and final resting place.

I attended a memorial service for the thirty-nine-year-old Reeves and Manuel at Nashville's Phillips-Robinson Funeral Home. At the service I met Bill Walker, a European orchestra leader whom Reeves had hired while touring overseas. Walker moved to the United States, arriving the day of the memorial service for the man for whom he had come to work.

Walker, after graduating from Sydney University in Australia, had been hired by RCA International. Part of his job was to make the RCA studio orchestra in Australia available to visiting RCA artists, such as Reeves. Walker also wound up writing the score for a Reeves movie and conducted the orchestra on a Reeves European tour.

"He worked on me for about six months to join him here in Nashville," Walker said.

En route to Nashville, Walker stopped in New York City to see a production of *The Sound of Music.*

"Steve Sholes, who was head of the country division of RCA then, he got me tickets, so I went and saw the show that night, and when I came out Steve was waiting for me to tell me that Jim's plane was missing," Walker told me. "Then I went on down to Nashville to see what's happening, and that's where it went from there.

"Upon my arrival, I was told by Chet Atkins that Jim Reeves was dead," Walker said.

Walker arrived in the United States with nothing. Due to contacts with RCA executives and studio musicians, such as Chet Atkins and Floyd Cramer, he eventually did studio work, and evolved into one of the city's most sought-after orchestra leaders. He eventually would lead the orchestra on Johnny Cash's network television show in the late 1960s and early 1970s, and today is orchestra leader for the "Statler Brothers Show" on The Nashville Network, the most popular variety show on television.

Reeves' memorial service was dotted with some of country's biggest luminaries of the day, including Eddy Arnold, Chet Atkins, Red Foley, Skeeter Davis, Floyd Cramer, Ferlin Husky, Webb Pierce, Dottie West, the Jordanaires, and many others. But, despite all the talent, not one note was sung. Recorded music was played and relayed by speakers posted in trees for the overflow crowd on the lawn. I guessed that no one sang or played because no one felt he could.

In September 1992, while doing research, I came across a letter written to Trudy Stamper, the former director of public relations for WSM and the Grand Ole Opry. The letter's author had intended it to be a condolence for the survivors of Patsy Cline, Hawkshaw Hawkins, Cowboy Copas, and Randy Hughes. The author knew that Trudy would make copies and send them to radio stations across the nation.

It read, in part, "I trust everyone is returning to normal after the terrible tragedy. I cannot, for the life of me, understand why such dear human beings and such needed and loved ones have to be taken away, and especially in such a tragic way. I'm sure their families will just never recover from this, and there is left a void in our facet of life that will never, never be filled." The letter was signed, "Sincerely, Jim Reeves."

In the spring of 1993, Mary Reeves told me that she was "investigated" by a newspaper in the Republic of Sri Lanka, an island in the Indian Ocean off the southeast coast of India. The journalistic probe came about fifteen years after Reeves' death. RCA was continuing to release songs from its backlog of Reeves recordings, and some residents of the island were convinced the singer was still alive.

A Sri Lanka newspaper ran a front-page story, Mary told me, claiming that Reeves lived in an insane asylum, where he had been committed by his unsympathetic wife. It went on to say that Mary only let him out of the institution to record new songs, then returned him to incarceration, she told me.

"Is Jim Reeves Really Dead?" Mary said a headline screamed.

Reeves' single records were released as late as 1984, and in 1981 a "duet" was released with Reeves and Patsy Cline. Master producer Owen Bradley took each of their recordings of the same song and electronically blended them. The result was a hit version of the standard "Have You Ever Been Lonely?"

I asked Mary if she felt that recording lent fuel to the flames of rumors about Reeves' being alive.

"In some parts of the world, they'll never let him die," she said.

"In some hearts," I thought, "they never will either."

On March 16, 1991, another plane crash occurred that caused the country music family to grieve once again. This crash took the lives of Reba McEntire's seven band members and tour manager. Those deaths were suffered by non-celebrity musicians, those who make the music on the front lines and help make the stars what they are. Almost everybody in the doomed band had played in other Nashville bands. Those eight people, therefore, were known by hundreds of other musicians who dot Nashville's spectacular Music Row.

One could physically feel the collective grief along the row as well as the foreboding realization among the living, touring musicians who thought that any one of them could have been on that plane. Each had jetted through darkness to still another show hundreds of times. There is no telling how many millions of miles Nashville entertainers ride and fly annually. Life hangs gingerly in the balance, dependent on tires that don't blow out at highway speed, or planes that don't go down in foul weather.

Flying conditions were nearly perfect at 1:40 A.M. south of San

Diego, just a mile north of Mexico. Subsequent investigations by the Federal Aviation Administration were inconclusive until the week of September 13, 1992, when the FAA officially attributed the crash to pilot error. As the plane was ascending, it failed to climb high enough to clear a mountain top. It was turning, and while flying slightly on its side, one of its wings clipped the mountain. It cartwheeled at 200 miles per hour and slammed into the earth. The passengers were engulfed in a ball of flame, and mercifully died instantly.

That did little to lessen Nashville's grief.

"I cried all morning," said country star Kathy Mattea, in a copyrighted interview hours after the crash with *The Tennessean*. "It's all of our worst nightmares come true. We think about it every time we fly. Your band is absolutely like family."

Reba was not in the aircraft because her husband, Narvel Blackstock, had persuaded her to stay in San Diego, where she and the band had performed only hours before the accident. She was not feeling well, and he said she should get a good night's sleep, then fly the next day to meet the band for a show in Ft. Wayne, Indiana. She did not sing publicly for five weeks, then dedicated one song to her fallen friends on the Academy Awards Show.

She resumed a full touring schedule the following July.

Reba personally organized a Memorial Service at Christ Church in nearby Brentwood, Tennessee. She asked Johnny Cash to speak. He did so after the recent death of his mother. He told me that closing his mother's coffin was the hardest thing he ever did, and he felt emotionally ill-equipped to deliver eulogies so soon after his own loss.

But his baritone resonance rang its comfort through the sanctuary whose mourners overflowed into the parking lot. Outside, reporters hungry for news were contained by police from the crowd in space across the street. Photographers used zoom lenses to try to photograph from fifty yards the faces of the brokenhearted as they walked sobbing from the church.

Jennifer Bohler, Reba's publicist, said her office was inundated with requests to help from members of Nashville's music community. One of the most conspicuous gestures of outpouring came from C. K. Spurlock, Kenny Rogers' agent. He organized a massive benefit show whose proceeds went to the families of the fallen. He paid for all production expenses himself, and the library of stellar talent performed free of charge.

I was the master of ceremonies for the sold-out crowd inside Nashville's Municipal Auditorium. "Nashville Now" sent "Star-Catcher," its remote interviewing service, to the show. Each act was asked to do no more than fifteen minutes. Many canceled paying engagements elsewhere and paid their bands salaries and transportation expenses to perform on a show that raised $100,000 that was divided among the survivors.

Entertainers on the program included T. Graham Brown, Ricky Van Shelton, Patty Loveless, Gary Morris, Eddie Rabbitt, K. T. Oslin, Willie Nelson, Exile, the Oak Ridge Boys, and Kenny Rogers.

Reba said she was not sure she would attend the show but showed up unexpectedly and sang an a cappella rendition of "Sweet Dreams," the giant hit by Patsy Cline. Ironically, Reba had closed her San Diego show with that same song. It was the last her band ever heard her sing.

I've never felt the presence of mass emotion more than I did as Reba's solitary voice consumed the sprawling hall filled with the bereaved. The last note echoed into stillness, then there was silence, save for the sounds of muffled crying throughout the hall. When the crowd left the arena, you could hear the shuffling of feet against the concrete floor. There was no talking, just the unspoken agreement among all on hand that music is a sweet but unsatisfying solace during the traumatic interlude in this fragile and temporary thing called life.

Grief is felt, not measured. It would be pompous to suggest that people today wouldn't hurt as much as those who ached when seven players on the Grand Ole Opry were taken by death in sixteen months. But back then in our business, everybody mourned the fallen. Today, with its outrageously rapid expansion, it's foremostly a business, and few people know each other well. Everybody in the business knew somebody in Reba's band. There was a time when everybody would have known everybody. And, it seems to me, contemporary artists who might feel pain won't take time to express it. I can think of a famous quartet that didn't attend the funeral for the manager who built its career. I'm also thinking of a popular vocalist who didn't go to his father's funeral because he had to shoot a video that day. The absenteeism at the funerals for Dottie West, the talent manager Dick Blake, Keith Whitley, and others was obvious and sad.

The 1991 Country Music Association's annual awards show aired only weeks after Dottie's death, but not one member spoke her name. President George Bush, as the ceremony closed, mentioned her in one fleeting sentence. The CMA oversight was unintentional. Someone just didn't think, and therein the tragedy lies. The absence of even a token tribute set off letters of grievance that were published in Nashville's morning and afternoon newspapers.

The bigger-than-ever country music industry has not grown without a price. Music mindful of humanity has given birth to an industry that often is not.

Bigger is not always better.

SEVEN

I am a fan of the Los Angeles Dodgers.

I love professional baseball and never cease to be amazed at how refined its play and promotion have become. Months are spent on the ramifications of modifying the infield-fly rule, or changing the formula in the lineament applied to an outfielder's glove from one climate to another. Players have lawyers, who have lawyers. Owners have legal staffs.

Yet somewhere among the innovations in America's favorite pastime, baseball's businessmen sometimes overlook the obvious: The game is essentially hitting, catching, and throwing. Failure to develop the fundamentals to their maximum before focusing on fine-tuning is futile. It's like applying a better bandage to a cancer.

A similar analogy can be made in country music. Once the anthem of barn dances, the music is now sung in hallowed halls for kings and queens. Promoters focus on bolstering the industry through increased television exposure, more motion pictures, commercial endorsements, and political affiliations.

At the core of all of this, however, the movers and shakers often overlook the task of improving the time-honored, indisputable heart of the industry: the song.

It doesn't matter how sophisticated the marketing if the product is inferior. I hear a lot of hit songs today. I hear few that I'll hear five years from now. The magnitude of the country music industry has bred a love affair with hit songs whose popularity rises fast but falls faster.

Among my most cherished memories are the tales of how some of the great hits became standards. Country music is often, simply, stories set to music. Here are a few stories behind the stories.

In 1980, the singer and songwriter Mel Tillis appeared on my radio show in the wake of a giant song he had written for Kenny Rogers and the First Edition called "Ruby, Don't Take Your Love to Town." The tune was inspired by an experience Mel had at the age of thirteen, when he lived in his native Pahokee, Florida.

Young Tillis was discovering firsthand the mysteries of life through the wide eyes of a boy whose body was changing. He thought a lot about the romance he had not yet experienced. He observed the older boys and young men who had the opportunity to do regularly what he yearned to do for the first time.

A young couple moved into a house behind the Tillis household. "It was," he recalled vividly, "across Cat Alley, next to Pool's Grocery and Miss Chandler's Chicken Farm."

Tillis timidly befriended the couple, but he was nonetheless wary. At night, when he lay before the open-window darkness, he heard the orchestra of Florida's insects, tarnished by the couple's bickering. They fought, Tillis told me, long, loud, and hard.

He no doubt wished that the objects of his new affection felt similarly about each other.

As Tillis' relationship with the couple deepened, he learned they had met while the man was recovering from a World War II wound in England. He was brought there from Germany, where the woman had been his nurse.

Eventually, he took her as his bride, and took her to the United States, where the injury flared up again. Surgeons tried an experimental "spinal tap" intended to modify the man's central nervous system.

It did. He was left paralyzed for life.

"It's hard to love a man whose legs are bent and paralyzed. And the wants and needs of a woman your age, Ruby, I realize." So goes Tillis' lyric.

The inquisitive Tillis eventually surmised that much of the couple's fighting had to do with the man's inability to perform sexually. The woman left the crippled man alone at night when she went to town, presumably to seek other men.

Tillis wrote about the woman's prolonged grooming, torturous to the man's crying eyes.

"You've painted up your lips and rolled and curled your tinted hair. Ruby, are you contemplating going out somewhere?"

In the song, Ruby never answers the question. In real life, she didn't live to do so.

Tillis never told me whether he actually heard the gunfire that took the life of Ruby, whose first name Tillis changed. In an effort to make the song commercial, Tillis also changed the song's reference to war to the Vietnam Conflict.

The real husband killed her, then killed himself. Twenty years later, their story was heard blaring from car radios that passed their graves. And millions bought Tillis' composition of "Ruby, Don't Take Your Love to Town."

Johnny Cash, in 1955, went to Sun Records producer Sam Phillips in an effort to get a recording contract. Then he went back. Again, and again. After the sixth attempt, Phillips gave Cash an audience simply to get rid of him, Cash figured.

Cash, who would go on to sell millions of records about prisons, drugs, killings, and the like, initially presented himself to Phillips as a gospel singer. The first song Johnny Cash ever pitched was entitled "Belshazzar," and had to do with the Old Testament king.

Phillips told Cash that the song was better than another tune Cash had with him that day entitled "Folsom Prison Blues." The latter became the second-biggest record Cash ever had.

The two rocked along through Cash's recording infancy, with Cash often acquiescing merely to retain the shaky recording agreement he had fought so hard to obtain.

Not long afterwards, Phillips produced another new song with Cash called "I Walk the Line." The title was suggested by Carl Perkins after Cash played it for him. Cash wrote the song when he was in the Air Force.

While Cash was on one of his first concert tours he heard "I Walk the Line" on the radio.

"I thought it was awful," Cash said. "I called Phillips and told him to please not release any more recordings of that song."

Thirty-five years and a thousand recordings later, "I Walk the Line" remains Cash's biggest hit. And Cash never again called Phillips to tell him he was wrong about a song.

Singer-songwriter Rodney Crowell began dating Rosanne Cash, John's singer-songwriting daughter.

Rodney and Rosanne had been living together and eventually were married, but not before Rodney went to visit the man who would become his father-in-law.

Rodney was, in fact, summoned by John, because John had heard that Rodney was sleeping with his daughter. When Rodney arrived at John's Jamaican estate, he assumed he would share Rosanne's bed, but instead, he overheard Rosanne crying. She had been made quite aware that her daddy didn't want her boyfriend sleeping with her. An irate and bellicose Cash called Rodney in and told him he could not sleep with Rosanne under the Cash roof.

Rodney, young and impetuous, told Cash that to do otherwise would by hypocritical. He said he slept with Rosanne elsewhere, and intended to sleep with her here.

"Son," Cash said, whose mammoth frame towered above Rodney's, "I don't know you well enough to miss you when you're gone."

Rodney was gone from the bed of Rosanne Cash until he walked her down a matrimonial aisle. And he eventually wrote and produced some of the biggest songs ever recorded by Johnny Cash.

The songwriter Mickey Newbury refuses to collaborate with other writers. To do so, he said, would mean to write on command, and he can only write when inspiration moves him. It doesn't move him often, as he only writes two months a year, he told me.

In 1968 he was moved not to write but to arrange. He did this spontaneously on stage before hundreds of people, many of them celebrities.

Newbury was performing at the opening of the Bitter End West, a trendy nightclub and listening hall in Los Angeles. He decided to sing the South's Civil War marching anthem, "Dixie," after he failed to persuade Joan Baez, also on the program, to do the number. When the club's owner discovered his plan, he told him he couldn't because the song might agitate the anti-war sentiment that was sweeping the nation during the Vietnam War.

A defiant Newbury introduced "Dixie" anyway by saying that he was going to do a song that had been banned in Georgia. Since the First Amendment had not been repealed, and freedom of speech was exercised heartily during pro- and anti-war rallies, who banned the song, and on whose authority, I wondered?

So I called my friend Zel Miller, Governor of Georgia. I told the Governor what Newbury had said.

"Ralph," Miller said, " 'Dixie' hasn't been banned in the state of Georgia."

He said the only thing of which he was aware that even remotely resembled Newbury's claim of a ban was the song's removal from the repertoire by the Georgia Red Coat Band, a pep band at the University of Georgia. Miller said he had no idea why the university band no longer played "Dixie."

"I want to do a song President Lincoln requested on the steps of the White House," Newbury told his west coast audience.

He eased into the lyrics, "Oh I wish I was in the land of cotton . . ." and a woman in the back jumped up and began to clap along, in march time, having no idea Newbury was going to sing the selection at ballad tempo.

Newbury said at first there were snickers, but they yielded to silence as he continued to sing. Then he sensed electricity in the room.

His wife was sitting in the front row next to the singer Odetta, who began to weep.

"I was moved that she, being black, would understand what I was doing," he told me.

So Newbury, without premeditation, then went "right into what I could remember of the 'Battle Hymn of the Republic.' " At the conclusion, Newbury's mind flooded with the memory of Harry Belafonte's version of "All My Trials," a Negro spiritual written by a Jamaican slave. Again, without hesitation, he sang this song as well.

Newbury changed only the tempos, not the lyrics, of the songs. At the conclusion of this spontaneous composition, the place erupted into applause.

Newbury subsequently recorded the songs and called them "The American Trilogy."

He was called a Communist and racist for his efforts.

"I got hate letters from the left and the right, but the 'Trilogy' was performed at both the Democratic and Republican conventions by Andy Williams and Wayne Newton respectively."

Newbury's recorded version was a hit, but the song's popularity skyrocketed after it was recorded on a live album by Elvis Presley, and incorporated into one of his television specials.

The Newbury recital marked the only time in my recollection when someone took others' songs and blended them before others to shape his own hit record.

Hardly a year passes in Nashville without one songwriter suing another for plagiarism. I think most of those who are charged are innocent. Songwriters hear so much music their minds become saturated with notes and combinations. Who can help subconsciously assembling something they heard consciously a long time ago?

A more comprehensible case came to light with "Duelin' Banjos," one of the most famous instrumental songs ever to emerge in country music. The song became the sound track for *Deliverance,* the blockbuster motion picture starring Burt Reynolds.

The melody was born in the mind of Arthur "Guitar Boogie" Smith. He performed it as a part of his stage act with Don Reno. Smith played the guitar part, and Reno, as if retaliating, tried to upstage Smith's guitar with a banjo riff. Smith put the arrangement on a 78 rpm record in 1955.

A copy of the record became a gift to Eric Weissberg, Smith told me. Weissberg performed the song in *Deliverance*. Smith saw the movie, heard the song, and felt like the victim of theft.

He called a lawyer for Warner Brothers, the producers of *Deliverance,* and told him he wanted compensation for performance rights from the movie and subsequent airplay. He also wanted the publishing rights to the song that Warner Brothers had allegedly stolen from him. The attorney was unreceptive, so Smith threatened to sue.

He was told by the lawyer that such a lawsuit would only be a nuisance.

"You have neither the time nor the money to sue Warner Brothers," the lawyer told him.

"I've got the time, and I'll get the money," Smith retorted.

Witnesses were subpoenaed and testimony was heard intermittently for fourteen months. Weissberg reportedly even brought his old 78 recording to court.

Arthur "Guitar Boogie" Smith, who wrote a tune for a 1950s stage act, spent $125,000 of borrowed money to retain ownership of his creation.

A judge and jury agreed he was right.

Smith has never told me how much he was awarded in damages, although informed sources tell me it was $7 million.

Ironically, one of the depositions was filed by a Warner Brothers executive who said he didn't pay much attention to copyright infringement of the song. He said he didn't think it or the motion picture would ever become popular.

Good songwriters can innately recognize good songs, no matter who wrote them. I've heard writers express more excitement about new songs they've heard than about the new songs they've written.

Johnny Cash told me about a number of songs he heard in his living room during a "guitar pulling," an informal gathering of songwriters who pull the guitar from each other to perform their new tunes. They had earlier eaten dinner at Cash's house.

In the space of one evening in 1968, Cash heard Kris Kristofferson premiere "Bobby McGee," Joni Mitchell debut "Both Sides Now," Shell Silverstein introduce "A Boy Named Sue," and Bob Dylan present "Lay Lady Lay."

Cash left the next day to record a concert live for an album inside San Quentin prison. His wife, June, suggested that Cash take with him the words to the song he'd liked so much, "A Boy Named Sue."

"No," Cash told her, "I don't want to. There is no way I could record it, I don't even know the song."

June, nonetheless, insisted that Cash grab the lyrics.

Cash arrived in San Quentin and walked on stage to a mob of hysterical prisoners. He sang a new song he had written about prison injustice called the "Ballad of San Quentin." The men became overwrought and demanded that he sing it again, because they identified so intensely with the lyrics. After Cash's second rendition, the prisoners jumped on top of the tables. They cheered endlessly and deafeningly. Cash told me he thinks he could have incited the men to riot with only a word of encouragement.

During the chaos, the words to "A Boy Named Sue" inexplicably popped into his mind. The more the men cheered, the more Cash thought about that satirical verse.

He impulsively snatched the lyrics from his guitar case, asked his guitarists, Bob Wootten and Carl Perkins, to begin the number, and he read the song aloud as the tape recorder rolled. This spontaneous recording of a song Cash was not familiar with became his greatest hit of 1969.

Had his wife not demanded he take the song with him to the concert, or had Silverstein defaulted on the previous night's dinner date, Cash might not have ever recorded one of the biggest novelty numbers in country music history.

Kris Kristofferson was once asked which of his compositions were his best.

"The ones where I just held the pen," he said, meaning that the inspiration was so overwhelming that the song just wrote itself.

Marty Robbins told me about a moment of inspiration that was, he said, as intense as spontaneous combustion. And, combined with a bit of extrasensory perception, it made for one of the eeriest experiences I ever heard about that resulted in a hit record.

Marty used to drive from Nashville to Phoenix each year for Christmas. At one point on the road he saw the lights of El Paso, Texas, and thought he would like to write a song about that city. He had no idea for a theme or story line and dismissed the thought until the following year during the same week at the same place on his Christmas sojourn.

Again, the thought went out of his mind and he drove through El Paso, and spent Christmas in Phoenix.

The next year, he had the same compulsion in precisely the same circumstances. He told me he interpreted the urge as a sign, and began to recite out loud,

> "Out in the West Texas town of El Paso,
> I fell in love with a Mexican girl"

The song is one of those stories set to music. It has a beginning, middle, and end, and more lyrics than any other song Robbins ever recorded. Yet he never stopped driving and he never made one note. He wrote and committed the song to memory simultaneously.

Shortly afterwards, he recorded it, and "El Paso" became the biggest hit he ever had.

It's no secret that Merle Haggard served time in prison. He was released in 1961 in California and a short time later began pursuing his music career in earnest. This was long before he started piling up his forty-one number-one records.

Haggard, who I think is the best overall singer-songwriter in the annals of country music, told me about walking restlessly up and down the California streets where sunlight, conspicuously absent behind prison walls, fell on his guilt. He just knew that everyone was aware he was a convicted felon who had done time.

"So I went through the ninety-day period after I got out where you don't feel right."

I didn't know what he meant.

The ninety-day period, Haggard told me, is the slang convicts use to explain the amount of time required to feel acclimated outside after being inside prison walls.

"A convict's life is still in prison," Haggard said, "but he's no longer there."

Haggard said he underwent extreme paranoia about simple things such as his haircut, and shoes crafted from paper that were made in prison. And all the people he had known on the outside before his incarceration were absent, taken by divorces and deaths.

Haggard, a proud man, felt his disorientation increase because he was depending on his brother for financial support. The kid who had always managed to earn his own way, through means as varied as picking cotton to stealing, was now society's stepchild.

So he wrote and sang about his experiences, and "Branded Man" became one of country music's biggest hits about prison life.

> *"I'd like to hold my head up, and be proud of who I am*
> *But they won't let my story go untold.*
> *I paid the debt I owed 'em*
> *But they're still not satisfied,*
> *Now I'm a branded man out in the cold."*

■

"It was the hardest thing I ever did in my life," Mac Davis said, referring to a segment on his old network television show where he wrote songs on the spot. He would ask a member of his studio audience at random to give him an idea. Then, before millions of people, he would instantly pen a tune about it.

Davis wore a silk shirt each time he performed that segment, which had to be thrown away afterwards because his sweat ruined it.

"People remember that part of that show more than anything else about my career," Mac told me. "To this day they walk up to me and they say two things: Didn't you used to be Mac Davis? and, Did you really make up those songs that quickly?"

The first night Mac introduced his impromptu songwriting skills, he received an idea from a thirteen-year-old girl. She wanted Mac to write a song about "pink polka dots on my nose."

> "Pink polka dots on my nose, on my chin a great big freckle. They may not make my daddy mad, but a hickie on my neck will."

Not exactly Shakespeare.

Mac fell into mild controversy in 1974 during the heat of the women's liberation movement.

"Each libber who came to my show looked like Helen Reddy in a Green Beret outfit," Mac said. One militant liberationist demanded that he write an impromptu song about burning a brassiere.

> "My girlfriend burned her bra today
> It really was a shame,
> Cause she ain't exactly Dolly Parton
> That sucker hardly made a flame."

Mac received a mountain of angry mail over that one.

Mac was born and reared in Lubbock, Texas, where he spent his childhood with a black youngster as his best friend. The friend became an inspiration for Mac's more serious song writing. Mac and his pal often played in a Lubbock suburb, "Queen City," where poverty prevailed, and Mac was always glad to leave the place at day's end, and wondered about the welfare of his buddy, who had to spend his nights in that dungeon. Even as a lad, Mac saw the futility of poverty and realized that people who lived there were so void of opportunity, they very likely could never leave.

So, when he was grown, Mac wrote "In the Ghetto," which Mac, Elvis Presley, and others made into a giant hit.

> *"As the snow flies, on a cold and gray Chicago morn,*
> *Another little baby child is born, in the ghetto."*

Mac tells a compelling story about his early days in songwriting when he owned a music publishing company with Nancy Sinatra. Nancy told Mac how she left notes for her husband under his pillow that read, "Whoever finds this, I love you."

Mac started thinking about a song involving an orphan girl who left notes like that around town, hoping a reader would adopt her. Mac worked up a rough draft and played it for a friend.

"Wait a minute," the friend said. "Is this 'Whoever Finds This I Love You'?"

"Yeah," Mac replied. "How did you know?"

His friend told Mac the song had been written twenty-five years earlier and offered to show Mac the original version.

"I don't want to see it," Mac replied, "I don't want to be accused of stealing a song. I'll write my own version."

Shortly afterwards, Mac ran into Joe Nixon, another friend for whom he sang the rough draft.

Nixon asked Mac if the song was called "Whoever Finds This I Love You."

"How did you know?" Mac had to ask again.

"I've been trying to write that song for twenty-five years,"

Nixon said. "The story was in *Reader's Digest* twenty-five years ago."

That story, published when Mac was only three and which he had never read, was the real life story of what Mac had fictionalized.

Mac interpreted the scenario as a sign that he was meant to write the song, and he did.

"Whoever Finds This I Love You" became a big, big hit for him.

Some songs are written from inspiration, some are written from personal experiences, and a few are written on assignment. The song-writing business is just that, a business, where many writers report to work at a certain time, leave at a certain time, and are expected to pen a certain number of tunes in the interim.

It wasn't done that way until the 1970s, when music publishers faced increased demands for material from record companies and singers and began to ask for an increase in output from their staff songwriters.

Eddie Rabbitt was given one assignment along with the writers Even Stevens and David Malloy.

"We were called by Steve Wax, the president of Elektra Records, who said he was making a sound track for the movie *Roadie,* and he asked if we had any songs," Rabbitt told me.

Rabbitt told Steve he had no tunes, but asked what kind of song he was looking for.

"I want a song about driving," Rabbitt was told.

"Driving what?" Rabbitt asked.

"I don't want you to say," Wax replied.

"Driving to where?" Rabbitt asked.

"I don't want you to say that either," Wax said.

"Okay," Rabbitt said, "you want a song about a guy who drives nothing and goes nowhere."

So, while working on other songs in an attic on Nashville's famous 16th Avenue South, Rabbitt and his co-writers dabbled with the tune about driving. They didn't take it too seriously.

"Midnight, headlight, blind you on a rainy night
Steep grade, up ahead, making time . . ."

Rabbitt went to Colorado to record his new album and included the new, experimental tune. He loved the way it came out.

"I called Steve Wax and told him he could have the song for *Roadie,* but only if I could have it for my album too," Rabbitt said.

Steve Wax consented, and the song became a number-one country song, and a top-five pop song for Eddie Rabbitt, entitled "Driving My Life Away."

And Rabbitt, to this day, has not seen *Roadie.*

Willie Nelson has lived all over Texas and lives there today, as much as anyplace else. If you ask Willie where he resides, he usually answers, "Holiday Inns."

While living in Ft. Worth, Texas, years ago, Willie regularly saw a guy hanging around a street corner. The man had no legs but sat atop a platform on roller skates.

Willie watched him for years and observed how relentless the fellow was while hawking his wares, wrapping paper, pencils, and the like. The guy held forth in his part of the world, that street corner, in the face of a Texas Blue Northern snowstorm or a blistering July heat wave. And about the man Willie wrote:

"Pretty paper, pretty ribbons of blue,
Wrap your presents, to your darlin' from you
Pretty pencils to write 'I Love You,'
Oh, pretty paper, pretty ribbon of blue."

"Pretty Paper" ranks with "Blue Christmas" as one of the most requested contemporary Christmas songs on radio.

■

A song that ranks with "White Christmas" or "Jingle Bells" as one of the most popular Christmas recordings of all time is "Rudolph the Red-Nosed Reindeer." The song, written by Johnny Marks, will be forty-four years old in December 1993.

I last spoke to Marks in 1969 when 350 versions of the song had been recorded. At the time, more than 57 million copies had been sold in the United States, and 29 million overseas. Those figures have probably been increased by one-third.

Marks first wrote the song in 1948 after having pondered the idea for four years while serving in the United States Army. He decided his creation was the worst song ever written and discarded it. A year later he wrote the version that we know today.

He said the tune simply "came to" him while he was walking down the street in Greenwich Village near his home in New York City.

Marks and some people at Columbia each sent the new song to cowboy star Gene Autry. Autry played the song and promptly decided it wasn't for him. The legendary movie star had recorded big western songs, including "Tumbling Tumble Weeds" and "South of the Border." Autry reportedly told Marks that he didn't think "Rudolph the Red-Nosed Reindeer" went with his cowboy image.

Autry's wife disagreed and was responsible for his having the hit in a way similar to the way June Carter was responsible for Johnny Cash's having a hit on "A Boy Named Sue."

Mrs. Autry demanded that her husband record the song. She let him select one side of his forthcoming record, but she wanted "Rudolph" to be on the back side. The Christmas ditty was intended to be filler, not a hit.

Two weeks later, before the invention of television and its entertainment promotion, the song had sold a million copies. The year I last saw Marks, the NBC television network had produced an entire Christmas special around the song.

Marks has written many other types of songs. But, he told me, he can walk into any music publishing house and get a serious listen for anything he writes having to do with Christmas. In 1960, for example, Marks took twenty-five new songs to Decca

Records. Each song but one was turned down. Decca went for that one simply because it was a Christmas tune written by Marks. Millions of copies of "Rockin' Around the Christmas Tree" were subsequently sold by Brenda Lee.

History has been the inspiration for many hit country songs. The Battle of Waterloo, for example, gave birth to singer Stonewall Jackson's "Waterloo" in the early 1960s, and the World War II sinking of the German battleship *Bismarck* was the inspiration for Johnny Horton's "Sink the Bismarck."

The Nashville songwriters seemingly got away from their musical recording of history until Lee Greenwood wrote and recorded a song that was called the 1980s answer to the National Anthem.

"God Bless the U.S.A." was proclaimed by former President Ronald Reagan to be his favorite song, and has been sung at scores of political rallies, Republican and Democrat, since its 1982 creation. The song was sung at both the Republican and Democratic National Conventions in 1992.

Greenwood told me he was inspired to write the song in the wake of the 1983 ambush of a commercial Korean airliner over Russian airspace. At that time, Communism was still very much alive, and the cold war had not yet warmed. Korean flight 007 flew over Russian air lanes. Its lights were off, and it did not respond to attempts at radar communication.

A United States congressman was among the passengers who died. For weeks after the shooting, which was likened to the ambush of a school bus, the free world reeled with speculation. Was the Korean craft in actual violation of airspace, was it on a clandestine mission, or was it simply lost?

"I felt very attacked," Greenwood said. "But nobody did anything. We [the U.S.] said it was an atrocity, but nobody spoke out. That's why I sat down and wrote 'God Bless the U.S.A.' "

Lee has recorded some significant hit songs, but his signature has become his patriotic classic.

In February 1991, I heard Lee sing the song at Reagan's birthday party inside Merv Griffin's Beverly Hilton Hotel in Los Angeles. Griffin mistakenly told the audience that Lee had introduced the song on his program.

It's a little thing, but something of which I'm proud nonetheless. Lee, in fact, sang that wonderful anthem to the United States for the first time publicly on "Nashville Now."

The highest-selling record of all time is Bing Crosby's "White Christmas." The second highest is "Tennessee Waltz."

Red Stewart and Pee Wee King were riding in a car when they heard Bill Monroe sing "Kentucky Waltz." They simply decided the state of Tennessee should have a namesake waltz, and wrote one. Its writers had no personal experience from which the song was inspired. Neither was even in Tennessee at the time of its writing, and both felt the commercial music market, in 1947, contained too many waltzes.

Stewart told King that he had never written a song about Tennessee, and it was decided to do so then and there. Stewart smoked big, black cigars and had a box of cigars and a carton of matches in his car's glove box. He tore open the matches, and on the back of one of the boxes, Stewart and King wrote the lyrics to "Tennessee Waltz."

When asked who wrote the lyrics and who wrote the melody, King simply said, "We both did."

Red Stewart and Pee Wee King were the first to record their new composition. Patti Page had the biggest recording of the song in the 1950s. It was published by Nashville's famous Acuff-Rose Publishing Company, and, of course, there was a lawsuit disputing authorship and copyrighting. Acuff-Rose won.

When I last interviewed Stewart and King, in 1992, approximately 300 artists had recorded "Tennessee Waltz." One of the first was Cowboy Copas, who declined to buy the song for $25.00. More than 55 million copies had sold. They had earned one and one-half cents each for each record sold, and were talking about how much more money they would earn off the song when they could renew their copyright, in 1997, and derive a higher rate of pay.

Their sales income from the classic does not include the millions of dollars they have earned from airplay.

Ironically, the artist who didn't record the song was the one they wanted the most—Elvis Presley. His manger, Col. Tom Parker, had once been the road manager for Stewart and King.

"I said, 'Tom, why don't you get Elvis to cut it?' " King told me.

"It's not his type of song," Parker told King.

"I took that to mean no," King said, and the subject was never broached again.

I don't think there has ever been a more honest song than Dolly Parton's "Coat of Many Colors." The inspiration for the song came directly from her life.

"When I was eight," Dolly told me, "I got a coat of many colors made out of corduroy rags. I was from a large family, and we had no money to buy clothes. So people used to send us rags. I didn't own a coat, and Mama made a coat for me because it was the day for school pictures.

"I was so proud of the coat," Dolly said, "because Mama told me the Bible story of Joseph and his pretty coat of many colors. But when I got to school, the kids didn't think I looked like Joseph. They made fun of me and I cried."

When she was older, Dolly realized her poverty lay strictly in material things, and how incredibly rich in love she and her siblings had been. That thought became the song's ending.

"The first time I sang the song on television," Dolly said, "the actual coat of many colors was superimposed on the screen, and my daddy saw it and cried. I've had songs that made more money for me, but never one that meant as much."

Other songs, written from the heart and recollection, have added to the dignity of country music. These songs have imposed themselves upon their authors at any hour, anywhere, and in every circumstance.

There is no formula for great writing, and formula writing usually isn't great.

When I visited Nashville recording sessions in the 1950s and

1960s, a "standard" session was three hours. During those 180 minutes, with the time clock running, a singer and musicians were expected to record four songs. Many of Nashville's biggest classics, such as "I Can't Stop Loving You" and "Crazy," were recorded exactly that way.

Today, musicians and producers might work months on just one selection. The result will probably sell more than the older tunes, but it won't be remembered as long.

Perhaps that's because today's record producers, artists, and musicians are more technically knowledgeable than ever before. They create more from their heads and less from their hearts than their predecessors.

But no matter how refined it all becomes, commercial music success will always be traceable to the song itself. "It all begins with a song" is the official Nashville Songwriters' Association motto. No expensive electronics board, no sustained process of electronic over dubbing, and no inflated production budget will ever be as important to the creation of a hit song as a five-cent pencil, a blank piece of paper, and the uncertain hands that hold them.

EIGHT

Into the gracious, sprawling, and distinctly Southern home of Lynn Anderson (whose "Rose Garden" is an American standard) and her then husband Glen Sutton (composer of such hits as "Almost Persuaded" and "Your Good Girl's Gonna Go Bad") walked Jerry Lee Lewis. In tow were his sister Linda Gayle Lewis, a brother-in-law, Kenneth Lovelace, and other members of his band. This was a home where politeness reigned. The hostess and host were known for their sophisticated evenings entertaining the high and the mighty of the music world. Lynn told me she had been especially delighted to entertain Lewis, the founder, arguably, of rock 'n' roll.

Glasses were raised, polite conversation abounded, more glasses were raised quickly, someone said something someone else didn't like, and suddenly the home was a boxing ring. Flying fists, kicks, scratching, biting, and wild profanity were everywhere.

And then, for a minute, the battle came to a halt.

"Lynn," said Jerry Lee, panting, "I'm sorry about all of this."

While he was apologizing, the man beneath him gasped and coughed, his face turning red from Jerry Lee's grip tightening around his throat.

"I want you to know we'll pay for anything we break," he said. "But right now I'm gonna teach this son of a bitch a lesson!" And he pummeled the guy some more in the face.

Lynn and Glen tried to quiet down the human wrecking crew,

but seeing how futile this was, she and her husband abandoned the effort to break up the fight, and tried instead to move it. With the assistance of their domestic help, they somehow herded the combatants out the door and into the back of a waiting car.

"It was incredible," Lynn said. "This big white limousine was pulling out of my driveway. My front door was standing open, all the house lights were on, and the only thing you could see in the back of that car were flying arms and legs. They were still beating each other to pieces as the limo eased out of sight."

This story is typical of the freewheeling men and women who made up Nashville's music industry in the 1950s through 1970s. The industry settled down in the 1980s, and some contend it is actually refined in the 1990s. I'm not sure I'd go that far. But there were plenty of parties during those roaring thirty years that were not regarded as successful unless people wound up naked in a swimming pool, or were sprawled bleeding on the floor. Those guys were just flat-out rowdy.

A singer would stand on stage and sing gospel songs or family music, then retire almost instantly to the willing body of a woman he'd never met, and would never see again.

Back then things like this never made print, except on the rare occasions when lawsuits ensued. There were only a handful of rape charges and paternity suits through the years.

The behavior was an outcome of the stress coming from a bunch of overgrown boys and girls who couldn't handle success in an uncertain business where one hit song in no way guaranteed another. Some of the misbehavior was merely the by-product of boredom. But the activity was once as much a part of Nashville show business as fiddles and guitars.

Some 1960s and 1970s country stars drank to the point of serious intoxication. Some 1940s and 1950s country stars drank to the point of incapacitation. Those days remind me more of embalmment than drunkenness.

Bob Wills and the Texas Playboys were booked in a Las Vegas casino in the late 1950s. Wills got drunk and missed opening night. The Playboys worked the show, but were told by the promoter not to return the next night without Wills. Going on without Wills and not getting paid, or going on with him when he couldn't perform, was a dilemma the band had faced many times, from the 1940s on into the 1960s.

The band couldn't sustain itself financially in Las Vegas without income, so they decided to dress Wills and bring him to the show. Wills was as famous for his "Ah-Ha," as he was for his fiddle playing. The plan was to prop him up and let him yell occasionally. He couldn't play a note, but at least they'd get paid. They had done this before.

So Eldon Shamblin, the Playboys' rhythm guitarist, and Leon McAuliffe, the steel guitarist, began the arduous task of putting clothes and boots on him.

Wills was tied, inconspicuously, to a chair, and he just sat in a stupor, immune to the music around him.

Once in a while, someone placed a hand-held microphone before his face, and he yelled out his trademark "Ah-Ha."

Wills was too drunk to talk, but he kept whispering and muttering "sock . . . sock" whenever a band member got within ear shot.

After the show, the band got paid and Wills was taken back to his hotel, where he passed out. Just before losing consciousness, he muttered, "sock . . . sock."

As Wills lay snoring, McAuliffe struggled to remove his tight, patent leather custom boots. As the second boot came off with a grunt, a round ball-like object fell from it. Throughout the evening, a pitiful Wills, unable to speak, had to sit in great pain from a sock that had been wadded into the tip of his cowboy boot. His toes had been bent backwards inside the pointed toe. When Wills awoke, he complained that he was suffering from the worst hangover he ever had. The pain, he said, even went all the way to his feet.

Buddy Emmons is the best steel guitarist in country music. He has a line of guitars named after him, sold in music stores internationally, and is popularly regarded among musicians as a player's player. He was the band leader, along with Phil Baugh, for

"Nashville Alive," my variety talk show for Ted Turner's WTBS. There is no telling on how many hit records he's played his guitar.

Emmons is as modest as he is talented. He embarrasses more easily than a Southern Belle at her coming-out party. He'll never talk about sex or anatomy. He will say "bathroom tissue," but never "toilet paper."

He had played, off and on, for Ray Price, and was in the band in the late 1960s with Darrell McCall, then the most sought-after bass player and high harmony singer in the business. Darrell told me that in all the years he was Buddy's roommate, he never once saw Buddy in the nude, and on only one occasion did he see Buddy wearing a towel.

The band performed one Saturday night in Lufkin, Texas, and stayed overnight at a Holiday Inn. Buddy was using the shower and Darrell was awaiting his turn. Meanwhile, a fellow band member, Johnny Bush, stepped into Darrell's room and asked to borrow a hair dryer.

Buddy emerged from the shower wrapped in a towel.

"Where is the hair dryer?" Buddy asked.

"Bush has it next door," Darrell responded. "Why don't you use the balcony to get it while I take my shower?"

Buddy Emmons did something out of character. Knowing Bush's room was only a foot away, he stepped from his sliding glass door to Bush's. When Buddy was out of the room, the door eased shut and automatically locked.

The world's most modest man (and best steel guitarist) was left standing on the outdoor balcony of a Holiday Inn. He wore nothing but embarrassment and a towel. Darrell was laughing uncontrollably and refused to let Buddy re-enter their room. Then Buddy began to pound on Bush's door. Bush stepped to the glass, saw Buddy's predicament, opened the door slightly and yanked the towel from a trembling Buddy Emmons. Now he was naked.

Downstairs, the motel restaurant had filled with guests awaiting Sunday lunch. People dressed in church finery were sitting down while a naked and hysterical man squirmed upstairs. His so-called friends refused to let him in. The only shelter he could think of was the band's bus, parked a block beyond the restaurant. In order to reach it he had to sprint past the floor-to-ceiling windows of the eatery, which he did at breakneck speed.

The post-church crowd, pressed against the glass, was rewarded by the sight of Emmons running laps around the bus, searching frantically for an unlocked door or window. Emmons was shielding his manhood with his hands and screaming from the gravel denting his dancing feet. At last he found an opening, a port hole in the bus bathroom. This small window was never meant to accommodate human traffic, but the naked, panting Buddy Emmons crawled through it anyway.

He didn't return to the motel. Band members brought his clothes, toiletries, and other personal items to the bus, but he didn't say thanks. In fact, Buddy didn't speak to anyone on the bus for the remainder of the tour.

On another tour with Ray Price, this time in Omaha, Nebraska, Buddy retired to his room after a show to do some serious drinking. Larry Adams, Darrell McCall, and Buddy got into the tequila.

A drunken Adams walked onto the hotel balcony (balconies were Buddy's undoing) and dared Darrell and Buddy to follow him. Then he leaped from the second story to the frozen ground below. Darrell accepted the challenge and followed suit.

Both Adams and Darrell had been wearing western boots with thick soles, heavy heels, and steel reinforcement. Buddy was wearing bedroom slippers.

He nonetheless took the dare, jumped from the balcony, and broke both feet.

They took him to a hospital and Darrell huddled with the doctor.

"Doc," Darrell said, "you're probably going to put my friend's feet in a cast, but could you put the plaster all the way up to his hips? He's going to need a dramatic story to tell, not just that he broke his feet jumping off a balcony drunk."

Darrell got the doctor to do it, but really only because he wanted Buddy to feel miserable. It worked. Buddy flew back to Nashville with two leg casts that stretched almost to his waist.

But Buddy had the last laugh.

When Darrell went to see him a few days later, Buddy had taken a butcher's knife and cut the casts from his legs. He couldn't stand up and had to crawl on the floor.

He used the knife for another task as well. To carve. He found a small log and sculpted it into the shape of a lap guitar. He put in meticulous work on the details, carved in strings, tuning keys, and frets.

Buddy later had steel dyes made from the carving. The dyes, by the Dobro maestro, Shot Jackson, became the prototypes for the first Emmons guitars. The rest, as they say, is history. The next time Emmons jumped was for joy when he learned his guitar was going to be mass produced and sold around the globe.

Some time later, he shot himself in the hip. The bullet traveled down his leg and exited from his kneecap. He was practicing a fast-draw, and the pistol got hung up in his holster. Today, Buddy Emmons plays steel guitar for the Everly Brothers and enjoys his status as mentor to every steel guitarist in the world.

Friends say it's been years since he pulled a pistol, leapt from a balcony, or trotted around in the nude.

Ray Price was playing in Texas in the 1960s and a member of the audience requested a square dance. Neither Ray, nor anyone in his band, could call a square dance. But Ray felt obliged to grant the request because he was playing for a private party that included the mayor and many of the town's elite.

Ray asked over the public address if anyone could call a square dance and a hand was raised. The man walked on stage in front of the band, the members unaware the guy was drunk. The man turned to the fiddle player, Shorty Lavender, and asked him to kick off a square dance tune.

The crowd of rich folks, unaccustomed to waiting, was growing impatient. For them, the country music was a novel way of fund-raising, intended to benefit charity. The musicians were little more than court jesters for the evening.

As the man approached the microphone, he grabbed its stand for balance, placed his mouth too close to the screen, and screeching feedback filled the room. The band knew now that he was loaded.

Ray and Shorty were afraid to let the guy go on, but more afraid not to. The crowd clamoring for the square dance, after all, contained the person who was supposed to pay them at the end of the evening.

"What do you want to do?" Shorty whispered to the drunk, out of the microphone's pickup.

"Oh, I don't know," he said. "L-let's do Raggedy Ann-n."

Shorty hurriedly kicked it off.

He was sawing away on his fiddle, and the "caller" at last began his chant. He did fine up to a point—then began to improvise.

A few society women were standing at the edge of the stage when the caller yelled out, "Raggin' ReRag, Ragamuffin Rag em back you bunch of Ragged Ass Mother F——."

Such talk was horrifying in polite society in the 1960s. People quickly began to leave the hall, and Ray and the band feared they wouldn't get paid.

"I don't know him, I don't know him!" Price said into the microphone. "Come back, it won't happen again, it won't happen again!"

Ray's appeal was so desperate and rhythmic, the band should have kicked in and let it serve as a square dance call. A few people returned, the band ultimately was paid, and the career of the mysterious square dance caller began and ended on that rural Texas stage.

Touring musicians get goofy. The miles and monotony take their toll. The musicians become so bored that their humor thresholds fall to the level of a first-grader. They will laugh at anything that happens on the road.

"Some of these folks, after they've been out on tour a few days, would laugh at a car wreck," said Jack Watkins, the veteran guitarist for Ronnie Milsap.

That was particularly true when country stars played less sophisticated venues up until the early 1970s. Many times two or three bands, including their leaders, would be asked to share the same dressing room. This happened even in the Ryman Auditorium, which housed the Grand Ole Opry in Nashville until 1974. Three dressing rooms had to accommodate thirty acts during a five-hour period. Many acts had their own bands. In the men's dressing room, a rule was made up disallowing flatulence.

The rule was ridiculous and so was its enforcement. If anyone passed gas, he had to yell immediately, "Free jacks." If he didn't, somebody else yelled, "Plucks," and pinched the guy.

Pretty sophisticated! Meanwhile, a radio show was being broadcast coast-to-coast forty feet away.

The Grand Ole Opry players usually left Nashville on their buses after the Saturday-night performances en route to Sunday matinees and a week of touring before returning to the Opry. Ernest Tubb and his Texas Troubadours follow this schedule routinely.

Tubb was famous for his marathon poker games. He and his band would play cards for days. Other entertainers, whose buses drove behind Tubb's en route to the same venues, would get off their coaches just to ride with Tubb. Hundreds of dollars were won from and lost to Ernest Tubb.

The caravan of entertainers had been out for days, singing on stage, playing poker on Tubb's bus, and sleeping little in between.

A stack of money overflowed Tubb's table. He was betting heavily, his opponents were raising, and he was taking the wagering higher.

At last, with all that money scattered around, Tubb called the last bet. Emotions were high and sensibilities dulled as players began to show their cards. As they did, someone at the table passed gas.

"Free jacks!" the culprit shouted.

"Well, I'll be damned," Tubb muttered, "that sure beats two pair."

He folded, lost the bet he should have won, and never knew the difference.

Willie Nelson suffered from touring boredom as well.

Willie was the hottest act in country music in the middle 1970s and early 1980s, and he was playing a Las Vegas hotel where the touring production of *Peter Pan* had closed the previous night.

Willie had been on stage for about forty-five minutes and had not yet sung his hit, "Angels Flying Too Close to the Ground." The hotel manager was becoming nervous. He didn't like performers entertaining for more than an hour. Casinos want the crowd to leave the show room and return to the floor and begin losing money gambling.

Willie finally eased into "Angels Flying." Suddenly, there was a burst of hysterical laughter. Willie noticed the crowd looking above him, so he whirled to see Bea Spears, his bass player, in mid-air.

The bassist had talked the production crew into strapping him into Peter Pan's leftover wire harness. Spears was "flying" through the air, while pointing his bass guitar forward, as if he were riding it.

Willie got angry, the show ended, Spears was almost fired, and the crowd was royally entertained.

Hank Snow was on a stage inside an ice skating arena and was taking his bows while walking backwards. Hank was characteristically gracious, although drunk, as he eased to the back lip of the stage, bowing all the while. He bowed a final time and stepped backwards over a ten-foot drop. Fortunately, he held a giant Martin guitar about half the size of a small refrigerator. The instrument cushioned his fall and might have prevented permanent injury.

Snow, always the showman, climbed back on the stage to bow again before the gasping crowd. This time Snow left the stage with a rigid dignity.

The audience could see his lips mouthing the words "Thank you, thank you."

Snow was instead talking to Chubby Wise, a fiddle player and the only person who could hear him above the applause.

"God damn it," Snow said, "why don't you watch where I'm going?"

Not long after that episode, Snow was playing in Canada, his native country where he is still a hero. Canadians treated Snow the same way they would deal with a minister or head of state.

Snow was staying in a hotel and was spotted by the parents of a couple that were two-hour-old newlyweds.

The wedding attendants had been into the hooch, and therefore didn't notice that Snow had been there too.

"My God," one yelled, "it's Hank Snow."

"Howdy, friends and neighbors," Snow said, in a drawl that is second nature from years of using it on stage.

"Oh dear," exclaimed the mother, "would you say something over our children? They just got married."

Snow, guitar on his back, beckoned the young people into his hotel suite with their parents, where he performed an impromptu ceremony. He took it very seriously.

"I bless you, son, I bless you, daughter, and may your lives be filled with everlasting happiness," he said. "Now," he continued, still in character, "old Hank must bid you adieu."

He turned around, opened a door, and walked directly into a closet, where he remained until they all left.

Snow used to make home movies of his concert tours. His band members grumbled about having to go to his house to watch footage of the landscape they hadn't been able to escape for days on end. But they went, and Snow would introduce each segment and provide running commentary. He took this very seriously.

The vistas obviously were intended to be pretty and scenic, like a travelogue.

Darrell McCall, who was working a Hank Snow tour with

Faron Young, stole Snow's camera. He sneaked around filming piles of dog shit.

About a month later, Snow had guests to his Rainbow Ranch. The lights dimmed as Snow began to roll the reel of his latest home movie.

Instantly, he shut off the projector and turned on the lights.

Seconds later, Faron answered his telephone at home. The sound Faron heard was the famous, forced laugh.

"Ha-Ha-Ha-Ha," came the voice.

"Hello, Hank," Faron said, knowing he was upset.

"That God damn Darrell. I know he did it," Snow ranted.

Faron probed Snow and finally found out why he was upset. Faron offered to make Darrell buy Snow a new roll of film, but Snow declined. On subsequent tours, Snow always locked up his camera when it wasn't in use.

The correlation between craziness and creativity in the Nashville music community is well known. Some of the most gifted songwriters, such as Hank Williams Jr., Kris Kristofferson, Willie Nelson, Johnny Cash, Merle Haggard, and many others, also have the gift of zany senses of humor. Cash, for example, once bought 500 baby chickens and placed them inside an elevator in a Manhattan hotel. He then proceeded to punch the buttons that would make the elevator stop at every floor. Baby chickens rolled out on every level, but the majority of them overtook the hotel lobby.

The only thing that made Nashville entertainers less inhibited than alcohol was amphetamines in the 1960s and 1970s. Merle Kilgore, now the personal manager for Hank Williams, Jr., has made no secret of his chemical addiction, from which he successfully freed himself.

He took diet pills day and night, and it was ruining his marriage. His wife insisted that he go into a rehabilitation program.

After checking him into the facility, she told the doctor she had no idea where Merle hid his pills. She said she had scoured their house, from crevice to crevice, and had discarded every pill she could find. Merle had been hiding them inside the works of a portable record player.

While in the rehabilitation center, he went through a painful withdrawal. He had an immense craving for his pills.

He said to his wife and doctor, "I can do without my pills, but I can't do without my music. Please let me have my record player."

His unsuspecting wife delivered the pill-filled record player. His ploy worked.

Merle was hospitalized for ten days and was high and happy most of the time. One day he had his pills all lined up and was counting and playing with them and heard the approaching footsteps of a maid.

He quickly threw the pills into the bottom of a vase of flowers and left for lunch. When he returned, he went to the flowers, intending to have a little chemical dessert.

The maid, not realizing they were artificial flowers, had watered the flowers, and the water melted the pills. So Merle threw away the flowers and drank the water. Merle now refers to this institution as "Happy Acres."

Substance abuse was the stimulus behind some of the best songs ever to emerge from Music Row. Listen to the records of the 1960s and early 1970s and you'll hear how brisk and clean the rhythm guitars are. That's because these hyper-active players were wired on chemicals.

The making of good music wasn't worth the price exacted from drugs. I'm glad that the days of excess are behind my friends and me. I'm glad too that today's young artists seem to be too bright to participate in the self-destructiveness that once gripped an entire industry.

But there is no denying that the abusiveness launched some hilarious and memorable behavior. But I'd rather remember it than re-enact it.

NINE

Country music's recurring themes of God, home, and country have long been coupled with the opposing themes of drunkenness and adultery.

The Country Music Association's 1992 Song of the Year, for example, was "The Whiskey Ain't Working Anymore," a tale of a man who is undergoing diminishing consolation from a bottle.

There is no end of songs about maternal love and domestic order with a wife who is obedient to her husband. Feminists have taken issue with these musical depictions of subservient women. The trend began as early as the 1930s with Little Rachael, a female vocalist in the touring Roy Acuff Show. She was deceptively portrayed as the sister of Bashful Brother Oswald, the band's Dobro player. The public, men in the cast believed, would accept Rachael's traveling with men only if she was related to one of them.

The most famous song about spousal submissiveness is Tammy Wynette's "Stand By Your Man," which prompted even Hillary Rodham Clinton, during her husband's 1992 presidential campaign, to take umbrage at its message: A woman is wimpy. Ms. Clinton spoke disparagingly of this meek image during an interview on CBS's "Sixty Minutes." Her remarks ignited Ms. Wynette, who demanded, and received, an apology.

The country music industry to this day refers to its women vocalists as "girl singers," an identification that would not fly in the camps of women's advocates, or with such best-selling authors as

Germaine Greer and Gloria Steinem. Amid the chauvinistic tradition exists a handful of country music marriages wherein the women are the bread winners and dominant personalities. Their husbands often stay home while they travel on the road, usually on a tour bus loaded with men. Their husbands earn substantially less money, and generally take a backseat to their famous and often independent wives.

The husbands are targets of curiosity among fans, who rarely get a glimpse of the role reversal of the men behind the women. I am friends with three such men: Mooney Lynn, the husband of Loretta Lynn; Ken Dudney, married to Barbara Mandrell; and George Richey, Tammy Wynette's fifth husband.

I hope the following recollections give some insight into the unusual lives of Mr. Lynn, and the regularly but erroneously misnamed "Mr. Mandrell" and "Mr. Wynette."

Loretta Lynn was married at fourteen, pregnant at fifteen, and the mother of four at nineteen. During this span, Mooney Lynn discovered that his wife could sing "better than Kitty Wells," which is how he pitched her when he brought her to Nashville. Her 1976 autobiography, *Coal Miner's Daughter,* was a bestseller, and the motion picture earned Sissy Spacek an Academy Award.

The book and film portrayed Mooney as a two-fisted fighter and drinker who was not above knocking Loretta around. He used her customized tour bus with its white carpet and upholstery to go wild-hog hunting with the former "Hee-Haw" star and rodeo cowboy Lecile Harris. Loretta appeared regularly in 1992 in Branson, Missouri, where Mooney was asked why his wife continued to work years after achieving major stardom.

"I have to keep her working so I can afford whiskey," he replied.

The two have been married for forty-four years and remain fiercely loyal to each other. Mooney, in fact, is loyal and supportive to anyone he likes, as I discovered firsthand during a show in 1981 aboard the *Mississippi Queen* riverboat. We were appearing on the Conway Twitty Riverboat special. I had been asked by the show's producer to apologize on behalf of the cast and crew to passengers who might have been inconvenienced by our production efforts. I was doing just that and couldn't hear the woman heckling me from the rear of the room where Mooney sat after having consumed a few drinks. She was angry because our cast was videotaping and that was disrupting her leisure.

Mooney stood up for me, telling her in front of the other customers to let me do my job.

The irate woman called Mooney a "country asshole."

The only thing shorter than Mooney's height is his temper. He is as stout as the heavy equipment upon which he works and looks like a real version of Bluto, minus the beard. He is a stump in a cowboy hat and is as stocky as Garth Brooks will be in thirty years.

The woman wouldn't have insulted him had she known him as I do.

Mooney made his own path amid tables and chairs as he walked toward the woman. Her husband had the good judgment to leave the table before Mooney got there.

"I'll whip his ass," Mooney said of her innocent husband. The outspoken woman, who I later learned had ridden her wealthy father's financial coattails most of her life, continued to taunt Mooney, who was growing increasingly tempted to deck her. But he would never hit a woman—to whom he wasn't married.

Loretta, who was on stage with me, was hailed by a waiter.

"Ms. Lynn," he whispered, "could you come to the back of the room, please? Your husband is very upset."

She trekked to his belligerent side, and not long afterwards had settled him down. It took a while, however, to persuade him to leave the room.

His parting words, to paraphrase, were that no one was going to pick on Ralph while he was on stage if "I'm in the audience."

Although I didn't agree with his method, I found his actions somehow reassuring.

Mooney oversees and does much of the work on their 5,000-acre farm about seventy miles west of Nashville just off of Interstate 40. He also runs a recreational vehicle park and generally toils as diligently as he did when he was bulldozing timber back in Butcher Holler, Kentucky, where he met Loretta. His backwoods savvy far exceeded his book learning, as shown by his crafty bet with Butcher Holler residents that a four-wheel-drive jeep could climb a mountain. They had never seen or heard of a four-wheel-drive vehicle, and Mooney easily won the wager.

When he isn't working, he enjoys his whiskey, and doesn't care who knows it, not even a President.

Mooney was a friend of Jimmy Carter before he became the governor of Georgia. Mooney and Loretta, consequently, were invited to the White House for Carter's presidential inauguration. Mooney looked and acted like Carter's late, beer-swilling brother, who drew a lot of negative press for getting drunk and urinating on the White House grounds. Mooney, wearing a cowboy hat, was walking through the White House corridors when a television newsman mistook him for Billy Carter.

The reporter, without provocation, shoved a microphone into Mooney's face and turned on the television lights.

"What do you think about your brother?" he asked Mooney.

"I don't know, he's a pretty good ole boy," Mooney replied, not breaking his stride.

The camera crew was walking backwards hastily to keep up with him.

"Well, how do you feel about him now?" the reporter pressed on.

"The same way I always felt about him," Mooney said.

The annoyed reporter became more aggressive.

"Aren't you glad he's been elected President of the country?" he asked.

"I think you got the wrong guy," Mooney snapped.

"Who the hell are you?" the reporter demanded, the camera still rolling.

"Mooney Lynn," Mooney said.

The reporter yelled, "Cut, cut," and stared blankly at Mooney, who continued forward.

"Mooney who? Mooney who?" the crew chanted, as Mooney walked out of earshot.

The festivities continued at the Carter White House, which was largely dry. The President didn't drink and had no whiskey on hand for his guests, Mooney told me. Champagne and wine were the only alcohol. The macho Mooney would likely rather gargle than drink wine or champagne, sissy liquid by his account.

"I drink Tennessee drinking whiskey," he once told my radio audience.

While the President, his cabinet members, and various heads of state raised glasses in toast, Mooney eased out of the Oval Office and toward the White House basement. He was, he said, looking for the hired help.

He went into the kitchen, a flurry of helter-skelter activity in the mass production of appetizers.

He cornered a waiter and cook and insisted, "I know you got a little bit of Jack Daniel's in here someplace."

"No, sir!" was the immediate reply. "President Carter don't allow no drinking."

"You're lyin'," he thundered, "where's the whiskey?"

Again, passionate denials.

This scenario went on for a while, after which a timid waiter approached Mooney with a "Coke."

"I don't want no damn 'Coke,' " Mooney fumed.

"Try it, you'll like this 'Coke,' " the waiter said.

"Take it away," Mooney insisted.

"Try it," the waiter argued.

Mooney reluctantly tasted, then devoured the "Coke" that was mixed lightly with Jack Daniel's.

"But that's not the end of the story," Mooney said to me.

Mooney returned to the White House with Loretta when Ronald Reagan was President.

Mooney was standing in a reception line when he heard, "P-s-s-s-t, p-s-s-s-t." Someone was beckoning him from behind a curtain.

The cowboy approached the peeping eyes behind the floor-to-ceiling cloth.

"Mr. Mooney?"

"Yes, who is that?" Mooney asked.

"Comes to the basement, Mr. Mooney, we's got lots of whiskey."

Mooney followed the mysterious host and never told me whether he ever returned to greet the new President of the United States.

Mooney was my radio guest the day he told the story. I asked him which was his favorite Loretta Lynn ballad. She has probably recorded 500.

"I liked Loretta on these real touchy ballads, you know, heart songs," he said.

I persisted in trying to get him to tell me his favorite, but, except for "Coal Miner's Daughter," he couldn't think of one Loretta Lynn song.

I asked him why he married Loretta, and he told me he loved her. I told him that was the best reason of all. At the time of their marriage, Loretta had never been farther than six miles from home.

We talked about the motion picture, and I mentioned that a lot had been made of the fact that Loretta was sexually naive when they married. He told me that was hard for him to talk about, and I thought that was the extent of his answer, until he added that Loretta didn't hold back on sex but took a long time to learn it.

He was beginning to warm to the subject, and I was afraid he would say too much, so I changed the subject.

The groom waited nervously at the altar for his bride, who timidly approached the wedding party. The sanctuary was draped with flowers and lit with candles. The room was hushed, save for the barely audible hum of videotape cameras.

One publication set the price tag for this lavish ceremony at $100,000 (the groom later reduced the figure by about fifty percent). The couple recited their vows, written exclusively for this ceremony, as their three children looked on tearfully. The children were the symbols of their love, first consummated twenty-five years ago—the first time they recited their wedding vows.

After a quarter century of marriage, Barbara and Ken Dudney renewed their vows. It was a spiritual renewal for the bride, better known as Barbara Mandrell.

Unlike many men behind their celebrity women, Ken Dudney has assumed a higher profile than most before a nation enchanted with the couple's suburban, establishment image. If Ken and Barbie dolls lived, their last name would be Dudney.

While Dolly Parton talks freely of her open marriage to Carl Dean and Tammy Wynette lamented George Jones' drinking and reckless sprees, Barbara and Ken Dudney maintained the image of devoted purity.

Their union got off to a rocky start because her parents forbade her to see him for six months. She was dating Ken at the age of seventeen. They thought that her being underage had her swimming over her head in the sea of romance.

What else does the man do who stood by his woman during the births of their children, the ascension of her stardom, and the 1984 automobile wreck that stunned the nation and nearly claimed her life?

"I am really hard-pressed to say exactly what I do, 'cause I don't do anything," Ken joked on the "Oprah Winfrey Show." "A lot of people ask and I jokingly say, 'I'm retired, my wife works, why do I have to work?' I can see it now. The local newspaper when I die will say 'Local Do-Nothing Dies!' The crowd, they loved that."

Ken, in fact, is one of Tennessee's major sellers of log homes. He was the co-designer of their 22,000-square-foot log home mansion.

It is no small task keeping a residential, real estate–related business afloat during the recessionary 1990s. He also oversees the couple's cattle herd and much of Barbara's professional management. He once toured with her for about five months, negotiating with concert promoters and collecting the money. Ken, a man in midlife, recently returned to college, where he earned a degree in business management.

And he is the dominant parent in a marriage where Barbara, obviously, is the preeminent personality.

In May 1990, their son Matt had not been doing as well as Ken would have liked at Abilene Christian University.

"I am done," Ken told his son. "I am done paying for it. Matt, as long as you are succeeding in school, seeking a degree in something, I don't care what it is, water-balloon making, I don't care, then I'll keep you under my financial umbrella."

He stressed to Matt that just attending school wasn't enough, but that he must pass.

"In this home there will always be a place for you," Ken continued. "I will take care of you all of your life, if that is what is necessary. I will feed you, but I will not supply you with money."

It was tough love, and Ken said it worked. The following semester Matt's grade point average was higher.

He told his son that one of his greatest regrets was not having ever earned a college degree. He earned his own after their discourse.

I admire anybody who can enter the competition of a college setting as an adult, when study habits are rusty, and succeed. Ken earned his diploma after transferring credits from five different colleges that he had attended years earlier.

Ken left the United States Navy on November 1, 1969, and interviewed with several airlines for a job as a commercial pilot. He moved from California to Nashville to be with Barbara, who was by then well into her music career. He wanted to work for a major airlines flying out of Music City U.S.A.

But by March of 1970 he was the official first pilot of the state of Tennessee, flying the Governor at His Honor's will. He flew for seven years and four different governors.

"Why did you quit?" I asked him.

" 'Cause they sold the Lear Jet, for one thing."

"And you didn't want to fly another aircraft?"

"I wasn't there for the money. I hadn't been there for their money for a long time, didn't need their money. You know my wife was doing quite well in those years, and so I didn't need their money," Ken said. "I was there just to fly the Lear Jet, that was a lot of fun."

His jet was replaced by a propeller plane, and his dissatisfaction soared into the clouds, so he quit.

"So I told Governor Alexander point blank to his face he'd made a mistake because they sold that Lear Jet for $745,000, and he bought a King Air 100 for $745,000. It was a swap deal. The King Air was a big deal in the news because it carries ten people and could do more, and all of this kind of stuff."

Ken said the trade to accommodate more passengers was unnecessary because the state's average passenger load in the Lear was fewer than three persons, and the aircraft seated six. The Lear Jet was cheaper to operate per mile than the new King Air, and the Lear was faster in the air.

"I told Lamar Alexander many times, I said, 'You know, that was the dumbest thing you ever did, you know?' "

The Nashville press made a big deal out of the state's supposed austerity, but Ken stood up firmly to Alexander, who eventually became the nation's Secretary of Education.

Ken recalled one of the first trips he made in the Lear Jet. He flew Governor Winfield Dunn to Las Vegas, where he presented Jerry Lewis with a check for $15,000 for the annual Muscular Dystrophy campaign.

En route, the passengers began to talk about a popular motion picture of the day, *Deep Throat,* that dealt with a man with an unusually large penis. They were talking about this film with the Governor, and somebody said, "I heard that he had a fifteen-inch unit, you know, fifteen inches long," and Governor Dunn didn't blink. He said, "My gosh, I didn't know there were two of us like that in the world!"

I asked Ken directly what it was like being married to Barbara Mandrell.

"What I tell people who ask is that it is really great, and I say we have been married twenty-five years and I am only going to give her one more week and if she don't square up she is out of here. And they laugh and that is usually the way it goes."

Ken said the only time he thinks trouble surfaces in a celebrity marriage is when one side reminds the other who is earning most of the money.

"We talked about it on the 'Oprah Winfrey Show,' about how it feels to be married to somebody so well known, somebody who makes a tremendous amount of money, obviously more than you probably would if you had a normal job. And the only time I think that the people have problems, ego wise in situations like that, is when their mate, the one making all of this money, brings it up to them. Barbara has never once done that, you know. We are a union."

I've seen Ken Dudney act in ways money can't buy as a patient and long suffering husband to one of my best friends. By her own admission, Barbara can be temperamental. He stood by faithfully at her bedside during her prolonged hospital and home convalescence after the car accident. He adjusted to her personality changes that resulted from her substantial head injury.

I've seen him open his heart by simply biting his lip and recall specifically the night Ken, Barbara, Joy, and I went to a fashionable Nashville restaurant to hear inside stories about a television special Barbara produced in my honor.

Often, when Ken tried to tell a story, Barbara interrupted him, saying, "Ken, please!"

He became embarrassed but long ago adapted to the aggression of the woman he loves, and to whom he is faithfully devoted. In retrospect, we were having dinner on a tight schedule as Barbara had to get back to the edit bay at Opryland Productions, where she proceeded to edit my special for the rest of the night.

"We are a team and we've always felt that way," Ken told me. "We both raised the kids and we never had men's jobs and women's jobs. I probably changed more diapers than she did, and it is not because I felt I had to or anything. It is just a thing I wanted to do.

"To be married to her has its ups and downs, just like anybody else's, you know. There is no perfect marriages around that I know of, and she has moments of great joy and moments of great depression just like everybody would have. You have to be able to fight through the ups and downs."

Ken was astonished when he and Barbara were asked to join Dolly Parton for lunch at her home.

"Oh good," Ken told Dolly, "I will get a chance to meet Carl."

Dolly told him he might meet Carl, but Carl would not dine with Barbara or him. Ken found that kind of reclusiveness strange, and, as coincidence would have it, the luncheon date was cancelled.

"Have you ever been called 'Mr. Mandrell'?" I asked him.

"Every day, just about. It doesn't bother me. People only seem to have problems in show business and the entertainment field when they start feeling a little bit inadequate. Barbara has never made me feel inadequate."

Ken said he enjoys the way his wife identifies herself as Mrs. Dudney when she takes her children to school, or enters other non–show business arenas.

"She does it all the time," he said, "but it would not bother me if she said, 'I'm Barbara Mandrell.' It has never bothered me that she does have another name or that they call me Mr. Mandrell. I am just thrilled to death. It took a lot of years for people to recognize that name."

Asked to tell something about himself that Barbara didn't know, that she would be surprised to learn, Ken said there was no such thing.

Ken moved with Barbara to Hollywood in 1980, when Barbara had her highly successful variety show on NBC. He said the couple rented a house for $10,000 a month, and that the fee didn't include a maid. He also understood, he said, when Barbara didn't work one-night shows on the road during her network run. Doing the one-nighters, he said, was too strenuous for her.

He doesn't think there is much about him Barbara would change, except that she would like him to be about fifty pounds thinner, and complains when he only shaves once a day if they go out in the evening.

"I don't know what else I can tell you," he said. "It's been a pretty happy time together."

———————■———————

Tammy Wynette has been married to her fifth husband, George Richey, for fifteen years. They married after her marriage to Michael Tomlin fell apart after forty-four days.

Richey played piano at the Wynette-Tomlin wedding, and as his fingers touched the keys, his heart was with the bride.

"I knew I was in love with her then," he said.

Richey is an unusual show business spouse, because he too was in the business at the time of his marriage. He seems to understand, perhaps better than other companions, the strains that show business and fame can place on marriage because of his own experience.

It isn't well known that he has been a successful record producer and songwriter before and during his marriage to Tammy. He penned "The Grand Tour," a giant record for George Jones, Tammy's third husband.

Richey moved to Nashville in 1967 to work for Columbia Records with one of Nashville's most esteemed record producers, Billy Sherrill. Richey was a staff producer for Epic, a division of Columbia, and had acquired an impressive record of smaller labels.

He quit school at the age of fourteen to become a gospel quartet singer. He did so with his father's permission, contingent on elder quartet members making sure that Richey's secondary education was finished through tutoring.

That never happened.

Richey later sang in another quartet just before it was hired by Red Foley to sing background on his gospel records.

Richey was drafted into the Army at the unusually late age of twenty-five and decided he wanted to go into radio shortly after his discharge. He was living in Arizona when he walked unannounced into the Tucson radio station KTKT to apply for a job as a disc jockey. He walked out as an employee.

He landed the all-night shift. Nocturnal listeners seem to pay attention more than daytime fans. Perhaps that's because the night world offers fewer distractions. One of Richey's attentive listeners was the station's program director, who Richey never suspected was awake during pre-dawn hours.

Richey was doing a live commercial for Pall Mall cigarettes and decided to incorporate a little humor. As he read his text, he coughed uncontrollably. The program director was at the station within fifteen minutes and fired Richey on the spot for his satire. Richey wasn't even allowed to finish his broadcast shift and saw the sun rise on his unemployment.

He bounced into another station before applying for work at KAYO in Seattle. Richey was interviewed over the telephone by the general manager, who hired him, and told him to report to the program director.

The program director knew nothing about Richey, except that his boss had hired him, and he would have to honor that decision.

"So I went in and asked for the program director and when he came out I stuck my hand out and started stuttering worse than Mel Tillis ever did," Richey said. The director melted, thinking that his station had hired a disc jockey who couldn't talk.

Nashville has always had a "silent side," a segment of its entertainment community that is more successful than the masses ever know. Richey fits that group. He is hardly a household word, and will probably always be identified mainly as Tammy Wynette's husband, but he has produced some of the biggest songs ever to come out of Music Row, including Bobby Barnett's "Drink Canada Dry," John Wesley Ryles' "Kay," and Freddie Hart's "Easy Loving." He even produced an album by the beloved Tex Ritter.

Richey was also an immensely successful music publisher until he sold his company in 1977. Among the classics he published are "Blanket on the Ground" and Kenny Rogers' "Coward of the County" and "Lucille."

Richey met Tammy in Billy Sherrill's office. At the time, Tammy had been turned down by virtually every record producer and record label executive in Nashville.

"Billy's secretary had been transferred just that week to the coast, and he had no one in the front office, so Tammy just got to walk right on through," Richey said.

"Billy was doing what I've known him to do ever since I met

him," Richey continued. "He was sitting there with his feet up on the desk, waiting for lightning to strike.

"Tammy had no demonstration tape with her, so she used his guitar and did three or four songs live, right there. He told her that day he would sign her if she could find material."

Tammy would soon record "Apartment Number Nine," her record for Epic.

The song was a "cover," meaning that it had recently been recorded by another artist. I was co-hosting the All-Night Show on WSM with Tex Ritter when Tammy's record was released. Tammy visited my studio to promote the tune. She was young, inexperienced, and very nervous because it was her first time on a national broadcast.

Tex was a friend of Bobby Austin, the singer who recorded the original version. He teased Tammy on live radio, although she mistakenly took him seriously.

"Why did you record that song?" he asked her, and before she could respond, he said, "Did you think you could sing it better than Bobby? Do you think you did sing it better than Bobby?"

Tammy was speechless and stared blankly into the face of this recording industry icon spoiling her big-time radio debut.

Richey recently reminded me that I had intervened, telling Tex that Tammy had merely recorded the song from a female's point of view. I succeeded in getting him off her back, and Richey said I had made a friend for life.

Tammy later told the story herself during a Tammy Wynette tribute on "Nashville Now" in December of 1992.

Richey, after a long friendship with Tammy, began to date her in 1977, although he admits the first date was little more than a glorified pickup.

Richey had been drinking heavily with two women and stopped by the CBS recording studios where Tammy happened to be recording.

"I sat down and she came over to speak to me and kiss me hello and I just pulled her into my lap," he said. "I had had just enough sauce to have enough courage to say whatever I wanted to say and by this time I had fallen madly in love with her, but she didn't know it. And I said to her, 'Will you go with me?' and she said, 'Well, yes, but you will have to wait awhile,' and in my condition I thought, 'Well, what the hell does she mean, six months? What is she talking about?'

"She knew I meant right now, but I didn't realize that," Richey continued.

Richey said he ditched the other girls and hasn't seen them since. He took Tammy to a couple of different places in Nashville, and he said he knew that she loved him right away.

"Let me ask you something," I said to Richey in December of 1992. "You are all drunk and suddenly you are madly in love with Tammy. When did you actually fall in love with her?"

"I was in love with Tammy when she married Michael Tomlin," he snapped. "I recall sitting there at the keyboards and thinking, 'Shit, it is over for me. I won't have a shot.' "

"And how long did you date before you got married?" I asked.

"Until I could get a divorce. My marriage was a wreck, and I was not always living in my home. It was in May of '78 that I got a divorce and we married July fourth of '78."

Richey told me he never had reservations about Tammy's potential for marital stability because she had been married four times previously.

I asked George Richey the question I had asked of Mooney Lynn and Ken Dudney—what is it like to be married to a famous wife?

"Well, on the one hand, it's like being married to anyone that I loved by another name, in the times that she is my wife, and that is when she is not on stage. Being married to her creates no problem for me. I am often referred to as 'Mr. Wynette.' Instead of saying, 'Well, no, I'm George Richey,' I usually say, 'Yes I am.' "

"What is your role in her life today?"

"I manage her career and love her as much as I know how to love her," he said. "My wife is wonderful."

I have always contended that the greatest struggle in the entertainment industry is not among young artists whose careers are aspiring, but among established artists whose careers are declining.

Tammy Wynette has not had a significant solo record or won a major music award in years, and I asked Richey how his wife handled that.

"Ralph," he paused, "very honestly, I think it is Tammy's attitude that, 'If I never win another award, I have had my share.' That isn't to say that she doesn't want to cut hits in the future. I think she is a very contented woman, having had the career that she has had."

Financial difficulties have recently plagued Tammy and Richey. There was a request for bankruptcy. Richey told me there is much public misconception about it. People erroneously assumed the couple was broke, when they were not.

Tammy Wynette continues to perform as many as 200 personal appearances a year.

The ordeal was misrepresented, he said, because of the slanted coverage in the tabloids as well as Nashville's mainstream press.

I asked Richey if that was a source of embarrassment.

"I would be untruthful if I said no. Yes, there was some embarrassment, but on the other hand, my attitude is 'screw 'em.' "

Falling rain added to the confusion of rush-hour traffic on February 11, 1993, in Nashville where, at the posh Vanderbilt Plaza Hotel, perhaps two important and forty-eight not-so-important music business people gathered for the world premiere of a video documentary on the life of Patsy Cline.

It was an invitation-only crowd.

Patsy's music was playing through speakers in the vestibule. The songs were subdued. After the crowd had consumed several cocktails, the music was mostly lost in the noise.

The greatest female country voice of all time was reduced to background music.

At the center of the finger-sandwich set was a short and graying man, a high-energy live-wire who had participated in the documentary's production. He had, in fact, co-produced documentaries on Waylon Jennings, George Jones, and the Mamas and the Papas. He is also a former Nashville records promotions man of some renown, and for some time operated the now extinct Linotype machines upon which the nation's daily newspapers were printed.

But the credentials were never mentioned. Each time Charlie Dick was introduced, it was always as "Patsy Cline's husband."

Perhaps less is known about Charlie Dick than any other spouse of a famous Nashville personality. There are two reasons for that. The first is that his legendary wife has been dead for thirty years. The second is, whenever he's approached and asked about their time together he slyly shifts the conversation to Patsy only.

Charlie has been portrayed in two motion-pictures, including the Academy Award–winning *Coal Miner's Daughter,* about the life of Loretta Lynn, and *Sweet Dreams,* Jessica Lange's film of the life of Patsy Cline.

Charlie was depicted as a violent man who frequently beat his wife. He agrees to the beating part, but not the frequency.

"We had one fight where I smacked Patsy and she called the law on me, but we never had a knock-down, drag-out slugging match," Charlie told me in January of 1993.

Loretta Lynn told me she didn't think Charlie could whip Patsy, that Patsy would have clobbered him had he tried. I related this to Charlie.

"That's what Johnny Russell said," Charlie chimed in. "He said she would have taken a two-by-four to me."

Of the clash that Charlie called the couple's only brush with violence, he said he eventually went to bed and was awakened shortly afterwards by policemen.

"They took me downtown," Charlie recalled, "and by then it was Saturday morning about six o'clock, and when the judge finally opened the court he asked me what I did, and I told him and he said, 'If I let you go, will you come back on such and such a date?' I said yes.

"I had been bumming cigarettes off of a couple guys in jail, 'cause when I left the house I didn't have nothing, didn't bring my billfold, didn't bring a thing," he continued. "I promised those guys I would get them cigarettes after I got out, and they were in there hung over. And so I went to Tootsie's and got them cigarettes. I had credit at Tootsie's.

"And then Patsy did the Opry that night, and I went to the house and I stayed all night. Patsy came home the next day after spending the night with Loretta or Dottie and said her mother was coming, so I left for two or three days. About Wednesday or Thursday she called me to come have dinner with her mother.

"Patsy wanted to drop the charges against me, but the judge said, 'No, I am tired of these people swearing out these warrants and not doing anything about it. I want to see this woman,' the judge said. So I just sat in the back of the courtroom and laughed while she told the judge that she wasn't prosecuting."

Charlie first saw Virginia Patterson Hensley perform when she was a part of a minstrel show at the age of eighteen. He later ran into her at a dance and she told him she had just had a car wreck, and had no way to get to Washington, D.C., from Winchester, Virginia, to perform on the "Jimmy Dean Show."

Charlie told her he would drive her.

"But I didn't have a car either. Mine was torn up, and I didn't have a driver's license," Charlie recalled. "But I convinced one of my buddies to take us down the next night, and from then on, we just started and it never quit."

They began dating in April 1956, Patsy got a divorce in early 1957, and they were married in September 1957. The courtship was interrupted by Charlie's stint in the Army.

Charlie is an outspoken person. He might not tell all, but what he tells, he tells truthfully, no matter whom he implicates.

He touched on the runaway popularity of Patsy's first big record, "Walking After Midnight." He said the song was born on the "Arthur Godfrey Show," and established Patsy's career. She hated the tune.

"I think she didn't like it a hell of a lot because it was associated with the man who demanded to have the publishing rights on the 'B' sides of her records, and she also didn't think the words made much sense."

But the song resulted in a major recording contract for Patsy, and she and Charlie moved to Nashville. Charlie went to work in a printing shop.

Patsy went to the Hubert Long talent agency and asked him to book her personal appearances and manage her career. He balked, Charlie said, because he was managing Faron Young and Ferlin Husky, who didn't want Long expending his efforts on any other artist.

I was aware of a depression in Patsy Cline when she worried about the delay between hit records. Charlie told me what I sensed was correct, then went on to tell me something I'd never heard.

Patsy Cline wanted to become a regular member, not a guest artist, on the Grand Ole Opry.

"One day in 1960 she said to her manager, Randy Hughes, 'When am I going to be a member on the Opry?' He mentioned it to Ott Devine, and he said, 'I didn't know Patsy wanted to be a member.' So they signed her up, and I think that did more to bring her out of her depression than anything."

Charlie talked about the inaccuracies in *Coal Miner's Daughter*—how Patsy was shown riding on her bus when she never owned one. She had thought about buying one but died in the plane crash before the sale.

Patsy had heard a young singer on the radio in 1961 named Loretta Lynn. Patsy was recovering from a car wreck and asked Charlie to find Loretta and bring her to Patsy's hospital room. Charlie did and introduced one superstar to an up-and-coming superstar over a bed rail.

He and Loretta became lasting friends, and she once asked him to collect her concert fee for her after a show. Charlie did and proceeded to count the money.

"Don't count the money right in front of the man," Loretta whispered to him, because the counting implied the man was dishonest. Charlie went on with the counting anyway, and Loretta chastised him again.

"So I just stuck the money in my pocket and we went on down the road, and when I counted out the money for Loretta it was twenty dollars short."

Charlie Dick was listening to the radio in 1963 when Billy Walker entered the house. Before Billy could say a word, a radio announcer said the crashed airplane carrying Patsy Cline had been found.

That's how Charlie learned.

Charlie asked that the body be brought to his house where, in a closed casket, it lay in state while mourners came from throughout Tennessee. After a funeral service in Nashville, Patsy was moved to her final resting place in Winchester, Virginia.

Their Nashville house is still standing. But Charlie moved out.

"I got married again in 1965, and everybody who came to the house would say things like, 'I remember when Patsy did this, I remember when Patsy did that.' That wasn't doing my new marriage any good, so I sold the house."

He divorced in 1972 and hasn't remarried.

Charlie floundered for about a year after Patsy's death until Tommy Hill told him that Starday Records needed a promotions man.

"I didn't know what a promotions man was," Charlie told me. "Then I found out it was the same thing I did on the road with Patsy, meeting disc jockeys and bringing them records."

That lasted seven years until he became a maker of documentaries.

In January 1993, a touring play based on the life of Patsy Cline got rave reviews in Nashville. Charlie didn't go. Neither did he read, in its entirety, a posthumous biography published about Patsy years earlier. He said he started reading all the inaccuracies, then put the book down.

At the premiere of Patsy's video documentary, whose accuracy is ensured by Charlie's involvement, it was time to leave the foyer and enter the screening room. A few folks scurried to put down their cocktails, while others took theirs inside. Wine was served during the show.

And as the mass of bodies pressed into two doorways, the background sound faded and finally cut off altogether.

No one noticed that Patsy was cut short while singing "Walking After Midnight," just as no one knew Patsy hated the hit all along.

TEN

August 5, 1957, was another muggy Monday in Philadelphia. Teenagers gathered as they had for months in the studio of WFIL-TV to dance to phonograph records played by the disc jockey Dick Clark.

Clark, as usual, prepared his play list and pulled the day's popular songs for broadcast. But this time things were different, because his daily dance party was to be picked up by the ABC television network where it continued to run, weekly, for thirty-two years.

The history-making premiere and the controversial music it featured became a target of criticism.

"In the fifties many people feared and hated rock 'n' roll," Clark wrote in *Rock, Roll, and Remember,* published in 1976. "*Look* said rock 'n' roll dragged music to 'new lows in taste' and Elvis was 'vulgar.' A New York 'World Telegram' columnist said rock 'n' roll was 'contrived by corrupt men.' In an interview that ran in newspapers across the country, Pearl Bailey said, 'Those groups with the weird names just aren't in time. The kids are listening to bad music.' 'Variety' said rock 'n' roll lyrics were 'nothing more than dirty postcards translated into songs.'

"These attitudes were focused on 'American Bandstand' as the show was there for parents and critics to shoot at every afternoon on the network. And from the moment I first announced a rock record on the show, I came under fire as a champion of rock 'n' roll."

It's interesting to note that many of the publications that railed against the music eventually would earn millions of dollars selling advertising for it. The double standard has never been a stranger to entertainment journalism.

Clark went on to become an icon of American entertainment and a pillar of the American way of life. American parents, unaware of the explicit music yet to come, grew to have few qualms about entrusting the viewing by their children of G-rated Dick Clark. Like Richard Nixon, and the Rev. Billy Graham, Clark became one of the world's most recognizable personalities.

Imagine my jubilation when I was informed in 1991 that I could interview Dick Clark for a one-hour special, to be broadcast on The Nashville Network, and that he would interview me for a similar program.

Writers say the most difficult interview they do is with other writers. I felt similar anxiety toward Clark, although I knew he understood the interviewer's process better than the vast majority of personalities I've questioned.

Ms. Debra Brawner, an associate producer of "Nashville Now," came up with the idea for the interviews. She contacted Clark's people, and he and I have her to thank for the programs. Viewer interest was high, and each show was rerun, and the mail response was heavy.

To bone up for the interview I read the most recent book on Clark, published in 1978. I studied it, and gathered ideas for questions. Ms. Brawner hired the Nashville writer, Robert Wynne, a thespian and undiscovered Robert Duvall, and he filled out my interrogation sheet.

Someone likened the idea to country music's most famous broadcaster interviewing rock's. At least that was the premise.

Wynne got help from Clark's office, and as my office researched Clark's, and vice versa, our similarities began to surface. We had each been chain smokers who quit the same year. We each had had three wives and found marital happiness only with our last. And we each had been accused of looking younger than we are.

I was made comfortable by the things we had in common. I felt that the mutual respect Clark and I had would lubricate any wheels of uneasiness.

Fortified with much information about him, I took my wife, hairdresser, writer, and the show's producer, Debra Brawner, with me to meet Dick Clark, America's oldest teenager, at the Alamo Studio in Burbank, California, not far from NBC.

The night before the first session, where Clark would interview me, my associates and I visited the set of "Hot Country Nights," a network show he was producing. We watched Tammy Wynette and Sawyer Brown perform for videotape. Then we huddled inside the control room used for the "Tonight Show" to finalize plans for the next day's shoot. Although most of the talent had been on the other side of that window, some of it probably had drifted into that control room over the years. That realization charged the air. There was an invisible energy like the kind hovering over Nashville's Music Row and outside New York City's Brill Building.

On December 18, 1991, my interview began and ended with the most famous, non-singing voice in rock 'n' roll. Right out of the box, Clark disclosed that his rock career had its background in country. I knew then we'd be compatible.

"When I was on television in Utica, New York," Clark recalled, "I was 'Cactus Dick' and the Santa Fe Riders, and we were sponsored by the Rothbard Reupholstery Company. I remember it to this day."

"What did 'Cactus Dick' do?"

"I was the announcer on the show. I did a little bit of singing, badly. They used to make fun of me, you know."

"I believe as a disc jockey the first records you ever played were country," I said.

"Yeah. On the 'W-O-L-F Buckaroo' show in Syracuse, New York, but those were the days of Eddy Arnold and Roy Rogers. Who else would have been around in those days?"

"Hank Snow, Ernest Tubb?"

I asked him if he used wild, snappy patter.

"No," Clark said, "I played it straight. Country music has always been sort of my secret-service life. I mean, I put the first country music show on NBC back in the 60s, called 'Swinging Country.' They wouldn't give us any night-time visibility, so we put 'em on in day time. Then I opened a country music night club. I had a couple of country music radio stations I owned."

I talked to Clark about his early days on "American Bandstand" and realized more than ever that he was a real pioneer in exposing country music to a national audience.

"You know," Clark said, "the amazing thing in the early days of 'Bandstand' was that kids had virtually no musical prejudices. They would accept Carl Perkins and Conway Twitty, who in those days was a rock 'n' roller. Little did they know he was a latent country artist. Don Gibson would come on, Johnny Cash, Jerry Lee. There were no prejudices. We would just play all the music, and country was hot."

Dick Clark was not only a front-runner of musical integration but also of racial inclusion. His program was the first in the history of American television to show black and white couples dancing side by side, and eventually, blacks dancing with whites. The mixing met with consternation.

"When I inherited 'Bandstand,' in 1956, it was a segregated show in Philadelphia, a northern city. There were always black artists on the show performing, but never kids dancing together. I said, 'Now, we have no directive from anybody, nobody said do it, don't do it, whatever.' The producer just said, 'You know, someday we've got to let Negroes in here.' So we began to have a few kids dance and nothing much happened. The very first day I ever spoke to a black kid on camera, on the 'Rate A Record' portion, where it's said, 'I like the beat, it's easy to dance to,' that sort of thing, I ran to the control room to see if there was any reaction and there wasn't. Nobody cared and it happened like that."

The racial mixing of dance partners didn't come about until the 1970s.

———————— ■ ————————

The list of celebrities who appeared on "American Bandstand" reads like a roll call of popular music's hierarchy. Few people realize, however, that two names are conspicuously absent from the list, and they are the biggest names of all.

Neither the Beatles nor Elvis Presley appeared.

"They were giants," Clark said, referring to the Beatles. "Ed Sullivan brought them over. The same with Elvis Presley. They were too tight and wouldn't work for scale. We paid $155 for a performance in those days."

One time, a country performer came on Clark's set, asked about the performance fee, and then refused to entertain. He said the amount was too small.

"Who was it?" I asked.

"You'll never believe it," Clark replied. "It was Porter Wagoner. Here's this show being seen by millions of people, and the little girl who did the contract put it out in front of him and he said, 'Why, I've never worked for that in my life.' "

I was astounded to discover that Wagoner did not do the show, and even more astonished to learn that Lawrence Welk did. And I was surprised to learn how many non-musical legends appeared on the program, including Jerry Lewis, Bob Hope, and Jack Bailey, the moderator of television's old "Queen for a Day."

I would bet the average Nashville music scholar doesn't know that Clark was among the first television hosts to offer national exposure to Patsy Cline, Marty Robbins, and Jim Reeves. His Yankee teenage audiences were dancing to those artists as regularly as they were to Little Richard.

Even as a boy, Clark's background was curiously integrated, exposed to a cross-sampling of show business luminaries.

"My neighbors were Arthur and Kathryn Murray," Clark said. "My mom and dad lived on the second floor of a six-story apartment, and the Murrays lived on the third or fourth. They became close friends and began to raise their families. They were buddies."

"You've always had interesting neighbors," I said. "Ed McMahon?"

"He was truly my next-door neighbor," Clark laughed. "We shared a wall in Philadelphia."

That's all he said about the famous announcer.

"But Mrs. Murray gave me lessons on my thirteenth birthday to teach me how to dance."

"Did she teach you well?"

"No, and not her, personally," Clark replied. "I went to the studio and took the lessons, but I never learned to dance. I mean, I don't want to say it was their fault. I learned to do the waltz and the jitterbug. I was on the 'Arthur Murray Show' once doing the jitterbug and I won."

Dick Clark, whose dance show was the cornerstone to a personal fortune, told me that he doesn't like to dance.

"You fear that you won't do it well?" I asked him.

"Yeah," he said, "and after all these years, wouldn't you expect that I would have learned something that I could have danced to, and get out there. I danced in Europe for a good reason . . . nobody knew who I was."

Clark said surveys show that nine out of ten Americans know him, so he occasionally flees to Europe to find privacy, "and to do my dancing."

"You remind me of musicians I know who do nothing but play dances and can't dance a lick," I said. "You went onto a television show that was literally built around dancing. And there on that show you created all the very in dances of the day. 'The Pony,' 'The Stroll,' 'The Bop,' 'The Alligator.' I would think at some point one of those kids would have said, 'Mr. Clark, let me show you these steps.' "

Clark said he only danced a slow dance once a year at Christmas.

I watched as much as I listened to Dick Clark. I marveled at his on-camera composure, so rigid yet so natural. He seemed to exude warmth, albeit controlled, and put me as much at ease as he did our viewers. He had an easy persona that is given to only a handful of superb television personalities. Johnny Carson had it too.

Clark, like many accomplished men, had no reservations about laughing at himself. The singers who appeared on the early "American Bandstand" shows used to lipsynch their songs, as Clark freely admitted, and they occasionally did so to the tune of calamity.

"There is one famous incident. It involved a country artist, Jimmy Dean," Clark said. "In those days we were playing 45 rpm records."

Clark introduced Dean to his national audience. The applause rose and then fell, Dean stepped into the spotlight, and the record was spun. Out came the voice of Dee Clark, a black singer with a high voice.

Paul Anka once tried to lipsynch to a record that skipped. He stood there, mouthing the lyrics as if he had a stuttering problem.

At one point in his early career, Dick Clark was doing seventeen hours of live television each week. Today, the industry's highest-paid personalities, such as Dan Rather and Peter Jennings, do little more than that in two months. Clark was as durable as he was innovative.

"I've had children throw up on me, pass out on me on the air," Clark recalled. "If you can get through that, you can get through anything."

"American Bandstand," although a major chapter in the textbook of American television, was an incredibly low-budgeted show. Clark, the talent, the director, the stage hands, and all the others were paid from the $1,500 a week allotted them.

At one time, rumors circulated that Clark required his celebrity guests to "kick back" their performance fee to him.

"There were a lot of rumors like that," Clark said. "Let me tell you the story. We had fifteen hundred dollars a week to do the shows. So we took the fifteen hundred dollars and we would spend it. Then, if a record company said, 'we'll pay the artist,' we said 'fine.' Never did the artist have to give his check back to us. You'd have to give it back to the record company, so the word got out that I was getting the money back. Not true. Once we ran out of budget money, we'd let anybody pay their way on. The Mormon Tabernacle Choir paid their way onto the 'Today Show' and NBC. It was very common. It was called a 'check swap.' "

A record company, in other words, would pay Dick Clark to have one of its acts on his program. Clark paid the talent, who in turn gave the money back to the record company. The funds went full circle. Clark added that the federal government eventually took a dim view of the practice and ordered it halted.

"Wasn't 'Bandstand' a highly rated show?" I asked.

"Oh yeah," Clark said.

"Then why didn't they give it a bigger budget?"

"Ask the people who owned the network at the time," Clark said. "I think what happened was the show went on to replace old English movies. ABC was the third-rated network. It was barely a network, and we were on sixty-seven stations as I recall when we went on, competing against CBS with two hundred and NBC with two hundred. Yet it became the number-one show, so that meant we had to have huge numbers in the markets we were in. Eventually, they increased the budget, but those first two years were tight. That's the reason I went into the music business. I had to make a living. I did record dances and sock hops, seven nights a week at seventy-five cents a head."

Clark insisted that he and his wife paid taxes on all the money they received in cash. Many of the bills had been rolled tightly in the dancers' sweating hands. The Clarks applied an electric iron to the currency to make it suitable for deposit.

I've never entirely understood brotherly love, and never will, because I've never had a brother. But I noticed a sinking in Clark's demeanor when we talked about his brother, five years his senior, who was killed in the Battle of the Bulge during World War II.

The two had been close all their lives and had shared a room together.

"He was the athlete," Clark recollected. "He was taller than I, he was stronger than I, he was every young kid's idol. I wanted to be him so badly. I went out for the football team and they walked on me, you know, because I weighed a hundred and fifteen pounds, and I decided when they walked on my head, 'I don't think I'm cut out to play football.' So I swam because my brother was a swimmer."

The Army wanted to make Bradley Clark a teacher, but he insisted on being where the action was and became a fighter pilot. He was shot down during the famous Battle of the Bulge two days before Christmas. Clark said Christmas always carries a pall because of its nearness to the anniversary of Bradley's death.

Clark said his teenage years were particularly lonely in the wake of his brother's death. Insecure and broken-hearted, he sat with his grief and acne in his room adorned with athletic pennants that had belonged to his brother.

Because Clark had discussed his brother's death on a number of interview shows, servicemen wrote to Clark. One pilot thought he shot down the plane that shot down his brother's.

"Do you think, had he lived, that you might have worked for him?" I asked.

"No," Clark replied, "it would have been vice versa. I mean, we were Mutt and Jeff, Abbott and Costello, the Odd Couple. He was everything I wasn't. I wanted to be like him and he said, 'You don't understand.' He was a placid, quiet, very loving, wonderful guy, and I was this crazy little runt of a kid, you know, full of vim and vigor, who would tackle the world. And all he said was, 'We'll never be the same, so why don't you just do what you do and I'll do what I do, and we'll love each other,' and I learned a little bit from that. You can't be somebody else."

Sensing that the interview was becoming melancholy, I decided to change the tone and abruptly asked Clark about teenage love.

"Oh boy," he said, "that's what you call a change of pace."

"Dick, you got married when you were a teenager, didn't you?" I asked.

"No, no, no," he said. "I fell in love as a teenager. I got married when I was twenty-one. You know, actually you're right. Mentally, I was a teenager because, remember, back in those days twenty-one-year-olds were very unsophisticated."

Clark's first wife was his high-school sweetheart, whom he married after their college graduation. They went to separate schools.

They were divorced after nine years.

"What happened?" I asked.

"She fell in love with another man."

"Is this because at the time you were so distracted by 'Bandstand'?" I asked.

"It probably had something to do with it," he said. "That would be the logical explanation from the outside. After our divorce, she said we never should have gotten married. She wasn't sure she loved me when we did get married, but she did it because we talked about it for so long and everybody expected us to get married."

"She said that to you?"

"Yeah."

Her statement didn't do very good things for his head, he said, and I added that rejection is not fun. He agreed.

Like so many smart but unwise men, Clark sought solace in a bottle.

"I drank a lot to put the pain away," he said. "I was making a movie at the time and a guy would drive me from Philadelphia to New York where the movie was being shot, and I had a terrible hangover each day."

Clark and I talked about children, the role of his heavy work schedule taking time from his offspring.

"Chet Atkins once told me," I said, "if kids did everything their parents told them there would be no progress."

"Kids will never do what their parents tell them," Clark said, "so it's an academic question. I mean, they're always gonna rebel against us. I get these reunions now of the kids that used to dance on 'Bandstand,' some of the old ones are pushing fifty, some of 'em are over fifty, and they hit me with the same stuff I heard when I was a kid and they were kids. They were saying the same things their parents said about the dreadful music, that rap music is awful, the heavy metal stuff. They go on and on."

Clark surprised me by talking about his angry days, the dark side of his public image as Mr. Nice Guy.

"I almost didn't graduate because I didn't want to give the dollar deposit back on my locker key and I said to the principal, 'When we gave you the dollar, you said we could have the dollar back when we graduated and now you say we gotta give it to the school fund. I won't give it to the school fund. I want the dollar back.' I was the president of the student body. He said, 'Here's the dollar.' I said, 'I don't want your dollar. I want the school's dollar.' "

We moved from Clark's teenage years to failed marriages and on to his workaholism. Clark, for years, had been rumored to be a taskmaster.

"I'm not as demanding as I used to be," Clark said. "When I was younger, I didn't have patience, because I didn't understand that everybody's not the same. I said if I'm working this hard and I'm this crazy, why isn't everybody else, and I would get impatient. I've gotten, I hope, a little wiser now. I realize that certain people have other attributes."

I asked Clark how he developed his work ethic, and he said it wasn't developed, but simply innate to him.

"I've been this way since I was a child, long before I was aware that my brother was a big influence. I had a shoeshine stand when I was four or five years old. I didn't need the money, but it looked like fun. I had a deal where you could have one shoe shined for three cents or two shoes shined for a nickel. Now that shows you what kind of a mind was going on in that kid's head. I mean the kid was obviously an entrepreneur.

"I also sold two lines of magazines. As I grew older I had a little restaurant in my mother's living room. Still later I picked corn, hoed cucumbers, worked in a chicken box factory, counted traffic, was a short-order cook, a disc jockey, a bed maker, and a pot and pan man in a kitchen. I had a lot of funny jobs."

Clark explained that as a traffic counter he and a partner stopped produce trucks. As Clark's partner talked to the driver, Clark stole fruit and vegetables from the back.

"But I think the statute of limitations has run out," Clark laughed.

The produce scuffling perhaps tells something about Clark's financial frugality as an adult. He admits some people think of him as overly thrifty.

"I'm frugal in a strange way," he said. "I'm a spendthrift in others, so I learned to fly first class because if you don't your heirs will. I've spent money in my life. I've spent a lot of it. I give a fair amount of it away as you should when you make a lot of money, but I hate to waste it. I went out to buy Christmas presents the other day. I looked at a shirt for one of my kids and they wanted a hundred-and-some dollars for the dumb shirt and I said, 'You can't spend that kind of money on a shirt, let's get out of here,' and my wife drags me back and says, 'You know, there are places where you can spend more,' so I get crazed."

Clark's third and current wife, Kari, worked in his office for three years before his romantic inclinations surfaced. They began dating and eventually lived together for seven years before their marriage, which has lasted for fifteen.

Today, he calls her his best and only true friend. Clark told me working seven days a week prevents a social life and close relationships, except for the one with his wife.

"This woman is the most delightful, upbeat person you'd ever want to meet. Maybe she might rival your wife, Joy. She and I are perfectly matched in every regard, even though we are different ages. She's thirteen years my junior. We share the same interests, enjoy the same food, the same travel quirks. She's always upbeat, she's always in an extraordinarily happy frame of mind. I don't know how she does it, but she can put up with me."

Clark underwent a severe emotional and psychological scare when he thought he was going to lose Kari Clark to cancer. He learned a lot about himself and his true priorities.

"It was a scare," he said. "It appeared as if she might have ovarian cancer with a minimal chance of survival."

Clark was in the hospital in Burbank when his wife underwent treatment.

"I went into the chapel and I prayed to God, and I said I wanted to apologize because I'd prayed before getting into the formal place to pray. I said, 'Please forgive me because my very first thought when I thought I might lose her was how will I be able to go on.' That's the wrong thing to think, but it's a human thought. Then I began to pray for her."

Clark told me that the greatest thing Kari does for him is to make life fun. I saw him involuntarily smile as he said it.

"Could you enjoy all of your success without somebody to share it with?" I asked.

"No. That's the secret. It really doesn't matter. Take things in order. If you've got health, the next thing you hope for is some kind of activity you can get involved in that may give you enough money to live on, and then if you can find someone to share it with, that's the ultimate success."

Clark told me that Kari's main complaint about him is their limited vacations. He said he wouldn't take any vacations were it not for Kari.

"My daughter used to chastise me," Clark said. "She made the same accusation you did . . . 'You're a workaholic.' Workaholics never stop, they work twenty-four hours a day, seven days a week. I work because I love it. I don't find it to be work. My daughter was working on a film. I said, 'You're doing seventy or eighty hours a week on this. You're working too hard. Why are you doing it?' 'Because I like it,' she said. That's the difference."

Clark's second marriage ended after nine years and set him off on a drinking binge.

"You were devastated, you went to the bottle, and I know that Connie Francis and Bobby Darin were part of your support group."

"Yeah," was all he said.

We talked about family structure, and the values American teenagers had during the heyday of "American Bandstand" and their values today. Teenagers routinely wore coats and ties on "Bandstand."

Clark surprised me when he said the dancers were ordered to dress that way. He also pointed out that adolescents of the 1950s saw their parents as important people in their lives. Youngsters today see their peers as the most important.

"It's just been a slow evolution that's been speeded up with technology and communication and everything else," he said.

Clark, known for his own meticulous grooming, said he had a hard time handling the personal appearances of the 1960s hippies, although he continued to play the music of their role models.

"I couldn't relate to that," Clark said. "I'm trying to think how old I was in the '60s—mid-thirties, forties—something like that. I was too old to be into drugs. I was from the alcohol and cigarettes generation. I didn't understand it. I couldn't relate to it, so I faked it.

"I just sorta went along and staggered through. I am very square. I give that impression. I'm odd. I happen to appear to be square, but you don't get to be this old and remain stupid."

Clark agreed with the hippies' anti-war posture. He thought his stance had to do with the death of his brother in the military.

Clark, a founder of rock 'n' roll, astonished me by saying he enjoyed rap music and didn't find it offensive. I personally resent its repetition.

Clark thinks white youngsters comprise the greatest part of rap audiences because artists are making statements that white teenagers understand.

I think his assessment is thoughtful but incorrect. His tolerance for the glorified noise is a west coast point of view.

Our interview got touchy when I raised the issue of disc jockeys accepting money to broadcast records. The ugly term for the practice is "payola." Mentioning the word to a disc jockey is like saying "fire" to a lumberman. Clark was characteristically direct in his response.

"I'm sure most everybody thought Dick Clark was really on the take and making a fortune on the side taking payola when payola became a big issue in the newspapers and on television," I said. "Did you take payola?"

"No," he said. "I paid payola. Now let me explain why I say that. It was not illegal in those days. It was later to be called commercial bribery, and it's against the federal law now. It goes way back to the old days of sheet-music sellers bribing piano players to play their songs in the Woolworth stores, even to somebody paying a band leader to play the song on a midnight radio broadcast, so it wasn't new. When I went into the music business I made enough money, so it was totally unnecessary to accept money to play records.

"Now when I was called before the congressional investigators [who asked], 'Did you take money?' What they couldn't understand was that I had very little respect for politicians. It's a very difficult job, I think, to have terrible compromises to make, and I don't want to be anti-politician, because somebody's got to do the job. But the quality of labor that you find in that job is subject to question. They saw a guy in his late twenties, who at that point was making somewhere between a half million and a million dollars a year and said, 'Obviously he's a thief.' "

Clark was grilled by Congress for two days, after which it was concluded that he was simply a successful entrepreneur.

"I used every single opportunity I could to make money," he said. "I managed artists, I pressed records, I did tours, I owned labels. I did everything I could think of to turn a dollar, and it was all legal, but nobody ever had to pay me to play their records so Congress said, 'Get out of here!' "

I had asked earlier the one question that is posed to Clark more than any other.

"How do you look so young?"

"I have answered this for twenty years," he said. "You select your parents very carefully. It's all in the genes. It's nothing you can do. I'm the luckiest man in the world. It all started with 'Bandstand,' being surrounded with kids. You have a youthful approach. If you've got things to do every day and unexplored adventure to get into, you're going to stay young. What makes you old is when you atrophy. Your thinking and your musical tastes don't change and the food you like, the same friends and the same travel plans. You can't let that happen. That's what's right for me."

"Ever had a face-lift?"

"No, but I wouldn't stop in a hot second," he said. "You do what you gotta do."

If I had been a baseball player, I would have been thrilled to get an interview with Mickey Mantle. I'm a broadcaster. Getting an interview with Clark was, for me, the equivalent of a priest interviewing the Pope. I'm not exaggerating.

I've done interviews that were more controversial, a few more candid, but none more revealing about the person behind the image.

The most powerful medium in history is television. Clark is arguably the most powerful man in the most powerful medium. For an hour, that man's mind was mine for the probing. I'm a better broadcaster for what he said; a better person for what I heard. And felt.

Thanks, Dick. Thanks.

ELEVEN

According to the *Tennessean,* Nashville's morning newspaper, 250 celebrities and music business personnel gathered inside the city's historic Ryman Auditorium on November 9, 1992, for a singing, hand-clapping, laughing, and dancing occasion.

It was a spectacular funeral. More accurately, it was a memorial service, as "funeral" implies the presence of a body and mourning. Deferring to the wishes of Mary Miller, Roger's widow, the service was a celebration, except that the life of the party was gone.

Roger Miller had been cremated days earlier in California where he died on October 25, 1992, about a year after being diagnosed with throat cancer. In his final days, the disease had spread to his brain, and death was imminent.

> *"We are pilgrims on a journey through the darkness of*
> *The night*
> *We are bound for other places, crossing to the other*
> *Side."*

Those words, written by Roger for his 1985 Broadway musical, "Big River," were distributed at his service.

I saw people there I hadn't seen in years, time and travel having kept us apart. It's a pity that some separations are so pronounced that they're interrupted only by death.

There were larger-than-life photographs situated around the Ryman stage. An old WSM microphone sat center platform. It had long since been retired, but was brought out for the occasion. Many past greats, Hank Williams, Jim Reeves, Patsy Cline, and Roger Miller, had sung through the chrome relic.

I've attended many celebrity funerals. I've never attended a memorial service, however, that produced as many tributes to the deceased as this one for Roger Miller.

Eulogies came from, among others, Chet Atkins, Johnny Cash, Jessi Colter, David Huddleston, Waylon Jennings, Garrison Keillor, Kris Kristofferson, Don Meredith, Willie Nelson, David Steinberg, Marty Stuart, Mel Tillis, and me.

Steve Wariner, accompanied by Chet Atkins, sang "Amazing Grace." His clear tenor filled the sprawling old hall. It was the first time he had sung the song in Nashville since August of 1991, at Dottie West's funeral.

Footage was shown of various Roger Miller television performances, including a guest shot he did with the late Stringbean on the old Porter Wagoner Show. A bouncy teenager, Dolly Parton, was also in the scene. Another clip showed Roger singing before 80,000 people at "Farm Aid 1984."

"In America, everybody is—but some are more than others." Those words of Mark Twain seemed appropriate since Roger wrote "Big River," a Tony Award–winning 1985 Broadway musical adaptation from Twain's writing. So I shared the passage.

Several entertainers sang, followed by the Music City Mass Choir. The proceedings ended and a number of us adjourned to Tootsie's Orchid Lounge, the landmark Nashville watering hole from where many luminaries, including Roger, launched their careers. Roger hung out there in the late 1950s looking for work as a musician and a songwriter.

In 1957 he landed a job playing fiddle for Minnie Pearl (Mel Tillis played rhythm guitar) and he wrote songs for Tree International, which would become the world's largest country music publishing firm. He remained with Tree for thirty-five years and was its most prolific and long-standing writer.

Watching the projected images of Roger in his prime reminded me of interviews I had done with him. I remembered the night he recorded "King of the Road." I attended the session, and recall his jubilant mood following the success of "Dang Me," his first number-one record.

Roger had won five Grammy Awards the previous year, and he appeared on my "Opry Almanac" show on March 8, 1966. One of the Grammys was for Song of the Year, as his "King of the Road" was pitted against "Taste of Honey" by the Tijuana Brass, "The Shadow of Your Smile" by Tony Bennett, and "Yesterday" by the Beatles.

Roger won.

The March 19, 1965, issue of *Time* magazine cited the song's lyrics and called the song "the hottest item on the current pop charts."

"The things I tried to do like somebody else always came out different," Roger told the magazine's interviewer. "It was frustrating—until I learned I'm the only one that knows what I'm thinking."

At the time of the interview, Roger had recorded twenty-five songs. All but one was his own composition.

When the largest news periodical probed him about his background, he told the reporter his parents were so poor that he was made in Japan. When pressed about his singing, he replied that he sang through his nose by ear.

Ten months earlier, he had been on the cover of *Life,* and the magazine ran a list of his one-liners.

"My education was Korea, Clash of '52." "God's house is the heart of a child." "Everyday is Saturday to a dog."

Roger was one of the first singers to garner major press attention for country music, which until then was covered mostly by small publications close to the industry, and trade music publications. The morning he did "Opry Almanac" he had recently learned that he would be given his own prime-time variety show on NBC, and that it would air in color. Color was a big indication in 1966 of the network's seriousness about the program.

Roger's personality was perhaps the greatest enigma in country music. He was goofy one minute, pensive the next, and bashful all the time. The morning I tried to get him to talk about his Grammy Awards I failed. I wound up having to put words into his mouth, and he was commercial music's most prolific writer of the day. He was visibly nervous on the set, squirmed, and looked downward.

"Were you sitting on pins and needles when you found out you were going to get your television show?" I asked.

"No," he said, "I'd been sitting on the edge of the bed."

The call with the news came at 8:30 A.M. Roger talked to the NBC official and calmly hung up.

"Come here," he said to his wife.

"I can't," she replied, "I'm changing the baby."

"Bring the baby," he said.

She walked over to him, and he was so enthralled, all he could do was recite the show's time slot.

"Monday nights, Monday nights," he babbled.

Roger had earlier done one network special. It garnered a whopping forty-five percent of the evening's national television viewership.

About the same time, Roger was invited to New York City to the office of Otto Preminger, the foremost motion-picture producer/director of the day.

The two exchanged pleasantries, and Preminger was interrupted by a telephone call. He asked Roger to pardon him for a minute, during which Roger fell asleep. Preminger re-entered the room and found Roger snoring.

Roger Miller appeared on network television regularly two years before the "Glen Campbell Goodtime Hour," and three years before the "Johnny Cash Show." His show failed after one season due to ratings. He blamed the failure on his own creative stagnancy, and blamed that on an addiction to amphetamines. Later he would tell the Oklahoma Legislature, addressing the need for drug reform laws, that pills limited his career and almost ruined his life.

The only thing predictable about Roger was unpredictability. He simply didn't do things like other people, and it cost him. It nearly cost him his life, he claimed, when he tried to get into an apartment he was sharing with singer-songwriter Bill Anderson. Having forgotten his key, he entered through a window.

Bill saw a shadow sneaking into his dwelling and fetched a pistol, Roger told me.

"Boy, that could have set back country music" was Roger's only opinion about the incident. In talking to Bill about the incident, I found that he didn't recall it the same way.

"Roger didn't live with me," Bill said. "It might have been a situation where Barbara [Roger's wife then] had kicked him out of the house and he was staying over. But I had come in earlier and had parked my car about three blocks away. There were a couple of girls in town from Atlanta that I didn't want to see, so I was trying to make it appear as though no one was at home. I was asleep and was awakened by the raising of the window. In the darkness, I saw a hand under the window, and then I saw a head and shoulders. Somebody was coming through. I didn't get a gun. I grabbed the closest things to me, and that was a pillow and a big alarm clock. The clock was so heavy it could have really hurt somebody."

Bill threw the pillow over the prowler's head. He raised the clock to batter the man's skull when he heard a muffled "Hey, Bill, it's me, it's me."

Roger had arrived.

Roger owned a Lincoln Continental, but preferred to drive a three-wheel motor scooter in the early 1960s. He drove the contraption into a tree, demolished it, and was injured.

Roger felt no guilt about the mishap because, after all, he'd been up for three days. The schedule was routine for a Nashvillian in 1963, he felt.

Roger was a spokesman for the rowdy faction of country music fans, perhaps in a way not heard since the hobo ballads of Jimmie Rodgers, who died in the 1930s.

His song "Dang Me" spoke for the "Bubbas" and "Leroys" who comprised the pool-playing, beer-drinking, pickup-driving, good ole boys of 1963: "Sittin' around drinkin' with the rest of the guys. Six rounds bought, and I bought five."

A year later, the British Invasion stormed the United States and knocked the few country artists who actually crossed over onto popular surveys off the charts. But not Roger. He held on with "England Swings," "Engine, Engine Number Nine," and, of course, "King of the Road."

Roger was the first country star to take a hit record and parlay it into a national business. He opened a "King of the Road" lodge in Nashville, and three others elsewhere. The inns were successful for a while but ultimately failed, like Conway Twitty's mobile-home lots and Minnie Pearl's chicken stores. Roger lost a ton of money, but his graciousness was an example to other Nashville artists who would eventually lose from behind a desk money they had earned behind a microphone.

In 1987 I told Roger that people frequently asked me "whatever happened to Roger Miller?" "Big River" had opened on Broadway two years earlier, but a lot of country fans don't pay attention to Broadway. The show had celebrated its 900th performance a week before our conversation, and Roger had written all of the songs.

He became the first country star since Will Rogers to go to Broadway and paved the way for other stars such as Larry Gatlin and Mac Davis.

Roger undertook "Big River" at the urging of Yale professor and Broadway producer Rocco Landesman, according to the *New York Times*. Roger quit school after the eighth grade and was sought by an Ivy League educator. I thought that was a wonderful irony.

"To set the record straight," Landesman said, "at that time there was no producer Rocco Landesman. There was just a kid with a dream and Roger took it on as a risk and because of Roger Miller there is now a producer Rocco Landesman."

Landesman, in April 1993, said that he had been a lifelong Miller devotee, and asked him to write the seventeen songs for the production after meeting Miller, who sang for him personally until 5 A.M.

Landesman casually, rapidly rattled Roger Miller lyrics as easily as he would recite his mother's maiden name. In evaluating

alter Ralph Emery, taken in 1934, at one year old. (Author's collection)

My first WSM publicity shot taken in 1957, when I was twenty-four. (Author's collection)

ere I am receiving my first "Disc Jockey of
e Year" award in 1961. (Author's
llection)

Gene Autry, left, interviewed by Ralph Emery inside Nashville's Jackson Hotel in 1962. Looking on is George Hamilton IV. (*Author's collection*)

A summer night on the *All Night Show* in 1971. I am surrounded, left to right, by Crystal Gayle, Doyle Wilburn, Teddy Wilburn, Peggy Sue, Loretta Lynn, Jay Lee Webb, Merle Haggard, and the late Wayne Raney. (*Courtesy of Wanda Raney Sutherland*)

The late Jim Reeves during one of his final recording sessions for RCA in Nashville, Tennessee. (*Photograph courtesy of the Country Music Foundation*)

Hawkshaw Hawkins, photographed at the March 3, 1963, benefit performance for Cactus Jack Call, is seen singing for the last time. (*Mildred Keith*)

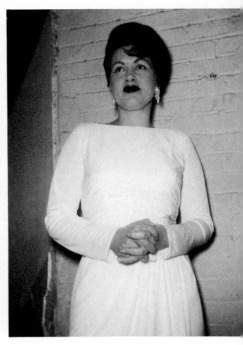

This picture, taken on March 3, 1963, is believed to be the last ever taken of Patsy Cline in concert. (*Photograph courtesy of the Country Music Foundation*)

This photograph was snapped seconds before Pat Cline went on stage for the last time in her lif Moments earlier, she had been overheard whi crying, hence the tissue in her hands. (*Mildred Keit*

BENEFIT SHOW for "CACTUS" JACK CALL!

WSM GRAND OLE OPRY

Roy Acuff ● George Jones
Ralph Emery ● Billy Walker
Cowboy Copas ● Hawk Shaw Hawkins
Wilma Lee & Stony Cooper ● Dottie West
Georgie Riddle & Jones Boys
Geo. McCormick & Clench Mountain Clan

K. C., KANSAS, MEMORIAL BUILDING

TODAY—3 Big Shows, 2, 5:15 & 8:15 p. m.

Adults (all seats) $1.50, Children 50c—Tickets at Auditorium

Now you see her, now you don't. One of the mysteries surrounding the plane crash in which Patsy Cline died is why her name appears in the show's program but not in a newspaper ad on March 3, 1963, the same day as the show. (*Author's collection*)

WSM GRAND OLE OPRY

ROY ACUFF

GEORGE JONES

PATSY CLINE

RALPH EMERY

BILLY WALKER

COWBOY COPAS

HAWKSHAW HAWKINS

WILMA LEE & STONY COOPER

DOTTIE WEST

GEORGIE RIDDLE & JONES BOYS

GEORGE McCORMICK & THE CLENCH MOUNTAIN CLAN

— Masters of Ceremonies —

GUY SMITH   HAP PEOPLES   HERB HOEFLICKER

The clock from the plane that took the lives of Patsy Cline, Cowboy Copas, Hawkshaw Hawkins, and Randy Hughes. Note that the hands are stopped at the point of impact. The clock was given to me by the FAA investigator, Bill Whitmore, and may now be seen in the Country Music Hall of Fame. (*Author's collection*)

The late Roger Miller at the site of the airplane crash that killed the four great performers mentioned above. (*Photograph by Gerald Holly/Nashville Tennessean*)

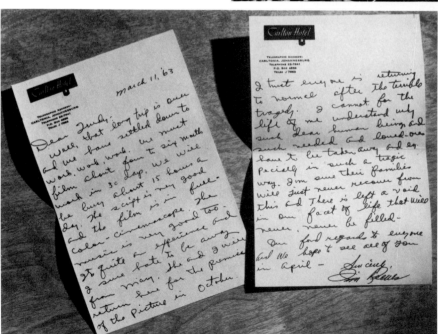

The letter of consolation from Jim Reeves written to Trudy Stamper, former director of promotion for WSM radio, regarding the deaths of Cline, Hawkins, Copas, and Hughes. (*Photograph courtesy of the Country Music Foundation*)

October 1970. A show simulcast over WSM-TV and WSM radio. From left to right, Tex Ritter, Merle Haggard, Roy Rogers, Ralph Emery, and Marty Robbins. Both Haggard and Robbins performed on the program with Ritter & Rogers in the audience. (*Author's collection*)

The audience segment of "Nashville Now" is one of the program's most popular attractions. An anonymous fan joins John Schneider and me during another sold-out live broadcast. (*Photograph by Jim Hagans/TNN*)

Loretta Lynn was co-host of "Nashville Now" during a Lynn family tribute, at which the singer was joined by her children. (*Photograph by Jim Hagans/TNN*)

Shotgun Red and Ralph Emery, two old pals, share a secret. (*Photograph by Jim Hagans/TNN*)

Randy Travis, while still recording as Randy Ray, first appeared on "Nashville Now" in 1984, when he still worked as a fry cook. He brought me a steak and lobster dinner that he had personally prepared. (*Photograph by Jim Hagans/TNN*)

A star-studded night in August of 1989 with Glen Campbell, Naomi Judd, the legendary producer Owen Bradley, Wynonna Judd, and Dinah Shore. (*Photograph by Jim Hagans/TNN*)

Vince Gill, on the left, joins the late Roy Acuff and me for fun on "Nashville Now." Acuff said that Gill's recording of "When I Call Your Name" was his favorite contemporary country song. (*Photograph by Jim Hagans/TNN*)

Shotgun Red and I recorded a children's album and sang Roy Acuff's "Wabash Cannonball." Our duo became a trio when we were joined by the man himself. The recording session marked the last time Acuff ever recorded "Wabash Cannonball," his biggest hit. (*Photograph by Jim Hagans/TNN*)

Willie Nelson, who has enjoyed a comeback as of late, is often asked where he lives. "Holiday Inns," he replies with a smile. (*UPI/Bettmann*)

A happy quartet. Former U.S. Secretary of Education Lamar Alexander, left, joins Larry Gatlin, Minnie Pearl, and Alfred Brumley, Jr., with me on "Nashville Now." (*Photograph by Jim Hagans/TNN*)

Chet Atkins, far right, was given his NARAS Lifetime Achievement Award on March 18, 1993, by Dolly Parton. From left to right are Harry Warner of BMI, Ralph Emery, Ms. Parton, and Gibson Guitar Co. President Henry Juszkiewicz, who presented Atkins with four guitars, including a one-of-a-kind instrument made especially for Atkins. (*Photograph by Alan L. Mayor*)

Ralph with Kenny Rogers and Travis Tritt at the 1993 Country Radio Seminar. (*Author's Collection*)

A big day in Joy Emery's life—Sunday, December 16, 1990. She graduated from O'More College in Franklin, Tennessee. (*Photograph by Mike Emery*)

Dick Clark and I "spin" records at the Alamo Studio in Burbank, California, on December 18, 1991. This shot was taken after the videotaping of "Dick Clark on the Record" and "Ralph Emery on the Record," two shows on which we interviewed each other. (*Photograph by Jim Hagans/TNN*)

Garth Brooks, center, joins "Nashville Now" producer Bill Turner and me to commemorate his first million-selling album. (*Photograph by Alan L. Mayor*)

Ralph Emery with Garth Brooks and John Anderson (with back to camera) at the Crazy Horse Saloon in Santa Ana, California on May 10, 1993. (*Author's collection*)

I observe President and Mrs. Clinton give the "S-o-o-o-u-u-i-i-e-e Pig" yell on the set of "Nashville Now." The yell is a part of the University of Arkansas' athletic cheer. Vice-President and Mrs. Gore also observe. The shot was taken during the 1992 presidential campaign. (*Photograph by Jim Hagans/TNN*)

On September 29, 1992, former President George Bush visited me on his presidential campaign trail. It marked the only time a sitting president ever appeared on "Nashville Now." (*Photograph by Jim Hagans/TNN*)

Above: Reba McEntire, left, joins Barbara Mandrell and me at the T-Lazy Seven Ranch after a day of skiing on December 23, 1992, in Aspen, Colorado. (*Photograph courtesy of the Joy Emery Collection*)

Left: Mary Chapin Carpenter with me about 90 minutes after she was named the Country Music Association's "Female Vocalist of the Year" in October 1992. Note her Bill Clinton/Al Gore button. (*Photograph by John Paschal*)

On June 8, 1988, O. B. McClinton posthumously received a star in the Walkway of Stars at the Country Music Hall of Fame. His widow, Jo Ann McClinton, is joined by son, Doyle, Bill Ivy, executive director of the Country Music Foundation, and me. (*Photograph by Don Putnam*)

My son, Dr. Steve Emery, joins his children and my only three grandchildren. From left to right are Stacey Emery, 13, Nathan Emery, 15, and Shannon Emery, 21. (*Author's collection*)

Joy and I and our sons: Mike Emery, left, and Kit Emery, who was discharged from the United States Air Force on May, 18, 1993. (*Author's collection*)

Roger's writing, he said, "It wasn't that he just didn't do things by the book, he didn't know about the book. He was an absolute original."

Persuading Roger to take on the "Big River" obligation, Landesman said, was hard. Persuading him to keep it was harder. Roger underwent burnout and was five songs short of his quota about six days before the play's opening.

"And we locked Roger into a hotel room," Landesman said, "and we tried that old trick, 'You are not coming out until you write a song.'

"Roger wasn't very happy about this," Landesman continued, "and finally after a while he emerged. He was really, really pissed off, and he says, 'I thought you guys were looking for a Rembrandt.'

" 'Yes,' " I said.

"Well," Roger said, "Rembrandt takes time. But if you want Earl Scheib, you got Earl Scheib."

Mary Miller told me Roger handed Landesman the song, said he was going home, and did. The song Roger had written was "Government," the highlight of John Goodman's performance in the show. It was the song that made John Goodman a star, according to Landesman.

A year after the play premiered, Roger went to New York City to play "Pap," the father of Huckleberry Finn in the production. He took the place of Goodman, whom Roger had handpicked for the role. Goodman went on to become a network television star as the husband of Roseanne Arnold on "Roseanne," and to play Babe Ruth in a feature film about the legendary slugger.

In the wake of "Big River," Roger was offered various theatrical options. He had considered writing an adaptation of John Steinbeck's *Grapes of Wrath* and doing a one-man show similar to shows by Lily Tomlin, Jackie Mason, and later Waylon Jennings in his solo production "A Man Called Hoss."

"You live in your mansion in California, and we don't see a lot of you," I said to Roger in 1987.

"I'm a private person," he replied, tersely.

"What does that mean?" I asked.

"It means I never made private first-class."

The answer was witty, satirical, and evasive. It was vintage Roger.

Roger Miller, with the possible exception of Glen Campbell, was the only country star to make it big without ever going on the circuit of road house, one-night engagements.

"I've never had a bus," he told me. "Had a jet for a while, like to ate me alive financially. I got to looking at Willie Nelson and a lot of people. Their buses are like their homes. They're wonderful. They're not like the old Faron Young buses of twenty-five years ago that just had seats in them."

He seemed astonished to learn that modern touring coaches contained VCRs, showers, microwave ovens, and all the other creature comforts.

"Used to be that the bathroom was a little hole in the floor and you'd raise the flap," Roger told me. "And if anything was hanging . . . whoo!"

I was afraid of what he might say next on the air, so I pointed out that he was the only country star who lived in Santa Fe, and asked him why.

" 'Cause it's close to my house," he said.

Roger Miller was also the only country star to launch his career from a fire station.

"I was on the fire department in Amarillo, Texas, and had been there a few months in the summer of 1957. My wife was pregnant and I wasn't making a good living. Ray Price came through one night, and I was backstage visiting with Jimmy Day, the steel guitarist, and I was singing and trying to pitch my songs. Van Howard was singing duets with Ray and was about to quit the business. Ray heard me and said, 'Boy, you can sing high.' He said, 'Would you like to come to work with me.' I said, 'Ho-ho-ho-ho.' He must have thought I was impersonating Santa Claus. He called about a month later and I sang the harmony on his show to 'Heartaches by the Numbers,' and he recorded one of my compositions, 'Invitation to the Blues.' "

Earlier, Roger had joined the Minnie Pearl Show with Mel Tillis.

"Mel was carrying around his guitar in a tow sack in those days," Roger told me. "He couldn't afford a guitar case. He couldn't talk enough to order in restaurants, so he'd always have a grilled cheese sandwich (Tillis' stutter was pronounced in the 1950s).

"You mean he couldn't say 'hamburger'?" I asked.

"He couldn't even say 'Melvin,' " Roger insisted. "Someone would ask him his name and he'd look at me and say, 'Tell 'em.' "

Roger Miller not only became one of the industry's most successful song writers, he also became one of its most successful song finders.

He was the first to record songs that later became giant hits for other artists, including "Little Green Apples," "Ruby, Don't Take Your Love to Town," "With Pen in Hand," and "Me and Bobby McGee."

"I just think I saw the glory of 'Bobby McGee,' " he said. "The guys singing on the chorus I put together are Mickey Newbury, Kris Kristofferson, and Billy Swan."

"Roger, you know that Kris is not a good singer," I said.

"Sings like a duck," Roger replied.

Roger is one of the few country personalities who seemed to wear every hat. Was he a songwriter, recording star, live entertainer, stage performer, television host, or stand-up comedian?

I recall the first time I had ever seen him on television. He was with Groucho Marx, and Roger actually got the best on the razor-witted legend.

"I remember the introduction," Roger recalled. "I heard him saying, 'Here's a guy that they say is wonderful, but I've never heard of him.' He introduced me, I came out, and he said again he'd never heard of me. I told him I'd never heard of him either, but that I'd read his brother Karl's books."

"Karl Marx," Groucho replied, "wasn't one of the Marx brothers."

"He looked at me funny, but I think he liked me," Roger said.

That was about 1963, a year after Johnny Carson became host

of the "Tonight Show." He used to take Tuesday nights off, and Roger was his substitute.

Roger, in fact, appeared on the "Tonight Show" the second night Carson was host.

"Was he nervous?" I asked.

"He was shaking so much people thought he was waving," Roger replied. "I told him, 'Hey, we're gonna be all right.' "

"You were trying to console Johnny Carson?"

Roger smiled and said he had done that. He subsequently performed on the "Tonight Show" about 100 times.

The first night Roger carried his guitar onto the set Carson asked him where his case was.

"I smoked it," Roger said dryly. Carson roared for half a minute. Not many entertainers, particularly country singers, alluded to the popularity of rolling "funny" cigarettes in the mid-1960s.

Roger was incredibly loyal to his friends. Roger once told me "Faron Young has a heart as big as his mouth," and said it with love, because Faron had given him a job when he was a big star, and Roger was a fledgling.

He would always stick up for Faron and other friends, whether or not they were in the right. It sometimes got him into trouble.

I was once broadcasting from the lobby of Nashville's old Andrew Jackson Hotel at 2 A.M. and Roger came along. Ray Price's wife came in unescorted, and a stranger got fresh with her. Roger leapt to the rescue. A ruckus started and eventually the police evicted Roger and the intruder. They re-admitted neither. Roger consequently missed his chance to be on my All-Night Show, which is why he came by in the first place.

Kristofferson told me about a night Tillis was playing a dive in Nashville's Printer's Alley and struggled to sing over the shouts from a guy who kept yelling, "We want Roger Miller."

Roger calmly walked over to where the guy was sitting and seized his throat. "You want Roger Miller? You've got him."

The heckler rose, and towered, all six-feet, six-inches, of him, over Miller.

Kristofferson rushed to the scene and barged into the fracas. A lot of huffing and puffing went on, and then he spun around in time to see Roger's back exit the door.

"Roger has left the building!" Kristofferson shouted.

The giant turned to him and asked, "And what are you going to do about it, little man?"

Marty Stuart, the singer, told me about a time Roger was pulled over by a policeman for speeding.

Roger pleaded to be let go, saying he was late for Red Foley's funeral.

Foley had been dead for twenty years.

The football legend, Don Meredith, related at Roger's funeral that when he was unemployed, he grew weary of people asking him what he was doing.

"Tell them you've been selling American jewelry to the Indians," Roger advised.

I could write an entire book of Roger Miller anecdotes, but I think that is best left to Mary, his widow, or other survivors.

Like almost everybody at his memorial service, I had not seen Roger in a while. I had spent too much time saying, "I need to call Roger Miller," and not enough time doing it.

One of the last people to visit Roger was Waylon Jennings, who struggled to lift Roger's spirits. Waylon said he was talking rapidly and aimlessly, and that Roger saw through it.

"I guess I wore him out," Waylon recalled. "He said to me, 'Boy, you look awful. Why don't you go home and take a nap?' So I did."

Tex Ritter had a big hit a while ago called "Hillbilly Heaven." The text dealt with all the country music legends who had passed away. The song could be re-worded with nothing but the deaths of legends from the 1980s and 1990s. These deaths remind me of my own mortality, that someday I'm going to visit that microphone in the sky.

Naturally, I'll look forward most of all to visiting the man my faith calls the King of Kings. One of the first questions I'll ask is what He thinks about the King of the Road.

I expect it will be my first time to see God smile.

TWELVE

Every successful organization has unsung heroes, men and women behind the men and women who take the bows and make the boasts. A production assistant at "Nashville Now" is such a person, an irreplaceable vertebrae in the productive backbone.

Ms. Connie Dickerson has worked her way through the corporate ropes for five years. She is unimpeachable and unflappable.

I thought.

Following his wish, Roy Acuff was buried less than eight hours after his death on November 23, 1992. About thirty-six hours later, I pulled onto the winter-darkened lot of "Nashville Now," where Connie was jabbering in a rapid manner that simultaneously exhibited fear and fascination.

A stream runs between the house where Mr. Acuff had lived and the "Nashville Now" studio. In the wake of his death she believed the stream had turned red. Blood red.

"Our secretary, Raquel, went out to lunch," Connie said after she calmed down. "When she came back in she and Jodie Tweed, our intern, came to me and shouted, 'Connie, Connie, the river's red in front of Mr. Acuff's house.' "

Raquel wouldn't hush until Connie moved toward the water to behold the mysterious flow. The secretary insisted that Connie use a cup to capture the crimson liquid.

As a security guard watched, the three women bent to their knees on the frozen Tennessee tundra. They scooped up the gurgling water whose color they feared had turned red as a foreboding affirmation of the death of the King of Country Music. Mr. Acuff was the Father of the Grand Ole Opry, and the man who more than any other epitomized the world's longest-running radio show.

Connie apprehensively dipped her glass into the water and then raised it toward the clouds. Its contents were clear.

Nothing would calm the two, however, and they began to plead, "But it *was* red, it *was* red!"

God told Moses to strike the waters of the Nile with his rod and He turned it into blood to convince the Pharaoh that the hand of God was upon Moses. Mr. Acuff, in the minds of some, dominated the Opry with a jurisdiction that was not only repeated, but also revered—as if it were actually sanctioned by God.

When people looked to Mr. Acuff for leadership, they always looked up.

I listened skeptically to Connie and suggested that someone had dumped a contaminant into the stream.

"Why would anybody put something in it?" Connie replied.

"To get people like you upset," I said.

Then Connie began to recite other events that preceded my arrival that day.

She had told a staff writer about the "blood red" stream. "Stranger things are happening," he told Connie. "The copy machine is making double-sided copies. Sometimes, nobody even touches it, and it spits out copies of things that aren't even there."

A fluorescent light flickered on and off all day, and finally yielded to darkness. A maintenance man changed the bulb and made other adjustments, but to no avail. The light stayed inexplicably out.

The writer lightheartedly suggested to Connie that the ghost of Mr. Acuff was playing with the light.

"Oh yeah?" Connie said. "Mr. Acuff, is that you playing with the light?"

The light came on instantly. She and the writer fled the room.

Beginning to believe what she didn't want to, Connie darted to the out-of-whack copy machine and hit the "five" button for five copies of a letter. It turned out five blank pages.

"Mr. Acuff," she implored, "quit playing with the copy machine."

She again hit the "five" button, and five perfect copies emerged.

"Now look, Ralph," she said to me, "the stream turned blood red without explanation, the light came on when I told Mr. Acuff to stop playing with it, and the copy machine started working when I told him to leave it alone."

Roy Acuff passed away in his sleep due to congestive heart disease at 2:35 A.M. To some people, he has not died.

Mr. Acuff perfected the performance of country music the way Hank Williams perfected its song writing. Mr. Acuff's credibility was Lincolnesque.

Do I believe the copy machine and fluorescent lights malfunctioned? Yes. Do I believe it had to do with Mr. Acuff's death? No. Do I believe the stream turned blood red? I believe some people believe it did.

It all has to do with the jarring effect of the death of the man who performed at the Opry almost every Friday and Saturday since 1938.

"When I appeared on the Opry in February of 1938, I was a very nervous person and I didn't do good," Mr. Acuff said, in 1988. "My fiddling wasn't any good. But I sang the 'Great Speckled Bird' and the audience applauded. I got four or five encores on it the first time. My voice was new to the public. They had never heard someone that reared back and sang with an open voice. Most people back then were crooners. I was different, but the public accepted me."

Indeed. He became the highest-paid member of the Opry in the early 1940s.

There are two things about Mr. Acuff that almost anyone who

ever turned on A.M. radio knows: His best friend was Minnie Pearl, and he *was* the Grand Ole Opry. He was identified with it as indelibly as the President is with the White House.

There are two other things about Mr. Acuff that few people know: He once fired Minnie Pearl and he once quit the Grand Ole Opry.

Mr. Acuff hired Minnie as the comedienne in his road show in early 1941, the year she joined the Opry. He fired her in April of that same year.

"Minnie, you are not fitting into our little act," Minnie quoted Mr. Acuff.

"I know I'm not, and I'm so sorry, but I can't help it," she responded.

"I know you can't," Mr. Acuff replied. "You're going to need a little more experience, but I can't keep you because it is an expense to me and I am not making all that much money."

Minnie remained a part of the Opry cast and developed her skills. She became a part of the Acuff Show again within months.

On April 6, 1946, Mr. Acuff walked away from the national radio broadcast that he had made famous, and it him. At that time, the Opry management required Opry entertainers to appear every Saturday night, the only night the program was broadcast. Mr. Acuff, however, could earn more money as a touring performer. In 1941, he earned $100 for a one-night road show. In 1946, he was still earning $15 for an Opry performance.

His request for a raise was denied, and local newspapers carried glaring headlines dealing with his departure.

Mr. Acuff went to Hollywood to make a motion picture, and while there, developed physical problems. He returned to Nashville for surgery. While hospitalized, Ernest Tubb visited him, one of the hottest singers of the day, and Opry general manager Harry Stone, both of whom asked Mr. Acuff at his bedside to please return to the Opry.

He did, but not as host to the Prince Albert segment of the show, which had formerly been his. That portion had been taken over by Red Foley, and Royal Crown Cola became Mr. Acuff's sponsor.

———■———

In 1982, Opryland officials had a brick, two-story house built for Mr. Acuff that was literally in the shadow of his beloved Grand Ole Opry. He ate, slept, and breathed on the Opry grounds.

"From that point on he was really part of the family out here," said Bud Wendell, who is the president and chief executive officer of Gaylord Entertainment, owner of the Opryland Complex. "We did his laundry in the Opryland laundry. The hotel and the park delivered his meals. He saw the inner-office memos and mail, and he drove a golf cart around the park. The corporation paid for his house, and there are no plans for it yet, but there are thoughts of connecting it to his museum."

No one else in country music was ever pampered as much.

He was given a birthday party by the Grand Ole Opry annually, and made no secret of the fact that he hated getting old. On his eighty-fourth birthday, he stood before a men's room mirror with his penis protruding.

"Happy birthday, you old son of a bitch," he said to his face. Then he looked down at his penis and said, "I'd wish you happy birthday too, but you died years ago."

Hundreds of mourners were at his gravesite before his body arrived. Even now there are usually a handful of mourners always there, even when the temperature drops after midnight.

Mr. Acuff died twenty days after a national election in which an elected Republican President was unseated after one term in office for only the third time in history. The Acuff death received as much play as the election in Nashville's morning newspaper.

Mr. Acuff unsuccessfully ran for the governorship of Tennessee on November 2, 1948. He lost to Gordon Browning by a count of 167,944 to 337,899. Mr. Acuff campaigned little, and his platform consisted solely of the Bible's Golden Rule. Ironically, he did not campaign in the primary election, which he won by a four-to-one margin over Robert M. Murray.

Mr. Acuff probably would have been elected governor were it not for his party affiliation. In 1948, "Republican" was a dirty word in Tennessee.

There was a time when it was virtually impossible to make it in country music without the blessing of Roy Acuff. No one crossed him. He resisted the playing of drums on the Opry, and they weren't heard on his set until he finally relented.

"No drums, please!" I heard him say on a live broadcast one night. The remark was unnecessary, as he had made his feelings public about drums many times.

He loved the saxophone of Boots Randolph, and told him that if a horn were ever heard on the Opry, it would be his. But he wasn't ready yet, and Boot's saxophone was long silent to Opry listeners.

Until country music became more of a recording than performing art, you couldn't get anywhere in Nashville without Mr. Acuff.

And he didn't always like me.

Mr. Acuff wouldn't share the same stage with me. In fifteen years, I don't recall his appearing on my All-Night radio show once, which began in 1957 and was the springboard to my career. My studios were only a few miles from his house, and other artists came from around the world for exposure on the program. When I did "Nashville Alive," the program that preceded "Nashville Now," it was picked up by Ted Turner's cable channel and Mr. Acuff was a part of the remote broadcast. But he wouldn't appear at the home base with me.

Then there was a change of heart. I don't know why. I talked to him, but I don't remember what was said. I only remember that his attitude whirled 180 degrees. He subsequently became complimentary of my work on "Nashville Now."

"That program is no good when you're not there," he often told me.

Shortly after Mr. Acuff's death I asked Wendell if he had any idea why one of the most influential men in country music had boycotted the man in its most influential media—radio and television.

He said it had to do with my using non–Opry members generally in the 1960s, and Buck Owens specifically. I had already faced up to the consternation of Ray Price for playing Buck's records when he lived in California. Price and a few others wanted me to play only Opry-based performers.

Mr. Acuff, on the other hand, staged a pout.

Wendell told me that he recalled going to Acuff's apartment, which was above his museum, and the King was railing about Ralph Emery and his perverted play list.

As I tell the people on earth now, and will recall for Mr. Acuff in Heaven, Buck Owens and a few of the west coast artists were making better music. I put them on the air for the way, not where, they made their music.

A few years later, I was routinely playing country music recorded in New York City (Willie Nelson), Los Angeles (Linda Ronstadt), and London ("Green, Green Grass of Home" by Tom Jones).

The only other reason Mr. Acuff might have gotten mad at me had to do with his multiple retirements. He'd quit the business, then unexpectedly return. During one "retirement" I asked Mr. Acuff how he was doing, and he said he was bored.

"I got so bored the other day I just got in the car and drove to Gatlinburg," he said. "You know you can't just sit around the house and fuss with your wife."

Perhaps I mentioned this quote on the air and Mildred heard it and was offended. She might have scolded him for being bored while around her, so much so that he had to take motor trips to Gatlinburg.

That's just speculation on my part, and I'll never know for sure why Mr. Acuff was so silent about his disdain for me. I know only that he was accustomed to always getting his way.

Mr. Acuff had the image of a benevolent grandfather, and it was well-earned. I've seen him sing on a show, sit on the edge of the stage signing autographs and posing for pictures, then get up only when it was time to resume singing for the second show. His generosity at times was limitless.

Mr. Acuff once walked into the Opryland corporate offices and wrote checks for $10,000 to three clerical workers who had been nice to him in his old age. He wrote a sixth check for $100,000 to Belmont College.

He toured overseas during World War II and the Vietnam War. He spent nights in battle zones behind microphones and days at hospital bedsides. He spent fourteen Christmases overseas.

He was a good man and knew it. How could he help it? Everybody placated him, and it was inevitable that he would become a little bit spoiled. Anyone would have, particularly in their temperamental senior years.

In his eighties, the King of Country Music seemed to have a mellow attitude toward most everyone, a change from the stories I had heard about the combative and competitive Acuff youth. I was very surprised, therefore, when "Nashville Now" attempted to salute the legendary Jimmie Rodgers on May 15, 1987, and Acuff was disrespectful of Rodgers.

Rodgers was the first country music recording star. He died five years before Mr. Acuff came to the Grand Ole Opry.

My guests on the Rodgers tribute included old-timers like Box Car Willie, Minnie Pearl, and Mr. Acuff, who was then eighty-five. Although Minnie and Roy were the most tenured members of the Opry, and Box Car was a show business veteran, none had met the legendary Rodgers.

"Tonight is a dedication to a man who has probably affected country music more than anyone in history," I said at the onset of the show.

I saw Mr. Acuff bristle.

My introduction was followed by photographs of railroads and the impoverished who lived along them during the Great Depression. The band played, and I delivered a five-minute narration about the pivotal role of the legendary Rodgers.

Mr. Acuff stiffened again.

"He died on May 26, 1933, in New York City," I continued, "two days after making his last recording. He ran out of time long before he ran out of songs."

Box Car Willie then sang the Rodgers classic "Waiting for a Train," and played on the hand-made guitar that was given to Rodgers on July 27, 1928, by the Martin Guitar Co. It is the only Martin Guitar ever given away, Box Car told the hushed crowd.

The moment was one of the most reverential in the history of "Nashville Now."

Having extolled the Father of Country Music, I segued to the King.

"And Mr. Acuff," I said, "was Rodgers an influence on you?"

"No," he snapped. "I wasn't that impressed."

Minnie Pearl, a trouper in the tradition of vaudeville, quietly gasped. She jumped in instantly to save the discourse.

"When I came to the Opry in 1940, people were still talking about Jimmie Rodgers," she said, smiling.

Mr. Acuff was silent.

"He was a medicine-show man like you," Minnie said to Mr. Acuff, trying to lighten his mood, and initiate, perhaps, an accolade.

"Oh yeah," Mr. Acuff said, "looks like I'd a met him."

Minnie's eyes met mine in mutual horror. But she was relentless in trying to do what she had come to do—commemorate Jimmie Rodgers.

Rodgers, she said, could charm a crowd with only a stool to sit on and a guitar to play. He needed no theatrical properties.

Mr. Acuff again fell into a slow, burning silence that was deafening.

She said that she had gone to the library at the Country Music Hall of Fame earlier in the day to do research for tonight's tribute.

"Did the book tell that he was a pretty mean type person?" Mr. Acuff said. "He was, he was a mean type person. He carried a pistol all of the time, didn't he?"

Minnie didn't know whether to be defensive, argumentative, or quiet. Mr. Acuff, after all, was her best friend and former employer. The world knew of their time-tested relationship. But people in the United States and Canada were seeing her fail at trying to honor one legend because of the attitude of another.

She pressed on about the reliability of reference books dealing with Jimmie Rodgers.

"I got most of my information from that town down there that he lived in," Acuff fired back. "I went to a barber shop and they said, 'We don't care nothing about him down here.' "

"Get him off of here," Minnie said, with loaded laughter.

At that point, as the videotape clearly shows, Minnie Pearl, sitting beside and behind Roy Acuff, put her hands around his torso. It was as if she was trying to be affectionate in order to drag out some affection for Rodgers.

She looked as if she feared he might come out of his chair in a tirade against a man who'd been dead for fifty-five years. Her eyes locked helplessly on mine, safely off camera, and filled with panic.

I pointed out that Rodgers must have been liked in his hometown of Meridian, Mississippi, or the "Jimmie Rodgers Day" wouldn't remain a successful annual event.

Silence fell on the set.

"Mr. Roy," I said, "you told me to get you off early so you can make the Opry."

Mr. Acuff stood and walked off the set, but not before giving an overdue and obligatory compliment to Rodgers.

"He was a liked man, he had a lot of friends," Mr. Acuff said.

Mr. Acuff, I feel, had the most dichotomous role in the Nashville entertainment industry. He not only performed hit songs, he published them. He loaned Fred Rose $25,000 in the 1940s to start Acuff-Rose, which became the oldest song publishing firm in Nashville. The firm published the hits of Hank Williams and countless other song-writing legends, such as Don Gibson, John D. Loudermilk and the Bryants.

The house, of course, also published the hits of Mr. Acuff, which sold over 30,000,000 copies back when the sale of 10,000 records would ensure a number-one country song.

The general public didn't know that Mr. Acuff was a fearful man, particularly after the death of his wife, Mildred, who died about eleven years before he did. Mr. Acuff was close to a Grand Ole Opry comedian, Stringbean, who, with his wife, Estelle, was murdered on his rural Tennessee farm. Stringbean had worked the Opry on a Saturday night when his assailants lay waiting for him at his house. They knew he was still on stage, because they could hear him on the radio in his living room.

Stringbean made no secret of the fact that he didn't believe in banks. He always carried hundreds of dollars in the top of his bib overalls. On the set of "Hee-Haw" he once flipped a fistful of cash into my face and said, "I love those residuals." When Stringbean entered his house, he was shot. Estelle fled, and was slain from behind.

Mr. Acuff never recovered and asked Wendell to build a house for him on the Opry grounds because he was afraid. After the construction and move, Wendell hired a security guard to walk Mr. Acuff to and from the Opry house and around the grounds.

In his final years, Mr. Acuff was virtually blind. He had no peripheral vision and his forward sight was severely limited. He complained to me about having to be hand-led through life. Near sightlessness frustrated the formerly robust man immensely. He hated not being able to drive.

He performed on the Opry just a month before he died. That night, as had been the case for years, he was led physically to his spot on the stage. He stood still, the curtain was raised, and he struggled to sing in a voice that was as broken as it was beloved. At the end of his set, the curtain was lowered and Mr. Acuff was walked back to his dressing room.

The crowds that applauded him never knew he hadn't seen them.

A week after Mr. Acuff's death I had four young country stars as guests on my radio show, Vince Gill, Lorrie Morgan, Joe Diffie, and Ricky Skaggs.

I asked each a question that had been asked of me by a newspaper reporter: "Do you think today's young stars can relate to Roy Acuff?"

"It's interesting how everybody's concept is what's great is new," said Gill. "And they have a tendency to forget where it came from. I have a great respect for him 'cause he's the first one. It's like inventing rock 'n' roll. Well, he invented country music."

Gill joined the Opry in August 1991, and won the Country Music Association's "Song of the Year Award" for "When I Call

Your Name," which is also the second most-popular country song of all time, according to an October 1992 survey by *Country America.*

He said Mr. Acuff stood beside him on stage. When Gill turned to Mr. Acuff, he noticed that eyes that couldn't see could nonetheless make tears. The newcomer sang while the legend cried.

"Seven or eight years ago, I was doing one of the television shows at the Opry and they were having a big cast sing," Gill continued. "It was a long day so I just laid down on the stage of the Grand Ole Opry and went to sleep. Roy told Marty Stuart that in all of his years that was the first time he'd ever seen anyone sleep on the stage of the Opry. It made Acuff mad. I never told him it was me."

Lorrie Morgan was the first person to perform on the Opry stage after Mr. Acuff died. She did a benefit show, unrelated to the Opry, a few hours after he was buried. I didn't know until she did my radio show a few days later that she had been a receptionist when she was a teenager for Mr. Acuff's publishing house.

"This last year, I went through bankruptcy," she said. "He called me over and said, 'All this stuff I'm reading about you, don't you let them get you down. You got your daddy's blood in you.' " (Lorrie's father is the late Opry star George Morgan.)

Skaggs was my third interview that day, and I posed the same question to him about young artists having an interest in Mr. Acuff.

"Roy was such an institution," Skaggs said. "He did so much to promote country music and to keep it in Nashville. When I was made a member of the Grand Ole Opry, I went backstage and Roy said, 'We've made you a member now so you'll never show up.' [Mr. Acuff always complained that Opry members spent too much time working the road to earn greater money than is paid by the Opry.] So every time I was at the Opry, I'd go up and say, 'Hey, Mr. Acuff, I'm here.' I wanted him to eat crow every time."

Listening to the eager youngsters and seeing their enthusiasm, I was struck by an obvious thought. I could have asked any one of those people to name their favorite artist and they would have said George Jones. At the time of these interviews, Jones was riding high on popularity surveys with a song called "I Don't Need Your Rockin' Chair." The tune contains background vocals by Garth Brooks, Vince Gill, Clint Black, Pam Tillis, Joe Diffie, and others in the hierarchy of young country talent. They all wanted to sing on the record because their favorite singer is George Jones.

Jones' favorite singer is Roy Acuff.

A few years ago I was making a children's Christmas album with the puppet Shotgun Red. We decided to do the Acuff standard "Wabash Cannonball," and asked Mr. Acuff to sing with us, and he consented.

He came into the dim studio and asked where the microphone was. It was almost touching his face.

Told as much, he said, "Oh," and launched into the verse that was the anthem of every working class tavern in America in the 1940s.

Mr. Acuff had surgery on his eyes in 1989.

"Will that make them any better?" I asked him.

"No," he said, "but now they won't get any worse. He didn't say what everyone on the Opry knew—that they couldn't get any worse without his going blind. Yet his spirit was relentless: His complaining was unheard.

I last saw Roy Acuff on November 5, 1992, eighteen days before he died. He had visited Minnie Pearl a few days earlier as she lay convalescing a year after her stroke.

"I'll see you in Heaven, Minnie" were his parting words to her. I called Minnie the day Mr. Acuff died and she was sobbing. Her short term memory, at that time, was not good. I shouldn't be surprised if one day she asks why Roy Acuff never comes to see her anymore.

I walked into Mr. Acuff's hospital room where he sat silently on the side of his bed. I felt sorry for him, a legend the likes of which show business doesn't produce anymore. Comedy had Jimmy Durante. The theater had Laurence Olivier.

Country music had Roy Acuff.

He was just a semblance of the man who had once entertained millions, received United States Presidents, and fostered the talents of Hank Williams. He sat listlessly, clothed only in the indignity of old age and a gaping hospital gown.

He had been in and out of the facility all year. He was released once just in time to dress and be driven to the Opry, where he sang one more time.

But on this day, he was dying. He didn't say it. He didn't have to.

Sinking winter sunlight glistened on his snow-white hair. It was as dense as it was fleecy.

"Mr. Roy," I said, "we all miss you. We're all praying for you."

He said nothing, except to thank me for coming. He never turned my way, our eyes never met, and I never again saw the face of Roy Acuff.

I know exactly how he looked nonetheless. And I will forever.

THIRTEEN

There are many unshakable associations, such as Babe Ruth and the New York Yankees, honesty and Abraham Lincoln, fireworks and the Fourth of July, and Chet Atkins and his guitar. When Chet plays a guitar, it's somehow almost irreverent for any other guitarist on stage to hold one. This high-school dropout somehow seems scholarly when he performs on his instrument.

It was Chet's playing that formed the foundation of the recording sessions that produced the sound that bred an industry. He, Don Law, and Owen Bradley were the principal architects of the world-famous "Nashville Sound" of the 1960s and 1970s. During that period Chet was the most active record producer in the world's busiest record company, RCA. When the public refused to buy the whine of steel guitars or the sawing of fiddles, he became the first successful producer to delete the time-honored instruments from country records. He replaced them with brass and symphonic strings. The move met with strong opposition, but it proved to be commercially successful. RCA sold more records under Chet Atkins' executive reign than anyone else's.

Chet, in 1973, became the youngest person ever inducted into the Country Music Hall of Fame. He was forty-nine.

"That's because I had cancer and they thought I was going to die," he told me. "The next year Owen Bradley was nominated and I said, 'Don't worry, Owen, it's in the bag, you have been sick.' He had had a heart attack, I think, and won.

"There was a lady that used to hang around the Grand Ole Opry and I'd see her and she would say, 'Hey, Chet, how is your cancer?' She would yell it all the way across the room. I wanted to say, 'Fuck you,' because I had eighteen inches of my intestines cut out. That was twenty years ago."

His sardonic analysis of illness and awards is typical of Chet, who is perhaps more misunderstood than anyone in commercial music. He has the image of a shy and retiring genius, but he also has one of the most hilariously dry wits I've ever encountered. To his friends, he's a walking frolic factory, a slow-talking mischief maker, a laid-back combination of George Goble and Garrison Keillor.

A friend had recently told Chet that Owen Bradley was Hank Williams, Jr.'s father. Chet called Bradley's office and told a member of his staff that he didn't know Bradley had dated, much less fooled around, with Hank's late wife, Audrey.

It's no secret that the Nashville Chamber of Commerce, Opryland USA, and other cornerstones of Nashville commerce are concerned about the growing country music community in Branson, Missouri. Thirty-one celebrities plan to have namesake theaters in Branson in 1993 where more than six million tourists are expected, many of whom once came to Nashville.

Chet, in 1990, was honored with an entire Nashville street named "Chet Atkins Boulevard" by proclamation of the City Council, in a ceremony officiated by the Mayor and Governor. In giving his acceptance speech, Chet said, in mock seriousness, that he would use this occasion to announce the move of Chet Atkins Enterprises to Branson, Missouri.

The Mayor grabbed his chest.

When Chet learned that I had plans to write a second book, he sent me a letter saying he didn't want to be in it, as I was so mean I would throw a "duck with a sore ass into salt water."

In 1979, when Chet's autobiography was published, he wrote in my copy, "Keep playing my records and you can become even closer to a semi-star."

Chet's crony in the 1950s was Robert Lunn. Chet was the

brains behind their rascality, and Lunn was the doer, and a ventriloquist to boot. The two were an off-stage version of Homer and Jethro.

Once, at the Astor Hotel in New York, a group of musicians was paid an unannounced visit by a Mr. Brown, then president of the Musicians' Local. Brown was checking membership cards.

"Mr. Brown wanted on line three," Lunn said, in a voice thrown elsewhere. Brown thought he was being paged and went to the telephone. Musicians carrying past-due union cards went out the door.

Chet and Lunn visited Tootsie's Orchid Lounge regularly when it was called Mom's, situated behind the Grand Ole Opry. Chet made up phony food requests for Lunn to order in a voice imitating the waiter's. In no time, food was piled high by the cook in the hole between the kitchen and dining area.

"Come get this God damned order," the sweating cook yelled at the frantic waiter.

"I didn't order the junk," the waiter replied.

The cook and waiter were about to come to blows as the tricksters slid out the back.

When the Opry was located in the historic Ryman Auditorium in downtown Nashville, its perimeters were often filled with would-be performers. Many came for miles with battered instruments and high hopes of getting a gig on the world's longest-running radio show.

Lunn would sometimes walk into Mom's, have a couple of beers, and strike up a conversation with one of the hopefuls.

"I'm the manager of the Grand Ole Opry," he would then reveal.

"You are?" was the astonished reply that always followed.

"Yes," he lied, "and you look like somebody who ought to be on the show. Do you want to audition?"

Lunn would then tell the eager aspirant that tryouts were being held between Mom's and the Ryman—in the alley.

"He'd say, 'Pick and sing for me,' and he would play right there in the alley," Chet recalled. "Then he'd say, 'Now can you dance?' and the guy would try playing his guitar and singing and dancing right there in the heat behind the Opry. There used to be a little privy back at the south end of the alley and Lunn said to one kid, 'Now, I can see you better if you get up there,' and he got him up on that tin roof, dancing and playing the guitar on the roof of the outhouse. That was a scream I'll never forget."

Crowds of curious on-lookers and other Opry hopefuls watched in astonishment. Some hoped they didn't have to go that far for a shot at the big time, and that the roof wouldn't collapse.

"Lunn was talking to a kid one night," Chet recalled, "and the kid was singing, and George Morgan, who was a practical joker too, came along and said, 'Mr. Lunn, I'm going to be off next Saturday' and Lunn said, 'Oh, God damn it, I pay you $10,000 a week, and you want to take off again.' "

The Opry, at that time, didn't pay $10,000 a year.

Morgan at the time was the hottest country singer in the nation, famous for his song "Candy Kisses." When the hopeful kid heard Morgan make his phony request for a furlough, he broke into "Candy Kisses" on the spot, hoping to get Morgan's job.

Chet, who played guitar for Hank Williams, has been a pillar of country music for almost half a century. Before the days of television, however, Chet's sound was famous, but his face wasn't.

He was sitting in Mom's one night when an angry young man walked in, loudly complaining about United States military involvement in Lebanon.

"He was going up the alley just cussin'," Chet said. " 'Those God damn people in Lebanon' and so forth and it was real hot in the summertime and I didn't have anything else to do. So I thought, 'I will talk back to him.' "

The man said, "I could go over there and clean those sons of bitches out if I was in the Army."

"Oh, hell, you're too scrawny, you couldn't whip anybody," Chet responded, "and he stopped and looked at me real mean."

Chet said the man was visibly humbled.

"All I am is a dishwasher at Linebaugh's," he told Chet. "But I can write songs real good."

By that time, a crowd had gathered around Chet and the dishwasher/would-be warrior.

"So I said, 'Well if you're a songwriter, sing one for me.' "

After more than four decades, Chet could still remember the guy's lyrics. One of the lines was " 'Your crazy heart has written the play for sad regret.' And he recited it like a stage play. Well, Webb Pierce's ears picked up, but Faron Young was the first to say, 'I want that song.' "

At the time, both men were immensely popular singers, and they began to argue about who would get to record the stranger's tune.

"Oh fuck you," the dishwasher blurted, "I have an appointment tomorrow with Chet Atkins."

And he stomped out.

Another time, Chet was on a cruise ship around Barbados with the songwriter John D. Loudermilk and their wives. Chet, who had grown a beard, decided he would go on stage and play guitar during an informal songfest.

He was approached by another passenger the next day.

" 'You're pretty good,' " the man said. " 'But you're no Chet Atkins.' My wife said, 'Tell him who you are.' I said, 'Hell no, I don't want to embarrass him.' I just told him I wished I could write material that good."

Chet has a serious side as well, devoted to what he believes is right. In that regard, he can be wonderfully relentless.

The songwriter Mickey Newbury was regarded as Nashville's first hippie during the 1960s, when many music business folks ate inside a pancake restaurant near Music Row.

The owner, who disliked hippies and beards, barred Newbury from coming inside, although he had been a faithful customer for years.

Chet got wind of the edict and posted a note on the bulletin board at RCA, asking personnel not to patronize the restaurant.

Chet is among the most even-tempered artists in a temperamental business I've ever met. He brings a low-stress presence to high-strung people. His tolerance is probably unprecedented on Music Row.

Chet was the producer, in the 1960s and 1970s, for the critically acclaimed singer and songwriter Don Gibson. Gibson had a reputation for personal insecurity and would even walk off stage without fanfare in the middle of his show if he felt his audience was unreceptive.

Chet said Gibson brought these same mood swings to recording sessions. Gibson had a terrible amphetamine habit and came to one session highly strung and wired. He wanted to record on his back with the lights off. Chet was non-confrontational, and recorded "The World Is Waiting for the Sunrise," one of Gibson's biggest hits, as Gibson lay down in the dark.

Chet also produced Gibson's "Oh Lonesome Me" and "I Can't Stop Loving You."

There were times when Chet's diplomacy wasn't enough to stop a rampage, but he was even diplomatic about the failure of diplomacy.

"Do you remember," I once asked Chet, "the altercation between Don Gibson and his wife?"

"It was his girlfriend," Chet corrected me. "She was on as many pills as he was. He and I had an agreement that if he was on pills and got in bad shape, we would call off the session and go home.

"So we were doing this session," Chet continued, "and it wasn't coming off, and he was just flying. I went out into the studio and said, 'Don, why don't we try it another time? It is not happening, and we'll wait until you get in better shape.' He threw his guitar on the floor and it bounced a couple of times and he took up a karate pose and said, 'Don't move, I will kill you, I'll hit you.'

"I didn't know what to do. I knew I couldn't run in front of all the musicians, so I just stood there and he could have broken my neck or something, you know?"

Gibson cooled off, and Chet began to console him. It worked with Gibson. Not so with his girlfriend.

"She slapped me right in the mouth!" Chet said. "Just, Wham!"

Chet Atkins was a man who gave loyalty. It was given in return.

He estimated that the biggest-selling record he ever produced was "The Three Bells," recorded by The Browns: Jim, Maxine, and Bonnie, a brother-sisters act.

Maxine was on hand when the whore gave Chet her hand.

"Maxine said, 'You can't slap Chet Atkins. You get your ass out of here or I'll whip your ass,' and she was screaming at her all the way down the hallway."

The studio turned into bedlam. Chet said, "I would have slapped her back, but I held my temper. Boy, it hurt though."

Few people realize that Chet Atkins had signed Dolly Parton to RCA, where she was a recording artist for eighteen years before moving to CBS. He did so because Chet trusts the opinion of others whose abilities he respects, and Dolly was recommended by Porter Wagoner.

Chet signed Waylon Jennings to RCA, the label for which Waylon made most of his greatest hits, and did so without ever meeting Waylon, or seeing him perform.

"I had heard a tape, and so many people kept telling me that I should sign him, so I did. And in Dolly's case, the way that happened was, Porter Wagoner told her that I didn't like her singing. And then he told me, 'Well, if she doesn't sell a record, take it out of my royalties.' He may have said something like that, I don't remember. But what really happened was, he did that to have power over her. I asked, 'Who are you going to get to replace Norma Jean [Porter's former duet partner]?' He said, 'Dolly,' and I said, 'Who is that?' He said, 'She writes for Fred Foster,' and I said, 'Well, can you get her?' I sent a contract over and that is all there was to it."

Chet said he had heard a recording of Dolly singing and decided to go with her as an artist because she was also a featured act on Wagoner's old television show, the highest-rated syndicated country music show in the nation in the late 1960s.

Chet fought against recording artists producing their own albums, a common practice today that has resulted in hundreds of number-one records.

"Waylon wanted to make his own records," Chet said, "and at the time, we had Bob Ferguson, Ray Pennington, Felton Jarvis, and Danny Davis as staff producers. I knew that if all the artists started producing for themselves, then all these guys would be out of a job. I was trying to protect them when I voiced my sentiments that I didn't think it was good for the artists to produce themselves. Well, I was wrong, but I felt real close to Ferguson and some of those guys."

Chet's discovery of recording talent is unsurpassed in Nashville. He also signed to RCA the legendary Charley Pride, the first black singer in country music, who has sold more than 30,000,000 records.

"When the history of country music is written, that will be my greatest social contribution," Chet told my radio audience several years ago.

"What happened was that Jack Clement [a record producer] kept saying, 'You have got to hear my black man sing,' " Chet said.

Chet took a demonstration tape of Pride singing to an RCA meeting in Monterey, California, and played "Snakes Crawl at Night," a tune that became Pride's first single record. Other RCA big shots flipped over the voice, decided it had a commercial edge to it, and urged Chet to sign the singer to the label.

"Then I told them he was black and that caused quite a commotion. They didn't know what the hell to say."

Some RCA executives feared that country fans, in 1965, wouldn't accept a black man singing what had traditionally been the white man's music. So those at the meeting, including Chet, decided to release the first record of their new artist on a major label without publicity.

"We decided to just put the record out on its own merits, and call it 'Country Charley Pride,' and Charley pulled it off great. He was nice to everybody and he was intelligent and people appreciated that."

Nobody banned the record, released during the turbulent Civil Rights movement, because Charley Pride was black.

Chet told me what few entertainers now can tell, personal stories about Hank Williams, Sr., who has been dead for forty years. In typical modesty, Chet began by saying he had little to tell.

"I don't remember much about Hank," Chet said. "When I first came here, we went fishing a couple of times, and we had gotten together and tried to write a couple of songs, and without any success. I was kind of intimidated by him. He was a big star and I was nobody, but I wish I had those songs we tried to write."

Pressed, Chet acknowledged having played on many of Williams' records, even on the ominous "I'll Never Get Out of This World Alive," released the year Williams died at twenty-nine.

"I remember thinking, 'Boy, you ain't just kidding,' 'cause he was in such bad shape. Sam McGee said Hank was so skinny that when he walked his ass rattled like a sack of carpenter's tools.

"He drank a lot and he took a lot of drugs, I guess," Chet said. "He'd come up and say, 'Hey hoss, listen to this!' And he would get right in my face and sing 'Jambalaya' or something he had just written and the bourbon would just knock you over. Really strong."

Hank would run his new material past Ernest Tubb or Hank Snow or Roy Acuff, and ask, "How do you like it?"

"Fine," one of them would say, "I want to record it."

"Too bad, you can't have it. I'm going to record it myself."

"In other words, he'd run it past one of them to decide if he wanted it for himself," Chet said, laughing.

I asked Chet to explain Hank's charisma.

"He was wonderful on stage. His body would sway and undulate with the music. It wasn't anything all that rhythmic, it was kind of like the wind blowing to the tempo.

"And he was temperamental. If somebody didn't like one of his songs, he would take it as an affront. If Mr. Sholes, the head of the country music artists and repertoire for RCA, turned down one of his songs, he'd go to him and say, 'Who are you to turn down one of my songs?' "

Chet is among the few Nashvillians still in the music business who worked with Elvis Presley in his early years. He played on Presley's first Nashville recording session. He even assembled the band for Presley's 1956 recording of "Heartbreak Hotel."

"I got the band together and played rhythm guitar," he told me. "That first session, Elvis came in and I remember he had on these blue pants with a pink stripe down the side that was kind of inside the pleats, and inside that was pink trimming. He was dancing around and having a good time and before you know it he split his pants and so they sent out to the hotel and got him another pair and he threw the old pair out in the hallway.

"The girl there, the receptionist, said, 'What are we going to do with these old pants?' I said, 'You better keep them, he's going to be the biggest star in the business.' She laughed and made fun. But a few months later she was trying to get on 'I've Got a Secret' [a television quiz show] because she had Elvis Presley's pants."

Years later, Chet recalled, Elvis would come to Nashville from Memphis to record. During these leisurely sessions he seemed to pay more attention to recreation than to his next record.

"He'd play piano awhile and then he would play guitar for a while and play drums awhile and sing hymns and finally he'd say, 'What do you want to record?'

"Freddy Beanstock was the liaison between his publisher and RCA," Chet said, "and he would go over and put a disc on the player and Elvis would say, 'I don't like that' or 'Let's do it,' and if they did it, they would copy the arrangement if it was good." The good arrangements were usually Otis Blackwell songs—for instance, "Don't Be Cruel."

While Elvis was frittering, the studio time clock was running, amassing expensive billing for union musicians who stood by idly.

"But Elvis was selling so many records that no one cared," Chet said.

At one session, Elvis was talking to Gordon Stoker of the Jordanaires, through an open studio microphone. Other musicians, including Chet, could hear their conversation. Chet had heard earlier that Elvis had been turned down for membership in the Grand Ole Opry. Elvis had done one guest spot for them.

At this particular session the rumor was confirmed.

"I really wanted to become a member of the Opry," Elvis told Gordon over the open microphone. "And that damn Mr. Denny said, 'We don't do that nigger music around here. Go back to Memphis.' "

"Out of his mouth he said it," Chet recalled. "I guess it must have been true. I never knew. I had heard it before, but I didn't know it was true."

Chet Atkins began playing as a child on a ukelele strung with screen wire. There was no money for guitar strings on his Luttrell, Tennessee, farm.

"Yeah, well it had some strings originally and they broke, they were cat gut and as one would break I would just pull a wire off the screen door and it was no trouble because we always had some animal, a dog or a pig or something, that would run through the door and it made a hole in it and then it was easy to rip off wire."

Chet's humor is a thin disguise for the loneliness he felt as a child. Chet's father approached him one day at the springhouse, a covering where milk and butter are stored in a stream, and told the lad he was leaving. It was that quick, that definite.

Chet tried to fill the void of his solitude with a guitar. For him, the instrument was not only music, but therapy.

"I would lean on the guitar for love," he said. "I never seemed to have enough of it, and I depended on it for the friendship I never seemed to find.

"I was shy and introverted and I just lived with a guitar," he told me. "Hell, I took it to bed with me. Anywhere I was, I would put my ear against it and just strum notes and listen. It sounded so great to my young ears when you hear all those harmonies and everything. I wish I could hear that well now.

"I always played with my fingers. We would take a toothbrush and at that time they were made out of celluloid, you would take it and heat it up and cut off a piece and cut it down with a pocketknife and put it in hot water and wrap it around your thumb and it became our own thumb picks."

Chet said that the only person who encouraged him when he was a lad was Azrow Thomas, an impoverished man who was deaf and mute. He'd gesture that Chet should keep practicing, then he'd pull out the linings of his pockets, indicating that someday Chet would have money in every pocket.

"It always amazed me that the only guy who thought I could make it couldn't hear me," Chet said. "Maybe that's why the others didn't encourage me. They could hear me."

Azrow would scream a certain sound when he wanted his mule to stop and yell another for it to go. Chet's brother learned the sounds. He hid in the woods and mimicked Azrow's verbal sign language and commanded the mule to go when it was supposed to stop, and vice versa.

Azrow, frustrated, would beat the animal.

One day, Azrow saw his tormentor in the woods and chased him all over Tennessee.

Chet saw Azrow twenty years after his first hit.

"He made motions like he was playing a guitar," Chet said, "and I felt good, 'cause I knew then he remembered me."

Chet was fired from many radio jobs in his early career because he was too shy to mix with other station personnel. He was a better player than a politician. Chet was once reprimanded by a friend for going on the "Tonight Show," the nation's premier talk show, and not talking.

Chet's shyness began to wane with his growing business. Today, he is confident and poised on stage. I first saw evidence of his unfolding personality on my television show "Pop Goes the Country," when he played "Stars and Stripes Forever" as a musical selection for the show, while simultaneously recording it for a live album. It prompted loud applause. The producer decided it was necessary for Chet to play the song again. The audience, naturally, didn't applaud very enthusiastically the second time around for something it had just heard. So right in the middle of his guitar chorus, Chet said, "Folks, come on, this is pretty damn good. Give me a little applause."

They did, and the noise was perfect for the live album.

Despite Chet's modesty of his songwriting talents, he was the only person with whom Boudleaux Bryant ever collaborated in songwriting, other than Bryant's wife. The Bryants penned most of the Everly Brothers' early hits, as well as dozens of number-one country songs that became standards.

"We came up with 'How's the World Treating You?'" Chet said. The song became a number-one hit for Eddy Arnold and Elvis Presley.

In the middle 1940s, Chet worked with the Johnson Sisters, identical twins, on WLW in Cincinnati, Ohio. The first girl he ever dated was one of these sisters, Leona Johnson. They were married in 1947 and celebrated their forty-sixth anniversary in 1993.

Chet said he was once fired from a radio job because there was a rumor that Leona was pregnant, but that she and Chet were not married. The truth is they were married, she wasn't pregnant, and no one bothered to ask them about the rumor.

"The first night I ever appeared on the Opry was with Red Foley in 1946," Chet recalled. "I don't know if I played a solo that night, but eventually I got a solo spot and I played for about a minute before the commercial break." The agency sent a notice down that they didn't need Atkins' guitar spot.

He had been fired again.

He returned after about five years as the guitarist with the Carter Family.

"I had my own show on the Opry later," Chet said, "and that's very unusual for an instrumentalist. The Opry is a very torturous place to play because the whole time you're on, bigger stars are in the wings and sometimes on the stage. It's like the fiddle player Benny Martin said, 'While you're on, people are looking at the ceiling wondering who is coming out next.'

"If you could play the Opry, you could play anyplace. The whole time you're on, kids are stepping on people's feet, and the vendors are in the audience hawking souvenirs."

The news of Chet's intermittent firings continued until 1960, when a Nashville newspaper reported that he had been fired from the Grand Ole Opry. Many people were stunned and upset, including Chet, but for a different reason. He had always played as a guest artist, not a staff member.

"I never worked for the Opry," he said. "I never signed any papers or nothing. In 1960 I got so busy producing records that I stopped playing the Opry, and the paper said a whole bunch of us was fired because we hadn't appeared enough on the Opry. I thought it was kinda funny."

Chet Atkins holds eleven Grammys and twelve Country Music Association awards. In 1993, NARAS (the organization that gives the Grammys) gave Chet a Lifetime Achievement Award, their highest honor. He is among the world-class musicians who attract the attention of other world-class musicians. He has performed with Arthur Fiedler and the Boston Pops Orchestra, and met Segovia. He was accompanied to the meeting by the Nashville guitarist extraordinaire Hank Garland, who asked Segovia if he might hold his instrument. Segovia declined, and Chet said he thought Segovia was "somewhat of an asshole."

Chet loved the late Fiedler, and recalled how the man, at seventy-five, spent intermissions from recitals drinking a boilermaker, then returned to his podium before one of the world's finest pop orchestras. He said Fiedler was a benevolent but firm taskmaster, and recalled his experiences with the maestro during the recording of a live album with the orchestra.

Orchestra members, Chet said, could talk to Fiedler, but only after making an appointment.

"One day, we were rehearsing and Fiedler looked over at the first-chair and the concert master wasn't playing. He says, 'Why are you not playing?' And the concert master said, 'Maestro, someone has my violin bow.'

" 'Well, what do you think I am, a retriever?' " Chet quoted Fiedler. "Give him back his bow!" Fiedler barked at the orchestra.

From an outstretched arm within the rank of musicians a bow was passed without explanation.

The orchestra couldn't see Fiedler when he looked at Chet and smiled slightly. Chet was charmed, and later toured with Fiedler and the orchestra.

Chet has his own favorite guitar players, including Nashville's Jerry Reed, who was a highly sought-after studio musician before he became a recording artist in his own right. Chet took Reed on a "Masters" tour with him as the opening act for Floyd Cramer, Boots Randolph, and Chet. Reed and Chet cut two duet albums for RCA and one for Columbia, and are close friends.

Chet has been named "Instrumentalist of the Year" several years in a row by the CMA. In the early 1970s, the award went to Reed one year, who was unable to accept because he was working as the summer replacement host for Glen Campbell's television show.

Chet agreed to accept the award.

He took possession on national television, thanked millions of people on behalf of Jerry Reed, then took Reed's award to his house and beat it with a ball-peen hammer.

Reed's wife, Prissy, was not amused.

"Well," Chet said, "I knew that Reed hated new guitars, he wanted guitars with scratches on them and cigarette burns. So I thought he'd appreciate the same type thing in his award."

Reed loved it.

With the exception of today's runaway country music popularity, the greatest commercial boom came in 1980 during the "Urban Cowboy" movement, made popular by John Travolta's motion picture.

As country music's audience began to expand, insiders were astounded by Chet's famous comment that country music was losing its identity despite its burgeoning patronage.

I couldn't believe that the man who had fathered the "Nashville Sound" in the 1970s to reach new audiences had criticized country music when its audience was growing even faster.

"Did you really say that about country music losing its identity?" I asked Chet.

"I may have said something or other," he said. "I have said a lot of things that I didn't know what the fuck I was talking about."

Chet plays only about thirty personal appearances annually these days. The strain of producing scores of acts with thousands of songs took its toll, and Chet stepped down as V.P. of A & R in 1980 at RCA, the record label he did more to build than anyone else.

"I was tired, man," he said, "I was tired."

I could hear the fatigue, even thirteen years later.

"When did you feel you had had enough of it?" I asked him.

He smiled.

"I came to work one day, looked down at my shoes, and they didn't match," Chet said. "I knew right then that I'd had enough."

FOURTEEN

On January 28, 1956, Tommy and Jimmy Dorsey led their band through the theme song for "Stage Show," a weekly variety program produced for CBS television by Jackie Gleason.

A young singer from Memphis, Tennessee, appeared on the program. It marked his television debut and sparked public pandemonium that prompted Gleason to ask him back for four more appearances within three months.

Elvis Presley's popularity was so explosive, it resulted in his appearing on the Steve Allen, Milton Berle, and Ed Sullivan shows that same year. Presley's last network appearance in 1956, October 8th on the "Ed Sullivan Show," drew 80 percent of the nation's viewing audience, according to A. C. Nielsen, the industry's respected ratings service.

On April 3, 1992, a singer whose voice and on-stage movements have been compared constantly to Presley's sang and danced on "Nashville Now." It marked his first network television appearance. He had wanted to be on the program for years, he later told me, and even hung around backstage on occasion, trying to garner the attention of those who book talent on the program. He had repeatedly brought them audio tapes, but to no avail. Both his manager and talent bookers felt he wasn't ready, and the rejection made him want the booking even more. When his debut came at last, his shirt was unbuttoned and his shoulder-length hair clung to the sweat on his forehead. His gyrations were as offensive to some as Presley's had been to others thirty-six years earlier. Billy Ray brought a contingent of fans from his hometown to ensure moral support and rousing applause. It worked.

When Presley premiered, he did so with a new music for a new audience. The artist and the public found each other.

By the time Billy Ray Cyrus made his debut, millions of people had listened to hundreds of thousands of rock 'n' roll compositions. Had it been 1956, Billy Ray might have been Elvis.

Garth Brooks enjoys a bigger career. Vince Gill enjoys a more critically acclaimed career. Clint Black has earned more awards.

But no one in the history of country music has ever enjoyed a more explosive debut.

Billy Ray Cyrus sold three million records in as many months. His first album surpassed the seven million mark nine months after it was released. It has now sold over eight million. It was announced the week of January 3, 1993, that Cyrus' "Some Gave All" album was the biggest-selling title by any artist in any field in 1992. On January seventh he was nominated for five Grammy Awards, the second-highest number of nominations ever received by a country artist in a single year, trailing only the six received in one year by Roger Miller in the mid-1960s.

Cyrus' "Achy Breaky Heart" video became the most viewed in the history of Country Music Television, and triggered a national dance craze not seen since the Urban Cowboy mania initiated by John Travolta twelve years earlier.

Rumors surfaced that Cyrus had been a male stripper in California. Not true. His only work in California was as a used-car salesman in the mid-1980s.

Country music has a wealth of great vocalists, songwriters, musicians and more. It has no shortage of sex symbols. With Billy Ray Cyrus, it instantly had a hip-swinging heart throb.

I've never seen an act, with the exception of Presley, that elicited such a sexual response from his audience.

So who is this hunk who at times has the sensitivity of a child, and usually the manners of a gentleman? Who is the teenage idol who won't take the time for a romantic relationship, but takes ninety minutes daily to lift weights? Who is the overnight success in denim and a tank top?

Depends on which night you mean.

Billy Ray spent hundreds of them commuting to and from Nashville on a five-and-a-half-hour journey from his regular engagement in Huntington, West Virginia.

"In 1989 I made forty-two separate trips out of the fifty-two weeks in the year," Cyrus said. "I would drive down to Nashville and I would stay Monday, Tuesday, and Wednesday and drive back to Huntington, West Virginia, and get up there just in time to drive straight to the club I was playing and get on stage and play there for four nights.

"Persistence was a very big part of it," he continued. "I would always read that persistence is to the quality of the character of a man what carbon is to steel, and I just kept on keeping on. And it finally happened."

Indeed. Cyrus was host to his own network television special in 1993. Much of the special was produced in Cyrus' hometown of Flatwoods, Kentucky, and in the small nightclubs he used to play in Ironton, Ohio, and Huntington, West Virginia, including the Ragtime Lounge.

Cyrus said he wanted to return to those places in the wake of his whirlwind success to ensure that he keeps his figurative feet on the ground. During production, he visited the cemetery in Flatwoods where he wants to be buried.

In early 1993 he made a video entitled "Romeo" with Dolly Parton, with whom he was linked romantically by the tabloid press.

He denied the reports and said he wished reporters who write for tabloids would channel their energy toward something other than damaging people's lives.

Cyrus had the same attitude about lingering press reports regarding his feud with singer Travis Tritt, who said that Cyrus had reduced country music to "an ass wiggling contest."

Cyrus said he had been out of touch with current events while recuperating from a long, hard road trip when the story broke. He said that he was enough of "a red neck," however, to have responded to the remark had he known about it immediately, but didn't specify what he meant. I got the impression that the robust Cyrus meant that, as far as Tritt was concerned, he might reduce country music to an eye-blackening contest.

On a major music awards show in early 1993, Cyrus was awarded for "Achy Breaky Heart."

In his acceptance speech, he told a network television audience that for anyone who didn't like the song, "Here's a quarter, call someone who cares!"

The line is the title of a Tritt hit, and was still another blow in the Cyrus-Tritt verbal feud.

The two took jabs at each other in the press and on national television to the degree that former *Tennessean* columnist Robert K. Oermann wrote a column calling for an end to the childish feud. But for a while, their verbal jabs prompted a lot of laughter on Nashville's Music Row, and among many country music fans.

In recalling other aspects of the building of his career, Cyrus related, "But I've got to tell you, I guess it would all have started as far back as 1988. Del Reeves, a Grand Ole Opry star and a very good friend of mine, came to Huntington and saw my show, and it was in January of 1989 that Del Reeves produced a song that I had written called 'It Ain't Over Til It's Over.' I took some money that I had saved up and made a 45 record. In the meantime, Del Reeves introduced me to Jack McFadden [Buck Owens' former manager], who was Del's manager. So in 1989 I made all those trips back and forth to try to get Jack McFadden to want to become my manager.

"And in the fall of 1989, I signed a management contract with Jack McFadden and in the spring of 1990, Jack talked Buddy Cannon from Mercury Records into coming up to see me at a show in Freedom Hall in Louisville, Kentucky. He gave Harold Shedd [head of Mercury-Polygram Records] a good report, and Harold Shedd came to see me two more times after that and that is pretty much it right there."

It was definitely happening, but happening slowly.

"It was all taking so much time," Cyrus said. "We are talking like months after Buddy Cannon had came to see me the first time. Nobody had still said yes or no. And I was just at the end of my rope, I just felt like I had to do something else. I felt like time was passing me by. And so I called Harold Shedd's office myself and his secretary Joyce was kind enough to make me an appointment for two days later, and I came down and she said I could have five minutes to see Mr. Shedd, and so I came down and I played him a tape of 'Where'm I Gonna Live When I Get Home?'

"Before he could say anything, I said, 'Mr. Shedd, I have a song that I want to play for you and this is my best song, and if this song isn't good enough then I need to do something else for a living, because my best isn't good enough.' "

Cyrus also played a rough tape he had made of "Some Gave All," which eventually became a title song for an album.

"At the end of that song," Cyrus recalled, "Mr. Shedd looked up at me and said, 'I believe that song could be a standard.' "

Shedd told the naive Cyrus that he would structure him a "deal."

"Does that mean he is going to let me cut the grass once a week or what is the deal?" Cyrus asked himself.

The deal called for an album whose first single was "Achy Breaky Heart." In a first-of-its-kind marketing scheme for country music, "Achy Breaky Heart" was released on music video to country dance clubs before it was released to the television market, and as an audio record. The video created an insatiable market for the audio before the latter was ever publicly available. When at last the record went on sale, the public didn't consume it, it devoured it.

The song was number one nationally within five weeks.

"The first time I heard the song, I fell in love with it," Cyrus told me. "It just hit me like a hit record should and we recorded the song, and the record company decided for that to be the first single off the album because the Achy Breaky dance craze had caught on all over the United States, Canada, and the United Kingdom."

Although the dance incorporates heavily Cyrus' on-stage movements, he did not invent the famous Achy Breaky line dance. That was the brainchild of Melanie Greenwood, the former wife of Lee Greenwood. Cyrus, in fact, doesn't even dance the Achy Breaky, but instead hops through improvised steps in his riveting stage show.

"We were having a meeting on the dance, exactly what it was going to consist of," Cyrus said. "Originally the dance was going to be a 'coupleless' dance, but I told people that a line dance would definitely be what's happening. Melanie put the hip thing in that I do on stage and people are doing it all over."

Cyrus drew a lot of press attention from reporters who predicted he would be a flash in the pan, a one-shot-wonder whose recording of "Achy Breaky Heart" would fade into obscurity shortly before he did.

He proved the press wrong.

Country fans danced all spring and summer in 1992 to "Achy Breaky Heart," then hummed along with Cyrus' "Some Gave All," a ballad he had written in 1989 about a Vietnam veteran. The man in question, Cyrus told me, had given all for his country.

"All gave some, but some gave all," Cyrus repeated the line to me, and said that his ultimate admiration is for people who give the supreme sacrifice, life itself, for something in which they believe.

"Some Gave All" was the number-one album in *Billboard* on the pop survey for seventeen weeks. "Some Gave All" was the number-one pop album when Garth Brooks' "Ropin' the Wind" was number two. The listings marked the first time in history that country acts had held the top-two pop slots.

Cyrus said he somehow believes that Hank Williams and Keith Whitley, both of whom died young, gave all for the music they loved. He told me that he had listened to Keith Whitley's last radio interview, done with me on my syndicated program on January 11, 1989. On that show, Whitley claimed to be drug-free. Four months later, Whitley was dead of an alcohol and drug overdose.

Cyrus wants the phrase "Some Gave All" as his epitaph on his tombstone. He wrote the song, drawn from the phrase, in about four minutes, while driving a car and speaking into a tape recorder.

"Could've Been Me" was Cyrus' second big single release. He didn't write the tune, and he almost didn't record it. But fate smiled his way.

"I wasn't supposed to hear that song," he said. "My producer, Joe Scaife, had brought me a tape to Asheville, North Carolina, and he was going to play me this song and when he played 'Could've Been Me,' he told me he had it on hold for another artist. By the time it finished playing I was already in love with the song. Then he said, 'Sorry, Billy Ray, but I have brought you the wrong tape.' I said, 'It don't matter, I love the song.' "

The producer told Cyrus once again he couldn't have the song.

"I felt like I had fallen in love with a married woman," Cyrus said. But he assembled his band anyway and rehearsed the song as if it were his.

"I just prayed, 'God, if it is meant to be, just let me record 'Could've Been Me' and a week later that artist that it was on hold for turned it down and Joe called me and said, 'Hey man, you can have 'Could've Been Me.' "

I was surprised at the reference to God, and asked Cyrus if he were a spiritual person. His answer was unexpected.

"I was brought up in a Pentecostal church," he said. "My Paw-Paw [grandfather] was a Pentecostal preacher. I would never want anyone to look at me and point a finger and say, 'Well, you hypocrite, you know, how can you talk about God and prayer, and I just hope that when people look at Billy Ray Cyrus that they understand that I am the first man to look in the mirror and say, 'I am Billy Ray, a walking, talking human being and I make mistakes too and I am just a man that is chasing a dream.' "

Cyrus' grandfather built the country church which the younger Cyrus first entered at the age of twelve. When his grandfather died, Cyrus didn't return until he was twenty-eight, and deep in the frustrations of the music business that had repeatedly rejected him.

"I was at the end of my rope," Cyrus said, "and I called Harold Shedd and said, 'I am at the end of my rope. I have got to have an appointment to come and find out the answers.'

"Two weeks prior to that, I was in Ironton, Ohio, and a voice within said that I needed to go to that little church in Flatwoods, Kentucky. I drove four hours to that church and there was a preacher in there, his name was Brother Don Atkins, and as I walked in the door, he was just shouting over and over, 'God loves a desperate man, God loves a desperate man!'

"I listened to him for an hour or so, and I realized that I was a desperate man, and I felt myself get out of that chair and I walked down to the little pew that I had knelt down at every Sunday morning as a kid, and I said, 'God, I'm a desperate man.' "

When Cyrus' "Achy Breaky Heart" went to number one, parishioners in that tiny church erected a sign. It read: "Jesus mends Achy Breaky Hearts."

Cyrus' recollections of his Flatwoods, Kentucky, church rearing included time spent as a lad singing in his dad's gospel quartet.

"We always sang, 'Swing Down Sweet Chariot,' " Cyrus remembered. "One time I was singing it and my tongue got caught between where my two front teeth were supposed to be, and I couldn't make any sound because my tongue was stuck between my teeth and that horrified me."

The youngster was traumatized and did not get back on stage for years.

Cyrus' weekly treks to Music City U.S.A. began in 1983. He knocked on the doors of record producers and music publishers until his knuckles were raw. In a career filled with ironies, another transpired outside the door of the Music Mill, the log cabin studios owned by Alabama, and the site where they made most of their hit records.

Cyrus was turned away.

"I rang the buzzer at the Music Mill," Cyrus recalled. "I wanted to bring in a record and play it for them, but the secretary got on the speaker phone and asked if I had an appointment, and I said, 'No, ma'am. I just want to leave a record,' and she said there was no soliciting.

"As I turned to the street, a Nashville tour bus pulled up with probably fifty tourists on it and the bus driver on a big old speaker phone said, 'This is the famous Music Mill where Alabama records their hit albums.'

"I remember looking up at this buddy that was with me and wondering why the driver didn't say about us, 'There, outside, is a couple of bums from Flatwoods, Kentucky, they won't even open the doors up for.' "

Eight years, hundreds of foiled tries, and thousands of prayers later, Cyrus was recording inside that same studio. During a break, he stepped outside for fresh air when a tour bus rolled past.

"And I happened to notice that one of the tour buses pulled up just like it did in 1983," Cyrus said. "And the tourists were inside it, and you could see the cameras going off and different stuff. My mind flashed back to the past when I wasn't even allowed in the building. Something inside of me said, 'You have got to do it.' "

"So I went and I opened up the doors and invited the whole bus to come on in and all the tourists came in and the bus driver, and they all took pictures of Alabama's gold records. A couple of them took my picture. And I wonder now, when they see me and when they hear my records, I wonder if they remember me."

The day I met Cyrus at the Music Mill he was signing autographs for starstruck fans outside the Music Mill. My assistant, Terry Schaefer, and I went inside the building to set up recording equipment while Cyrus remained outside with his admirers. Soon, he would begin his interview with me, and resume work on his second album.

I remember he wanted to wear a shirt given to him by T. Graham Brown for our interview. I thought it was curious that he would be concerned about what he wore while doing a radio show. We stepped over weights for his upcoming workout and put aside his duffle bag, which held a copy of the *National En-*

quirer. He maintained throughout our session the mild-mannered and polite demeanor that is enigmatic when compared to his macho mystique. He humbly asked Terry and me how he was doing, and he asked repeatedly.

When the session was over and the recorder was off, Cyrus asked for my advice regarding show business. I felt as though he actually wanted it.

I told him simply to always be himself. I think that advice was unnecessary.

FIFTEEN

The highest hope for a vocalist is a "career" record, a song that can establish him firmly with the public and his record company, ensuring big sales and big performance fees. A career record becomes the signature song of its singer.

The second most heralded country career record of all time is "When I Call Your Name," as voted by readers of *Country America* and *USA Today* in a 1992 survey. The song's popularity trailed only that of George Jones' masterpiece, "He Stopped Loving Her Today."

In the wake of "When I Call Your Name," Vince Gill was nominated for six awards by the Academy of Country Music. The awards show on NBC failed to garner one prize for Gill.

"I think Garth got them all," Gill smiled with characteristic good nature.

Gill had recorded earlier a handful of songs that got on the charts, but not in any major way.

"Why did MCA sign you?" I asked Gill.

"Because my producer, Tony Brown, believed in me. He used to play piano with Emmylou Harris, and I met him back in the middle '70s when he was playing with Emmylou and I was playing with someone else and we would wind up in the same joints together."

Brown had early on signed Gill to RCA, and when he moved to MCA, he took Gill along.

During the next two years, Gill was pronounced "Male Vocalist of the Year" twice by the Country Music Association.

I asked Gill if he was surprised that he beat Garth Brooks for the award. He said he was not.

"I take it with a grain of salt, because I think there is still Conway Twitty, George Jones, Ronnie Milsap, Vern Gosdin, and fifty guys who sing as well as I do. The award is really just a temporary kind of thing and popularity oriented every year. I am real fortunate that the records are going well for me right now. I feel different about the awards than most people do. A lot of people see Entertainer of the Year as the pinnacle award, but I see Songwriter of the Year as the best award."

I had never heard another entertainer say that, and Gill's priority toward the integrity of his craft pleased me. So did his humility.

I went so far as to ask Gill if he realized how good God had been to him; Gill sings, plays an instrument, is an athlete, is handsome, and has a winning personality.

I particularly enjoy his sense of humor. During the tribute to Minnie Pearl in 1992, Gill told me backstage at the Grand Ole Opry House that a member of Gill's band used to play with Elvis.

"Elvis couldn't stand to pee in front of anybody," Gill told me. "He took a bodyguard into the rest room with him to be sure no one saw him pee," Gill said.

The musician who formerly played with Elvis accidentally got trapped in the men's room with Elvis, and the bodyguard scolded him.

"Don't be looking at the King, man!" the bouncer implored.

"Now wouldn't that be a thrill?" Gill said to me. "Whizzing with the King!"

The genius of "When I Call Your Name" exists indisputably in its angelic harmony. Roy Acuff, just before he died, said the record contained the most beautiful harmony ever recorded.

And the question that bounced from coast-to-coast was, who is the girl singing harmony with Vince Gill?

"I just love the way our voices work together," Gill said. "Out of all the people that I have sang with over the years, you know, that harmony that her and I have together is pretty pure and I really love that. I don't think anybody is doing harmony like they used to, like Porter and Dolly.

"They made several records," Gill added. "They didn't just get together for a duet to have a hit and then you never heard from them again. I would like to see some of that get back into country music. I was a fan of those records. I don't think anybody is doing it, and I think that people enjoy duet records."

Gill's mysterious harmony-singer on "When I Call Your Name" is Patty Loveless. It's fitting. He sang harmony on eight of her hits, and on songs for Conway Twitty, Reba McEntire, Emmylou Harris, Rosanne Cash, and others.

One of Gill's great disappointments is that Patty Loveless decided to move to Epic Records in 1993, thereby eliminating any chance that they could become duet legends. He had hoped to do an entire album with her.

In 1991 Gill told me he had recorded or written songs with more than one hundred artists before striking major pay dirt on his own. And he raised that figure to two hundred when he and I visited in 1992. He played around Nashville for eight years before becoming famous.

(In the summer of 1989, Gill appeared either vocally or instrumentally on every number-one record that came out of Nashville.)

One of his songs, "Oklahoma Swing," rose to number eight on a national survey. He recorded it with Reba McEntire, who is also from Oklahoma.

"We knew each other socially but were not really close friends to speak of," Gill told me. "I 'demoed' this song and sent it to her, and said, 'I am getting ready to record for MCA, and I would love for you to come and sing on this record.' She misunderstood and thought I was pitching her this song, to cut for her recording session, and she said, 'No, I wouldn't be interested.' "

Gill and Brown decided to record the song without Reba and sent that version to her, contending she had misunderstood Gill's original proposition. Reba, pregnant at the time, didn't have a record of her own out, so she sang the duet with Gill, and the song worked.

I asked Gill how he found work during leaner days.

"The musicians' union has a board down there," he said. "And it is covered with names of guys that play and are looking for work. The thing about Nashville is that the musicians are separated into two categories—road musicians and session musicians. In some people's theory, the road musicians aren't good enough to play the sessions, and I think there is some of the guys that play the road that are definitely good enough to play sessions."

"It is real tough to crack into the session world. And you have got to go out and almost play the road for a while and prove yourself and do some things in that way before you can be heard or seen."

Gill was one of the most sought-after studio singers and guitarists in Nashville for years before his solo career went through the roof. He was an anonymous genius behind many monster records. But before "When I Call Your Name," the general public didn't know this.

"It is the record that I have been waiting to have for about seven years," Gill told me in September 1990. "I wrote the song with Tim DuBois [president of Arista Records, Nashville Division] and that thrills me equally that I have written my so-called 'career record.' You know everybody dreams of having one. With the sales and the popularity of this record I finally have hit the hanging curve ball."

Gill's voice is a critic's dream, as high as it is pure, with the clarity of a mountain stream. He is a tenor's tenor.

"In this day and age, there are not many high-singing guys. It is a very baritone-oriented business for guys right now with Randy Travis, Ricky Van Shelton, Clint Black, and all those guys. They sing fairly low and Mark Chesnutt, and all these guys. I got a tenor voice and so it is a little different in finding the right songs with the right melody and such that can really fit my voice."

Had Gill not made it with a song, he would have with a ball. A golf ball. He is a scratch golfer who almost pursued a career as a professional athlete. Instead, he received a call from a blue-grass band leader when he was eighteen years old. He packed everything he owned into an old car and left his native Norman, Oklahoma, and never looked back.

"I started when I was seven or eight years old with little sawed-off clubs in the garage that Dad would make for me," Gill said. "It was just a game that I immediately fell in love with, and the Junior Golf Program in Oklahoma was very supportive of the kids. Played all through school until I was eighteen and was sitting there deciding what I was going to try to do—go to college or try to play music."

"I don't know that I had to make a choice," he said. "It wasn't like Oklahoma State University was knocking my door down to come and play golf for them."

"You go out there and shoot 68, 69, every now and then, but I think the difference is that I could beat Greg Norman one out of twenty times, but he is going to beat me nineteen of them," Gill said.

"How long are you off the tee?" I asked.

"Extremely long," he said. "I guess that is my greatest asset, my distance. There is the story of this one hole down in Florida, and it is like 620 yards long. It is a par five and they had the guys from the 350 Club, all these guys like Mike Dunaway and Big Cat Williams, and all of these long-hitting studs who can hit it 350 plus. I hit this green in two, and they had their 350 Club down there and none of them could get home in two on this hole.

"One of my favorite times playing golf was with Lee Trevino," Gill told me. "We were playing a scramble and there was a gallery of two or three hundred people. Everybody hit and they forgot me and everybody started walking. I said, 'Wait a minute, there is one more.' You know, I caught it flush and smoked it about three hundred yards and straight down the middle. Right after I hit it, Trevino jumped back and said, 'God dang! Have I got to look at this all day?' And he said, 'You must spend a lot of money on golf balls, 'cause they burn up when they re-enter the atmosphere.' "

Gill said he consistently outdrove the master in this one game.

He added that his temper would have been a liability in the world of professional golf. He sometimes loses his composure on the course, where the act is suicide to his score.

I have never seen Gill in a disconcerting mood.

"Does your temper carry over into the music business?" I asked him.

"Every now and then, sure. There are times when you are not playing great or not having a great show. And it can work on you a bit, but I try to keep it in check. I'm doing a lot better as I get older."

He added that he gets angry at criticism when it is moved from the professional to the personal arena. I pressed him as to what he meant.

"If they attack what I believe in or what I say as not being the truth. I have been panned for speaking out against some things and people would say that they didn't feel it was genuine."

He said he was criticized for his support of the war in the Persian Gulf.

"It was in the middle of a stage show and I said I saw something on TV today that was pretty special. I saw the first POW come home and he came home to the city I was playing in, and I said, 'Man, that was just great.' And I said I really supported what those guys did."

A reviewer wrote that Gill was insincere. Gill was livid.

I had the opportunity to be a co-host with Gill for a Nashville golf tournament. During a press conference to tout the event in July of 1991, Gill announced that he was about to become the newest member of the Grand Ole Opry. His announcement was premature and inappropriate, since tradition dictates that the news come from an Opry official. The next day, a Nashville newspaper headline said, "Oops, Vince Joins Opry."

"I let the cat out of the bag a little early, and I hope that nobody was too put off by it. My intentions were very good. To me, that is the pinnacle of the reason that I wanted to do commercial music. The Opry was the church of country music and that was the ultimate goal to strive for since I was a little kid."

Gill has a cutting-edge wit that borders on sarcasm. It belies his otherwise laid-back persona.

I asked him about the legendary University of Oklahoma football team, known as much for the shady carrying on of some of its coaches and players as for its touchdowns.

"So you must be a big OU fan," I said.

"That's right," he said. "When we get them all out of prison, we are going to have a good football team."

Gill asked me in 1992 to appear with him and a bevy of celebrities in the video for "Don't Let Our Love Start Slipping Away." We were on the set for about twelve hours, and I appeared in the video for only a few seconds.

I complained playfully to Gill on "Nashville Now" about having wasted an entire day for such a brief appearance.

"And you certainly need more television time," he quipped.

"Well, I think I did a pretty good job in the video," I said.

"If you do say so yourself," he fired back.

Gill is unusual in a few other ways. He has a show business marriage, and the marriage works. He's been married to Janice Gill, a vocalist with "Sweethearts of the Rodeo," for thirteen years. One of Gill's biggest records, "Look at Us," is about their relationship.

"The story borders the song," he said. "It is kind of rare to see people stick together anymore, with the divorce rate pretty high and people not really sticking with it and outlasting everything. This song is saying basically 'Look at us, after all these years together, we are still leaning on each other.'"

Gill said, however, that he didn't know what direction to take with the song—to write that theirs was a model marriage worthy of public examination, or to invite examination of a marriage that was falling apart. He said he went with the more positive approach because he and his wife were getting along famously when he penned the tune.

Gill got married on his birthday. He did so, he said, so that he would never forget his anniversary. "I gave myself the best present I could for my birthday," he said. "She was the best present a man could get."

Before he moved to California, and before coming to Nashville, the fiddle player Byron Berline told him about Janice.

" 'There is this girl out there who plays guitar and she and her sister sing bluegrass and country music, and you guys would be the perfect couple. You are going to fall in love and get married,' " Gill was told.

So Gill asked her out. And he asked again. And again.

"I asked her to go out with me for two or three years," he said. "And she wouldn't. Finally, we lived together for a couple of years before we finally got married."

Gill is also married to the idea of musical perfection. His records are as flawless as his voice, and some have complained that they are so tightly produced, they sound mechanical.

Yet he remains a red-hot newcomer whose mega-hit was a legitimate country standard only three months after it was released.

Here's betting, however, that even bigger records will emerge from the mind and soul of Vince Gill. Newcomer or veteran, Gill is, in my estimation, one of the best vocalists to grace country music in years. If it sounds like I really like this guy, you're right.

SIXTEEN

On November 6, a crisp Friday night in 1992, the television set buzzed with previews of the next day's collegiate football clashes.

A bulletin flashed suddenly on the Cable News Network.

Out-of-focus footage, shot through a faraway lens, showed the speeding outline of an airplane in the dark. The plane skidded on a foamed runway as sparks shot out at 200 miles per hour.

The fuselage looked like a long, out-of-control sparkler.

The plane had crash-landed at the Nashville International Airport. While the number of passengers was not known immediately, the identity of one was confirmed.

Reba McEntire was on board.

Mentioning Reba's name in connection with a plane crash was the equivalent of saying "heart attack" to a cardiologist.

The mishap came only twenty months after the March 16, 1991, catastrophe when seven band members and Reba's road manager perished in a fiery crash on a California mountain side. The tragedy churned up reams of news reports and follow-up stories around the world. *People* magazine, on its cover, called the first crash Reba's "darkest hour."

But that horrible event was sudden. The passengers in the private jet were talking one second, incinerated the next. The recollection had to be unavoidable for Reba while her private aircraft circled the Nashville airport for one suspenseful hour, burning fuel in preparation for the crash that was inevitable. Reba spent sixty minutes, an eternity, recalling one tragedy while bracing for another. She didn't expect to die. Neither did she expect to live.

"I didn't know what to expect," she told me.

I knew she didn't want to talk about what she wanted to forget, but I also knew that her fans and my radio listeners would want to hear, firsthand, about the flying curse that some say plagues her.

"And when you got out of the crashed plane, you got into another one to fly to your concert?" I asked.

"Sure," she said, "when you have a car wreck, you get into an ambulance, don't you?"

An investigation by the Federal Aviation Authority revealed that a mechanic, during routine service of the aircraft, had left a flashlight inside the wheel housing, and the plane's nose wheel wouldn't come down for the landing.

"But I'm still curious to know how you felt, in the air, knowing you had problem," I asked.

"I knew immediately we had a problem," Reba said. "I heard it right after take off. I heard a 'crunch.' I looked at Narvel [Reba's husband] and said, 'Something's not right, the nose gear didn't go up right.' You know, you fly every night, you know what sounds right and what sounds wrong, just like with your car."

The pilot radioed the Nashville tower, and was directed to fly the jet slowly and close to the earth to allow examiners a ground inspection of the nose wheel.

"So we basically had to fly by and let them look at it and nothing panicked me one bit," Reba said. "And I never was bothered until we began to get close to the ground."

Then she saw the fire trucks and ambulances.

"Then it alarmed us, like this was major," she said.

Again and again the small jet flew over the runway, and with each pass, everyone hoped that the radio voice would say that the nose gear had descended.

"I looked at Sandy Spika and said, 'If there is going to be forty-five minutes before we land, are we going to have time to eat?' " But then she thought, "Kevin [the pilot] will have a heart attack if he looks back here and sees us eating instead of getting ready for what's fixin' to happen." "So I said, 'Okay, do you want to play another round of cards?'"

"Jeff Nix, the co-pilot, knew exactly what was fixin' to happen," Reba said, and added that he had recently been discharged from the Air Force where rehearsed crash landings were routine. "So we knew we were in good hands, and we landed."

The only preparation Reba made for the crash, she said, was to grab a pillow and hold it against her chest "like I see on television. And then I said, 'Well, you all may see me later, and you all may not.'"

When the fuel was at last virtually gone, lessening the risk of fire, the pilot plopped the plane onto its underside. Emergency vehicles raced down the runway in its wake.

The plane landed on its two rear wheels and sped down the runway in that posture until inertia set the ship on its nose, and the aircraft dragged along for a few hundred yards more.

The pilots, Reba said, struggled to keep the plane going straight for fear it would tumble end over end.

"We got off the plane and Sandy and I were looking around, making sure somebody got the catering off the plane 'cause we knew we were gonna have to get on another plane and go to Madison, but nobody got the catering."

"Were you afraid of anything, Reba?" I asked.

"Being killed," she said.

"But you seem very cavalier in your attitude. 'Do you want to play cards? Do you want to eat?'"

"It's better than sitting there white-knuckled and getting scared," she said. "We did ask each other, 'Do you want to go to the bathroom?'"

Reba's true emotions surfaced when the plane finally halted. She and other passengers had been ordered by the pilot to stay in their seats. He had told them there would be no interior lights, and that trying to walk inside the cabin would be hazardous.

"I looked over at Narvel and Narvel said, 'He's crazy if he thinks I'm gonna sit here in this seat while he's giving instructions. We don't know what's gonna happen after we get on the ground.' So when that thing stopped, we were all sandwiched at the door and we took out in a hurry!"

Three passengers, the pilot, and co-pilot all made a hasty exit.

The crash landing happened to be filmed because the vice-presidential candidate, Al Gore, was awaited by television news crews at Nashville International Airport.

Otherwise, no television crew would have been present, and the world might not have seen the event, as Reba had no desire to tell about still another aviation mishap touching her life. When she arrived in Madison, a news crew was waiting. She asked that they be escorted from the building since she didn't want to talk to them. She never mentioned the incident to the 9,000 fans on hand that night.

During a music video shoot for Vince Gill in 1992, I encountered Reba, who told me that she and her family were planning a Christmas ski trip to Aspen, Colorado.

I asked her to join Barbara Mandrell's family and mine, since we would be skiing in Aspen as well. Our three families, including all our kids, were joined by Dr. and Mrs. Newt Lovvorn, a friend who treated Barbara after her 1984 near-fatal car wreck. We gathered at the T Lazy-Seven Ranch to dine and dance. My youngest son, Kit, got on stage and sang with a band. He had no reservations about performing in front of Barbara and Reba.

A few days later we congregated on the slopes, and Reba, a novice skier, hired a personal instructor. She enrolled Shelby, her son who was then two, in ski school.

The independent spirit is typical of my friend. On the ski slope in Colorado, Reba mentioned to me casually a profoundly revealing attitude that has propelled her through life.

"I hate to be told I can't do something," she said. "My sister Alice is the same way. Tell her she can't do something and she'll do it every time, and I guess we're just alike."

"Oh yeah," I joked, "then let's go ski the back slopes."

That ended the conversation.

We did have, later, a serious discussion about fear. Reba at first told me she feared nothing, then said she feared for the welfare of her loved ones. And her second greatest fear was of snakes. The fear was nothing less than obsessive, and had been with her a lifetime, much of which was spent in the snake-infested pastures of southeastern Oklahoma.

"I stepped over a six-foot rattlesnake when I was little," she said. "We were gathering cattle across the hill from where I grew up. I was in the pickup and got out and there was a rattlesnake that was traveling. We were in open pasture and I walked right over him. I was looking up to where Daddy was bringing the cattle. I was straddling the snake. I looked down and began screaming so loud that Daddy had to leave the cattle. Daddy had to think I was dying for him to leave the cattle. You know, you just don't leave the cattle.

"I've seen my daddy kill rattlers in the mountains where we lived and their heads were bigger than his fist."

Another of Reba's fears was of horses. She didn't fear injury, but feared instead that she might not ride them well enough, although she once had aspirations of becoming a world-champion barrel racer.

"When you're afraid, the horse can sense it," Reba said. "And I am the daughter of a world-champion steer roper. I am the granddaughter of a world-champion steer roper. So when you go into the arena as a McEntire, to the rodeo arena, a lot of pressure is put on you. Everyone thinks, 'Well, she's a McEntire, she's gonna go out there and she's gonna win everything.' Well, I never did. Alice and Pake do. But I never was that good. And I think that was God's way of saying, 'Reba, you're not that good, quit this and tend to what I have given you the talent for.' "

I asked Reba if there was any money in becoming a professional cowgirl.

She said that there is today because rodeo has changed to allow commercial sponsorship of those who enter. When she was a child, however, a contestant had to sponsor himself or herself, and could not enter competition without coming up with the entry fee.

"But compared with what you're doing now, Reba, the money in rodeo is not a lot," I said.

"Nope," she said, "I'm really glad that I was not that good at it so I had to do what I'm doing now. And too, the longevity. I couldn't have done it as long as I can in the music business. This is the business to stay in."

Reba is among the more physical women in country music. She wasn't raised to be dainty, and was more comfortable in pickups than Porsches. She still rides horses on her Tennessee farm and dons denim in her office, as she once did on stage.

"I began to hear complaints from women who came to the concerts and told me they got more dressed up than I did, so I changed my look," she said, laughing.

She's told me many times about the closeness of the four McEntire children as they grew up. They accompanied their father to rodeos, and the entry fee exhausted family resources. The siblings rode in the backs of pickups, slept three in the bed, and fought as they frolicked—as a family.

The first time Reba was ever paid to sing, she sang with Pake. She was five and he was seven.

They were in Shane, Wyoming, with their other two sisters and parents. The six McEntires all stayed in one hotel room, devoid of even a black-and-white television.

Hundreds of cowboys had gathered inside the Cheyenne Frontier Hotel and congregated around the building's only television, in the lobby.

"So for a pastime you didn't stay in your room, you went down to the lobby," Reba recalled. "Everybody you knew was there because you just followed the circuit. It was Cheyenne one week and then you went on to Salt Lake the next, or you went up to Sheridan and everybody went to the same rodeo. And all the kids knew all the other kids and it was just a big happy family.

"And so one day Pake, who was a big show-off, was singing 'You Ain't Nothin' But a Hound Dog' for all the cowboys, and somebody gave him a quarter. So I went over to him and I said, 'Hey, you been making all the money here, why don't you help me?' And he said, 'Okay, what do you wanna do?' The only song

I knew all the way through, besides 'Please Mister Custer,' was 'Jesus Loves Me.' "

"So I sang 'Jesus Loves Me' and a cowboy gave me a nickel. It was the first time I was paid for singing."

It was a twentieth-century family with nineteenth-century loyalty. Members fought each other, but if an outsider fought one of them he fought them all.

"And I can remember Alice and Pake fighting so hard that Susie and I would call Mama at work and say, 'They're killing each other,' and we really thought they were," Reba recalled. "Alice would usually win."

A bonding among children of modest means in the rural South in the 1950s was stronger than the links of today's fast-lane siblings. With the proliferation of television, contemporary youngsters, even in the country, are often without the innocence their parents possessed.

That's why it was hard for Reba, Susie, and Pake to part ways. The sister and brother sang in her band during the 1970s, and Susie even sang on some of Reba's early hit records.

Dolly Parton saw the breakup of her own "Traveling Family Band," and other country entertainers, including Buck Owens, have seen their offspring come and then leave their shows without success commensurate to the family front-runner.

It has to be awkward, and the public never knows all of the circumstances surrounding the breakups.

I asked Reba if Pake had difficulty deciding to leave her bandstand and show business to go back to civilian life.

"I think it was real easy for Pake to make the decision," she said. "I think he wanted to go back home, to continue his ranching and his rodeoing and being with his family. When he was rodeoing and he could sing too, that was fine, but when he was singing he couldn't continue his rodeoing and his practicing and he really missed it.

"And I see Susie once in a while when she comes to my show. She and her husband have a gospel ministry, 'Psalms Ministry,' out of Atoka, Oklahoma. Susie sings and Paul gets up and preaches and they travel all over the United States. They've gone to Australia, they've gone up into Canada. And they travel more than I do and they take their kids with them sometimes, but now their kids are in school so they're leaving them home quite a bit. Susie and Paul have just signed a record deal and are doing very well."

Reba's older sister, Alice, works for the Oklahoma Department of Human Services in Atoka, and runs, with Reba's mother, Jackie, the "Reba Ranch House" in Denison, Texas. The facility is similar to the Ronald McDonald House. It provides housing for people whose family members are ill, in this case under treatment at the Texoma Medical Center.

The center had not been open very long when I first visited with Reba in 1993. She was holding a letter from a little girl, who had stayed at the Reba Ranch House with her sister and mother while her grandfather was hospitalized at Texoma.

The old man died, and the child had written Reba a letter of thanks, telling her that the medical staff was nice to her family before her grandfather went to Heaven.

Reba personally answered the little girl's letter. Reba had, days earlier, read for a part in the Gene Hackman–Tom Cruise movie *The Firm*. She had videotaped appearances on "Evening Shade" with Burt Reynolds and faced her typically grueling concert schedule. But she took the time anyway to thank a grieving child for saying thanks.

"I told her I was glad that her family was all together. I don't have a grandpa either anymore, I wrote her, and that it was really neat that they got to spend that time together before he did pass on," Reba said.

I told her that her gesture was nice but didn't belabor compliments about her kindness or her good heart.

"Well," she said, "it's a great thing to get to help people that have family in the hospital. Everybody is under a lot of stress then, and to be able to stay in a nice place is neat. All the people in the Texoma Medical Center have worked real hard to put this thing together."

———■———

Reba is among that handful of entertainers whose profile is so high, a first name is all that's needed. Yet her dramatic rise to superstardom had an uncertain beginning with an attempt to get some free tickets.

"I was trying to get my college buddies in free to a rodeo and Ken Lance [the owner of Ken Lance Sports Arena in Ada, Oklahoma] stopped me and said, 'Reba, I'd like you to meet a friend of mine.' So I met Red Steagall, a popular songwriter and recording artist in the 1970s. We talked for a while, and I said, 'Well I gotta go. I gotta get up there and sing the 'National Anthem.' So I did that, and that night after the rodeo we all went over to the Hilton. The Justin Boot party was going on and Red Steagall was there with all the cowboys and his wife, so Mom and Dad took us kids over there, you know, always promoting our singing careers.

"So I was standing around there, and I think it was Everett Shaw who wanted me to sing Dolly's 'Joshua.' So I did."

Steagall and his band tried to accompany Reba, but they didn't know the chords. So Reba sang a cappella.

Her mother pulled Steagall to the side and asked if he could help get her children into the entertainment world.

"Jackie," Steagall said, "I'm just writing for myself, I don't think I could do anything."

So Reba returned to college, Pake to ranching, and Susie to high school.

The McEntire telephone rang in January of 1975.

"Jackie, I've been thinking about this," Reba quoted Red. "I really can't get all three of the kids in, but I think I might be able to do something with Reba. Why don't y'all come down and let's cut a demonstration tape and then this summer I'll pitch it around and see what we can get done."

"And so we did," Reba said, "and in November 1975, Polygram signed me. So it was eleven months after I met Red for the first time that I had a recording contract."

She called Steagall one of the nicest men she had ever met, and said that he was incredibly loyal.

"He's your friend forever," she said.

In the winter of 1992–93 I watched Reba in her two-story, sprawling office complex about two miles from mainstream Music Row. About seventy-five people are on the payroll, including the band and singers who rehearsed as we talked. Our conversation that day was cut short by an expected call from a reporter with the British Broadcasting Corporation, the first of perhaps a hundred relayed that day.

"It never stops," Reba said, "it's endless."

I looked around at the corporate headquarters beehive and remembered that her childhood clothes were all "hand-me-downs." Somehow it pleased me to remember.

"My clothes came from cousins, and I mean it was like Christmas when the boxes came in," Reba said, smiling. "We had rich cousins down in Ft. Worth, Texas. Dorothy Markum's kids. They would send us huge boxes of clothes. And Alice was closer to Maria Jo's and Judy's age than I was and I'd wear those shoes that were three sizes too big. I'd wear pants that were two and three sizes bigger, just because they were the most beautiful things in the world to me. There was one pair of bell-bottoms, two pair black with rhinestones, and they were western bell-bottoms, and I about wore them things out.

"I'll never forget one day when I was in the bathroom, Daddy knocked and he gave me a five-dollar bill," Reba remembered. "And I thought, 'Big-time Christmas,' and thanked him very much. Daddy was not very flamboyant, and I'll give you a great example. Daddy would go to the rodeos and wipe the mud off his horse because he had just got it out of the pasture. He didn't have a nice stall barn, like I have now. And his horse would be caked after rolling in the mud and Daddy would wipe him with a tow sack. Everybody else would have all their curry combs and their brushes and clippers. And Daddy would go out with his horse still having caked mud around his ankles and his hocks and win the ropin'. And then Daddy would jump his horse back up in the trailer, and we'd go home, and the money he won would go to buy more cattle or buy land."

I recall one of the first times I met Reba, in 1981. She was wearing one of her father's world-champion belt buckles. She was rehearsing for "Nashville Alive" when someone entered her dressing room and stole the keepsake. Her nervousness of appearing on network television was overcome by the panic of the loss of the metal buckle.

Her emotions said volumes about the priorities of this woman. I put the word out, and the buckle was returned by a security guard, but part of it was missing. Reba asked no questions about where the guard had gotten the buckle.

Reba McEntire, unlike any performer I've ever met, can tell you where she was when, with whom, and where she'll be at what time in the future. She's a walking itinerary with a photographic memory.

Perhaps Reba's genius lies in the fact that her talent is matched by her fortitude. Both are awesome.

She was named the Country Music Association's Female Vocalist of the Year" annually from 1984 through 1987. That four-year run was unprecedented, and remains unsurpassed.

In the third year she was nominated, she was also nominated for "Entertainer of the Year," country music's highest honor. Music industry insiders deemed her a long shot.

In 1985, at the end of the awards show, Reba and other winners were loaded into a used van at the program's conclusion and driven to the Opryland Hotel to meet the press. She, and other stars, wondered aloud why they couldn't have faced reporters backstage at the awards hall, the Opry House.

She told her former manager, Bill Carter, that she felt as if she were being "herded" and that she and her colleagues resented the treatment. Once she arrived at the hotel, a popular tourist attraction, she was besieged by fans, and a mob scene resulted that interrupted the press conference.

Reba and Carter politely registered their grievance with the CMA, giving the organization plenty of time to work out other arrangements for its next winners' press conference a year later.

The CMA didn't change its plan for press coverage. It instead reacted negatively to Reba and her candor.

On the very year when she was nominated for the grand prize, she was provided no backstage pass and no backstage parking. I found out, thought the CMA was petty, and arranged for the reigning "Female Vocalist of the Year" to park in a space, and to have a dressing room, provided by The Nashville Network.

Reba, as I've indicated, won "Female Vocalist of the Year" and became "Entertainer of the Year" on the same night the CMA would have had her park in the fans' parking lot, or alongside the hired help. That would have been very difficult for someone so strongly embedded in the public eye. It also would have been a security hazard for Reba.

After she accepted each of her awards, she did not walk backstage. Instead, on prime-time television, she simply returned to her seat in the audience.

At the show's conclusion, when CMA officials wanted her to be hauled via van to the Opryland Hotel, Reba left the Opry House through a side door and walked to an idling limousine.

Two CMA representatives literally followed her to her car and begged her to get into a van bound for the hotel press conference.

She stood by her guns and refused to go.

"Reba would not budge on that, and I respected her decision and supported her totally on it," Carter said in 1993. Carter, who later became my manager, told CMA officials after the 1986 awards show, "Reba is going to the RCA party, and then she is going to [her] hotel."

Some folks may think it was snobbish of Reba to refuse to do the press conference anywhere other than backstage at the Opry House. But some folks don't know the pressures of being Reba McEntire.

As a result of her stance, the interviews today are done backstage, as they are after the Grammy Awards and other prestigious awards shows. And the general public is a winner. It derives the benefit of press coverage devoid of distractions that once came when celebrities and reporters fought fans and tourists inside the sprawling Opryland Hotel.

Reba remembers what she might like to forget: March 16, 1991. She was at the center of what was one of the most disastrous events in the history of country music. I had no intention of rehashing it when I saw her last. But twenty-two months after the fact, Reba kept returning to the split second that eliminated eight lives.

There were times I wanted to change the subject for her comfort. Yet, I felt ill-at-ease, avoiding the conversation she sought.

So I simply listened.

"People say to me, 'Have you gotten over the tragedy?' Of course not, I never will. But in my music, my emotions reflect in my music because if I'm really upset, really sad, that's what I want to sing. I don't want to do a happy song when I'm sad.

"So here, as we are pulling out of deep depression, of the losing of people that you love and you've gotten to work with and had so much fun with, and you want to pull out of it not only for yourself but for their families to give them strength."

"So you correlate this [her new album, "It's Your Call"] with the sadness."

"The day before we left on the tour of the weekend of the plane crash in '91," she remembered, "I was in the office at home and I was listening to this song of Skip Ewing's called 'Lighter Shade of Blue.' I put that song in the stack of the ones I love and we went on the trip. The plane crash happened, we flew home, and that night I walked right back into the office and I picked that tape up and I listened to it. I called Narvel and said, 'Narvel, come here, I think you ought to listen to this song.'

"And it was the plane crash," she said, "it was like that song knew this was gonna happen. And I couldn't put it on the album we did after that, and so I kept it, and it's on the new album, and it's been two years . . . and we've only turned a lighter shade of blue."

SEVENTEEN

On January 1, 1943, there was no Oak Ridge—no town, no name, and no people. Only two months earlier the Army had designated 59,000 acres of land in a valley between the Cumberland and Smoky Mountain ranges, the center of which was about eighteen miles west of Knoxville, Tennessee, as the Kingston Demolition Range, and all 3,000 residents of settlements like Scarsboro, Robertsville, and Wheat had been evacuated. A few construction workers had arrived on November 22, 1942, and at their suggestion the place was named Oak Ridge, after Black Oak Ridge, one of the five pine- and oak-covered ridges in the area.

Within two years, 75,000 people had moved there, and nobody—not even the majority of the new residents—knew why. But from the tight security at the guard gates, it was obvious the military was involved in a secret project.

It was a secret, all right—the best-kept secret of World War II. It was the Manhattan Project. The atom bomb.*

In 1943 the Allied forces were escalating the pressure that would, within two years, reduce Berlin to ruins.

The United States' atomic energy plant at Oak Ridge was running three shifts, twenty-four hours a day, to keep up with the

*Widner, Ellis, and Walter Carter. *The Oak Ridge Boys.* New York: Contemporary Books, Inc., 1987.

government's schedule to construct a top-secret bomb that might or might not be dropped.

To eliminate the smuggling of parts of classified information to the outside, civilian workers were sequestered. For weeks on end they labored, ate, and slept inside the arsenal that was both their place of work and home.

In support of the war effort, a gospel quartet called Wally Fowler and the Georgia Clod Hoppers from nearby Knoxville, Tennessee, frequently went to the Oak Ridge plant to entertain worried and weary workers free of charge. Don Light, who has managed the group twice in his career, told me the quartet's name was eventually changed to the Oak Ridge Quartet.

A number of singers came to and left the quartet while it toured churches and revival tents throughout the 1950s and 1960s. The group's popularity was helped by Fowler, who employed the group on a live show each Friday night over WSM in Nashville.

The Oaks and other groups in which Fowler had an interest played each Saturday night in Atlanta. Fowler used WSM to promote the Atlanta shows until station officials asked him to refrain.

"So Wally would sneak a plug for the Atlanta show in his radio prayers," Light told me. "At the end of the Friday night show, he'd pray, 'Lord, watch over these quartets as they travel to Atlanta, where they'll be performing at eight o'clock tomorrow night in the city auditorium.' "

In 1957, Wally Fowler had hit upon hard times and owed the members of the quartet between $2,500 and $3,000 according to Herman Harper, a bass singer with the group at the time. Fowler gave Smitty Gatlin ownership of the name in return for forgiving the debt.

In the spring of 1966, Smitty Gatlin announced he was leaving the group for a job as minister of music at the First Baptist Church in Dallas. His departure was a devastating blow to the group since he managed the group as well as sang lead. Herman Harper took over the management of the group.

The most difficult thing to do was to replace Gatlin, one of the best singers in gospel music. Their first choice was Duane Allen, whom they knew as the former baritone singer with the Prophets Quartet. He lived in Texas. They called and offered him the job. Duane drove to Nashville and went to Don Light's office. Light had been booking the group since 1965. The Oak Ridge Boys were in the next room talking about disbanding.

Herman Harper said, "If we hadn't gotten someone of Duane's caliber, we might have gone through with the break-up." After singing two songs in a rehearsal, Duane Allen was made the lead singer and a full partner in the Oak Ridge Boys. The Oak Ridge Boys now consisted of Bill Golden, Willie Wynn, Herman Harper, and Duane Allen.

Herman Harper left in 1968 and was replaced by Noel Fox as bass singer. Fox left in 1972. Both left to work for Don Light Talent as booking agents. Richard Sterban came aboard in 1972 to sing bass and does to this day. Willie Wynn left in 1973 and was replaced by Joe Bonsall, who continues as the tenor singer today.

The Oak Ridge Boys became the first gospel quartet to implement progressive arrangements, abandoning the traditional gospel rhythmic piano for arpeggios and improvisations, and implementing additional instrumentation, including electric guitar, bass guitar, and drums.

The resulting sound was a sharp contrast to the Blackwood Brothers, the Statesman Quartet, the Speer Family, and other conventional gospel groups of the day. The Oak Ridge Boys even began to dress fashionably, donning the 1960s popular bell-bottom trousers instead of polyester suits with narrow neckties, all the same cut and color. The Oak Ridge Boys were the first quartet to wear clothes that expressed the individual.

Controversy swelled within the evangelical circles that were the groups' bread and butter. Regimented, religious fundamentalists were resistant to the changes and said so in protests and angry letters. The anger really flourished in 1977 when the group recorded its first number-one secular song, "Y'All Come Back Saloon," a ditty about a woman who worked inside a honky-tonk and knew every song on the juke box.

The Reverend Oral Roberts spoke out against them and by doing so prompted more controversy than if he had become a male stripper.

But the Oaks knew what they were doing, and knew they were doing it right. For six consecutive years, the Statler Brothers had been the Country Music Association's "Vocal Group of the Year." They had been country music's only group for several years and their reign as the kings of four-part harmony was unchallenged until October 1978.

The Statlers, who today are still the act with the most awards in all of country music, were unseated as "Vocal Group of the Year" by the Oak Ridge Boys.

In accepting the award on national television, the tenor, Joe Bonsall, said that he hoped the Oaks could carry the award with the same grace and dignity with which the Statlers had possessed it for so long.

The tact and timing were brilliant. The Oak Ridge Boys had arrived. Not long afterwards, the quartet recorded an album with a cover showing the members emerging from a bus under a headline, "The Oak Ridge Boys Have Arrived!"

In 1978, Kenny Rogers was scorching hot in the wake of "Lucille" and "The Gambler." He had recorded earlier a duet with Dottie West, "Every Time Two Fools Collide," that topped the charts. He and Dottie were touring to promote the record and wanted another act on the package. Kenny selected the Oaks, and the show was country music's biggest box-office attraction that year wherever it played.

I was the master of ceremonies the night the show opened in Greensboro, North Carolina. A heckler in the audience blasted every act on the program, including me, and finally Rogers told the man, "Hey man, even a train stops once in a while."

Deafening applause.

I also remember how anxious Dottie West was to please Ken Kragen, Rogers' manager and tour organizer. This was Dottie's first work for a major Los Angeles entertainment mogul.

In the limousine after the program, Kragen told Dottie that he didn't want her to sing "The American Trilogy" again, and that he thought the pacing of her show could be improved. She listened intently and implemented each change he asked for.

I remember my own observations that night on the differences between the Oaks and Statlers. While the Statlers' show consisted of four men standing still and singing their hits, the Oaks were all over the stage, running and jumping through a maze of swirling lights and pyrotechnics. They just generated excitement.

Today's Oak Ridge Boys are Richard Sterban, Joe Bonsall, Steve Sanders, and Duane Allen, who, after twenty-seven years with the group, is the oldest Oak. Each member exhibits a loyalty to the organization that is almost unprecedented in the fickle world of commercial music. It's all for one and one for all. The Oaks are the four musketeers, their voices are their swords.

"All I ever wanted to be was an Oak Ridge Boy," said Allen, the lead singer. "The first time I saw them I was a disc jockey and a college student, and I sold enough tickets to charter a bus from Paris, Texas, to Ft. Worth to see the Oak Ridge Boys. I had sixty-five passengers, and that was enough for me to get to go free."

The singers are all married and each member celebrates a wedding anniversary from September 20th through September 23rd.

"It is a week when our local jeweler will do good business in September," Bonsall said. "His business may be in the hole the prior month, but he knows the Oaks' anniversary week is coming up."

"And we pay his bills for a whole year," Allen joked.

I visited the Oaks in late 1992 and realized then how many collaborations they have made with other celebrated artists. I'd speculate that no other vocal group has worked with so many singers, including George Jones, Ray Charles, Jimmy Buffett, Brenda Lee, Johnny Cash, Roy Clark, Con Hunley, Del Reeves, Roy Rogers, Paul Simon, Billy Dean, the Forrester Sisters, Larry Gatlin and the Gatlin Brothers, Bill Monroe, Hank Thompson, Buck Trent, and Lorrie Morgan.

And the Oaks were sought out by still another public figure, the former President, George Bush.

"I go back to 1963 with George Bush," Allen said. "My brother was the political arm of the Allen family. He told me about George Bush, and we campaigned for him every Saturday when he ran for Congress. We would go place leaflets in shopping malls. I didn't really run into him again face-to-face until we performed for President Ronald Reagan and we were on the White House lawn at the annual barbecue that is held for both sides of the House. We were doing a sound check in the afternoon and we saw this long, lanky guy running toward the stage, going through security.

"We had been hearing that we were his favorite group. He came up and said, 'I've got to go to Africa tonight and won't be able to stay for the show, so would you sing me a song or two?' We wound up doing a concert for George Bush on the White House lawn, him standing on stage requesting number after number. In fact, he would call for songs that weren't even our hits.

"He was coming up with album cuts from 'Room Service' and 'Together,' albums from the late '70s," Bonsall said. "He loved anything that had to do with the bass singing aspect."

Sterban is considered one of the world's finest bass singers. I've heard him hit subterranean notes that rattled the public address system. During the Republican National Convention in 1988, Bush was standing near Sterban as the Oak Ridge Boys sang the National Anthem. The President was caught up in the excitement of the music and moment and he began singing bass himself— into the ear of Sterban, who was trying to keep his own harmony correct on national television.

"Bush is up there just singing awful bass, right in Richard's ear, and that was the most unique experience," Bonsall recalled. "Wow, this guy could be President of the United States and he's singing in Richard's ear."

The Oaks campaigned for Bush during his 1992 presidential bid. They traveled aboard Air Force One during the final five days of the Bush effort.

"It was the very last day of the campaign, and the President came back to where we were sitting and said, 'Would you please come on up here, guys, and sing me some gospel songs?' We said, 'Sure man, of course.' "

On the night before the election, while millions of eyes across the globe turned toward the United States, four singers and the most powerful man in the world huddled inside a plane cabin, singing songs of Heaven while soaring through it. The Oaks told me they delivered an a cappella rendition of "Farther Along," "Swing Down Sweet Chariot," "Dry Bones," and "How Great Thou Art."

The minstrels and their one-man audience sat closely so that they could be heard above the engines' roar. Then the chief executive asked for a final selection, and requested "Amazing Grace."

The singers broke into song; the President broke into tears.

"Why do you think he became emotional?" I asked the Oaks.

Bonsall said, "I think maybe some reality was hitting. There was a real possibility that George Bush could lose this election. Everybody was crying, including the four of us."

The Oaks visited the White House four years ago and Bush took them on a tour of the premises, including the Oval Office and his personal workroom. Bush insisted on showing them the sound system where he listened to their songs. He hit a button, and sure enough, one of their tunes filled the room.

"And I will tell you something that really blew my mind," Bonsall said. "At the time while we were listening to his system playing at honest-to-God concert level decibels, there was setting there that red phone! And I thought, 'My God, suppose the President is sitting in here some night rocking out and that red phone rings, and he can't hear it! The Oak Ridge Boys could be the cause of an international disaster!' "

Only two groups had country music recording contracts when the Oak Ridge Boys came on the secular music scene, Allen said. Today there are forty-six. The Oaks' concert career has continued to flourish despite the absence of hit records. They continue to draw large audiences to the nation's largest arenas, including state fairs and sprawling theme parks, such as "Six Flags Over St. Louis" and "Six Flags Over Texas." Their popularity prevails de-

spite the departure of their longest-standing and most conspicuous member, William Lee Golden. He was the baritone singer
who sported near waist-length hair and a triangular beard whose
tip hung to his navel. He wore mountain-man attire and looked
nothing like the fashion plates of the rest of the group.

He was at odds with the other members and they had many ar-
guments over his attitude and behavior.

The Oak Ridge Boys with Golden on board recorded "Elvira"
and "Bobbie Sue," their two biggest records, then recorded six
gold albums, and one that went double-platinum, with sales in
excess of two million. These feats were particularly significant
because they occurred when country music was not nearly as
popular as it is today.

But, at the height of the Oak Ridge Boys' success, the other
three members kicked Golden out and replaced him with Steve
Sanders.

I asked Allen, Bonsall, and Sterban if they were willing to talk
about Golden's departure.

"Certainly," Bonsall said, "but I don't think that you just want
to write down that he just became such a pain in the ass that it
was hard to deal with him."

Bonsall said trouble surfaced when Golden, in 1981, wanted to
act as an independent concert promoter and promote a show in
his hometown of Brewton, Alabama, in which he wanted the
Oak Ridge Boys to appear. Bonsall said Golden offered to pay
the quartet $50,000, but the Oaks were willing to do the show
free of charge.

"We helped save his concert, and Golden, I think, held some of
that against us," Bonsall said. "Now he may say that he doesn't
remember any of that, but that Harvest Jam was a big-deal thing
that started to separate us."

Bonsall was right. Golden said he didn't remember any of
Bonsall's contentions surrounding the Harvest Jam.

Bonsall said the dissent intensified among the three members
when Golden wanted to record a solo album. The other Oaks
were against it.

"I had exercised an option that I had on a recording contract that we had," Golden said. "We were signed to MCA Records, and when we signed, which was one of the biggest contracts within the country of any artist at that time, when we signed that contract it also specified in the contract that MCA had us as a group and also had the contract on us individually in case that we decided, any member decided, to do a solo album."

Golden said the other Oaks never chose to exercise the option to record solo, although the lead singer, Duane Allen, recorded a solo album when the group was strictly gospel on Heartwarming Records.

Golden pointed out that many successful rock acts, such as the Rolling Stones, Grateful Dead, and Genesis, have members who record with the group and as soloists.

"I never wanted to steal any of the Oak Ridge Boys' deals or try to go in and hire people that they were using, to try to undermine what the Oak Ridge Boys had created as such," Golden said.

"Golden seemed to surround himself with a bunch of people all the time that told him he was better than us and we were his enemies," Bonsall said.

"We were having a business meeting, this is the next big blow," Bonsall continued. "We are having a meeting in here one day, all of us. Golden was an hour late for the meeting anyway. He came in, slammed his thing down on the desk, and told us, 'I am doing a blankety blank solo album and I don't give a God dang blankety blank what any of you think about it.' "

Golden denied the allegation.

Bonsall said the other Oak Ridge Boys felt they were in a no-win situation with Golden and his solo efforts.

"If this solo album does really good," Bonsall said, "he was probably going to quit the group because he thought he was better than us and say he was right, and if it doesn't do good, it is going to be our fault."

Bonsall said Golden became harder to work with when the album didn't sell well.

Golden, in his defense, said he wouldn't have left the Oaks, even if his solo album had been a success.

Sanders said the Oak Ridge Boys' record label became confused in its promotional efforts, not knowing whether to focus on the Oak Ridge Boys or on Golden as a soloist.

Bonsall contended that the situation deteriorated to the degree where Golden declined to talk to the other Oak Ridge Boys, and was speechless for months while riding the same tour bus with them.

I asked the Oaks if the standoff made performing difficult.

"Well, it does when you go for two months and never say 'hello' or 'kiss my foot' to each other," Allen said.

"So we set a timetable in motion is what we did," Bonsall said. "We went to Golden several times. I know I personally went to him many times and tried to say, 'Golden, look, what do you want to do? You know right now the Oak Ridge Boys have the world, you know, kind of by the butt. And we can make a good living for a long time. But yet you keep going against us all the time, what do you want?' He could never tell me. He would say stupid things like, 'Well, I am a rocker and I am this and I am that.'

"So the question is, did the Oaks really kick Golden out of the group?" Bonsall said. "Yes, we did! And we did it because he just, by God, he just didn't want to cooperate. It had nothing to do with long hair. It had nothing to do with being in with the Indians, or a mountain man, or none of that.

"And now let me tell you one more thing, Ralph," Bonsall continued. "That was another reason for us dismissing him. Golden was insisting for several years in a row, or spreading rumors, that he was either leaving or that we were breaking up. And it got so bad that promoters were starting to question whether or not to book us. The Domino Pizza guy would come to the house and say, 'I hear you guys are breaking up.' "

Golden, for his part, said he never spread rumors about the group's pending breakup.

Bonsall and other Oaks were visibly upset with Golden and they continued to complain about his "anti-Oak" behavior.

Bonsall said he then sent a letter on behalf of the group telling Golden he was no longer wanted in the Oak Ridge Boys.

"Two months before that," Bonsall recalled, "I sat with Golden up in South Dakota and I said, 'Golden, you know we have had a lot of times, good times.' And we have. I have had a lot of fun with Golden over the years off and on. He and I have had some good times. Him and his wife at the time and my wife and me had some good times. I said, 'Golden, I just want you to know, man, and this is for the good times, brother, I am worried about you because you are way out there on your own and listening to these people that ain't your friends. You don't seem to know who your friends really are. You have given us the hardest time, the hardest way to go, and I am a little worried about you, man.'

"And he looked me right in the eye," Bonsall said. "And with all the honesty that I have ever seen in his face, he got a little bit mean looking and said, 'Well, Joey, don't you waste any of your God damn time worrying about me!' And I said to him, 'You got it.'

"That's it!" Bonsall said. "I believed him, and believe me, I shut the door on his ass that night. That's it, we have got to move on now. You are out of here. That's how I felt. That is really how I felt then."

On September 16, 1982, a letter signed by Joe Bonsall, Duane Allen, and Richard Sterban was sent to William Lee Golden.

"This will be the most difficult letter we ever write," the text began. "Your mountain-man appearance is causing the group embarrassment."

The letter attacked Golden for wanting "to wear a dead animal" on Johnny Carson's "Tonight Show."

Golden told me he had, in fact, wanted to wear a skinned coyote over his head and down his back, but that he wanted to wear it en route to the program, and not on the telecast.

"Your hair and beard are much too long," the letter continued. "You need to clean up, bathe, and start smelling fresh."

Golden said he did not always bathe daily because the pressures of travel often prevented personal cleanliness as he would like it.

Bonsall acknowledged Golden's alleged use of drugs but said his behavior was irrational "whether or not Golden was ever doing drugs."

Bonsall and Allen said they felt Golden wanted an image of mastery, and sought a public persona similar to the singer–songwriter David Allen Coe.

Golden's public statements about drug consumption reflected badly on the other members of the group who were image conscious. Bonsall made reference to Golden having told a writer for *People* that he smoked and snorted drugs.

"The three of us were devasted over this, it makes us look like druggers," Bonsall said. He was going through customs at the Dallas/Fort Worth airport a year after the *People* article. "They nailed me and my wife to the wall," Bonsall said. "And went through everything we got, and you know what the customs guy told me afterwards? 'Okay, you're clean, but let me tell you something. You tell that long haired son of a bitch that he can snort and sniff all he wants, but we are going to get him.' Now I told Golden this and you know what he did? He went . . ."

At that point, Bonsall extended his middle finger.

I got the idea.

"But as far as drugs," Golden said, "they didn't like it because I admitted that I had smoked pot before, one time when *People* magazine came out." Golden added that he also told the magazine reporter that he had snorted cocaine.

"Bill, the best solution for us is for you to get with the program," the Oaks wrote in their letter of reprimand.

Bonsall went on to say, "I was the last guy in this group over here to be for making a change. I was the most maybe insecure of all. This little Philly boy thought, 'Oh my God, it's got to be us four guys . . . look what we've done.' I told that to Golden. I got on my knees to Golden. What do you want? It's got to be us. I was so insecure about it, I couldn't believe it.

"I felt it had to be us four," he continued. "Golden, Duane, Joe, and Richard. I didn't want to see it change, man. That's why I hung on for so many years, that's why we put up with one thing or another, because we felt like it had to be us, it was worth it, because we are the Oak Ridge Boys. But in the last year or two of that, I got so tired of everything, our guys got so tired of dealing with the problems all the time instead of working on our career. If you look at our career you will see when the Oak Ridge Boys started leveling some. You will see when we stopped moving forward, and it was during those two years because we were expending all our energy inward instead of outward, and that got to be real mentally claustrophopic for all of us. We're the kind of guys that gotta keep at least working hard to move forward and we weren't moving forward no more, we were spinning wheels."

According to Bonsall, in December of 1986, the Oak Ridge Boys closed their office, shut down their career, and asked Golden to make a decision about his future with the group. When a response was not received, in late February of 1987, Joe Bonsall, on behalf of himself, Duane Allen, and Richard Sterban, wrote a final letter to Bill Golden, terminating his job with the group.

Quoting Joe Bonsall, "We told him that he was obviously not happy here and that we would like to ask him to leave so that he can go and do that which will make him happy, so that we can go on and continue to be the Oak Ridge Boys, because that's what we want. Obviously that's not what you want."

During the course of these interviews with the Oaks and Bill Golden, I received a call from Steve Sanders, who told me that he had been present when Golden received the final letter from the Oak Ridge Boys. Bill was visibly upset. Soon afterward, to his surprise, Sanders received an offer from Duane Allen to become the group's new baritone singer. Before he accepted the offer he went back to Bill Golden to discuss what Golden's intentions were.

Golden said, "I will never sing with the Oak Ridge Boys again." Bearing that in mind, Sanders accepted the job. Golden had left the group after twenty-two years.

It has been written that into every life a little rain must fall. The same could be said of rain and careers.

The day the four Oak Ridge Boys temporarily became three

was painful for all involved. And on that day, in a twist of irony, the world's number-one country song was the Oak Ridge Boys' "It Takes a Little Rain."

Recorded months earlier, the record's resonant baritone was William Lee Golden.

EIGHTEEN

Garth Brooks, a rotund, balding, pudding-faced singer in too-long jeans and a hat that's too wide, has sold more records than Michael Jackson or Madonna.

Someone suggested to me that Michael Jackson should be asked if he'd like to record a duet with Garth Brooks. I replied that Garth Brooks should be asked if he'd like to record with Michael Jackson.

Brooks sold 28 million copies of three albums in three years. Sales figures, as of this writing, were incomplete for Brooks' last two albums, including a Christmas album. Each of his albums, however, continues to sell briskly.

No country singer, and for that matter, no entertainer other than the Beatles or Elvis Presley, has drawn more press in a shorter time span. Brooks has graced the covers of *People, Time, Life, Us, TV Guide, Saturday Evening Post, Forbes,* and *Entertainment Weekly* magazines, and there has been a mountain of press in most major American newspapers, from the *New York Times* to *USA Today.*

Taking nothing from his talents, much of his press success is due to his publicist extraordinare and co-manager, Pam Lewis.

His concerts sell out in hours, but Brooks once told me about working a show following the release of his first record on a major label. It was less than a sellout.

"In Anniston, Alabama, nine people showed up," he told me.

Shortly afterwards, Brooks was the opening act for George Strait in Jackson, Mississippi, where 17,000 people turned out.

"And a note came back that says, 'One of the Anniston Nine,' we're proud of you,' " Brooks said. "I ran back to the security guard and I said, who gave this to you? I want to see this person! And he said, 'I don't know, she just gave it to me and disappeared into the crowd.' It's things like that that make you want to go and say, 'No, man, stop, let's find her because she was one of the ones in the beginning.' "

The popularity of Brooks and Clint Black broke about the same time, in 1989. Brooks' first release, "Much Too Young to Feel This Damn Old," moved to number eight, while Black's "Better Man" went to number one. Many folks, myself included, would have bet that Black's popularity would have outdistanced Brooks', since the former has a better voice and is notably handsome.

I asked Jimmy Bowen, the most successful record producer in Nashville and the president of the label for which Brooks has recorded each of his albums, why his dark-horse artist surpassed the debonair Black.

Bowen said that Black's stage show, when compared to Brooks', was less charismatic and stressed that Brooks is one of the most dynamic performers he's seen in more than four decades in the music business.

"First of all," Bowen went on, "Garth had better songs. Clint just records his own songs, and he is not Roger Miller, as a writer."

Bowen added that Brooks recorded three albums during the time that Black recorded only one. He compared Black to "pop" acts who record so rarely that they break their own popularity momentum.

The Brooks-Bowen team almost didn't happen, because Bowen turned down the singer for a deal with a record label of which Bowen was earlier president, according to popular rumor in Nashville. Bowen acknowledged the story but told me it wasn't entirely true.

"When I had Universal Records, a joint venture with MCA,

Pam Lewis brought Garth to me, and I will never know if I would have turned him down or not," Bowen said. "At that point in time is when I was buying my way out of MCA."

Bowen said he negotiated for four months, during which he was prohibited from signing anybody.

He conceded that he was intrigued with Brooks after the singer came to his house and auditioned "live." He said Brooks especially tapped the interest of Mrs. Jimmy Bowen, who urged her husband to sign him to a record deal.

Bowen was also offered Alan Jackson. Bowen admitted that he would not have signed Jackson even if he could have, as he thought Jackson's work was "too country." He expressed no regrets at not entering a contractual agreement with Jackson, who became a superstar.

Brooks' second release, "If Tomorrow Never Comes," hit number one, and so did every single release thereafter, except for "We Shall Be Free" in 1992. The song advocated unconditional, brotherly love, and many disc jockeys wouldn't play it, thinking it alluded to the acceptance of homosexuals.

"It's a known fact from the tabloids that my sister is homosexual and I love her to death," Brooks told Barbara Walters on ABC, an hour before the March 29, 1993, Academy Awards Show. More than one billion people around the world watched the Oscars Show, so estimations were in the millions for the Walters telecast.

I wondered about the wisdom of Brooks' remark in defense of his sister. His sister, Betsy Smittle, plays bass in his band. He, in fact, has been quite generous with various family members, and reportedly bought his parents a ranch shortly after his success. That notwithstanding, most of us don't want our sexual persuasions known on national television, and we certainly don't want someone else making them known for us—relative or not.

Bowen disagreed about the song's diminished popularity having to do with its alleged resistance by radio programmers.

"That's bullshit too," Bowen said. "Radio didn't resist it, they played it for eight or nine weeks. They just didn't get any phone calls on it. People didn't like it."

"Do you think it was a homosexual thing?" I asked the legendary producer and music executive.

"No," he snapped, "I think America has just already heard that story [brotherly love]. It is not what they wanted from Garth. Here is a guy that sang about 'If Tomorrow Never Comes' and 'Friends in Low Places' and all these great songs. And in the last year he got to taking himself way too serious. You know, he is not the second coming.

"He has changed, Ralph, but who wouldn't?" Bowen continued. "It is incredible, but I think the biggest change comes when they get so big and it dawns on them that they are prisoners of it [fame], and they can't go here and there anymore. If you remember, Elvis went to drugs, the Beatles all went to drugs, Michael Jackson went into seclusion, and Garth has just become a control freak. He tries to control everything in his life."

"Why then, does he have a manager?" I asked Bowen.

"I have asked myself that many times," Bowen said. "I have asked myself that, and it's too bad, because from where you and I sit, he ought to be enjoying some of this."

Bowen said that Brooks' penchant to make all the decisions affecting his career reminded him of Frank Sinatra, whose recordings Bowen used to produce. He said that Sinatra was the total opposite of Dean Martin, who wanted to do only what he was supposed to do, then delegate other duties to employees or associates.

Brooks is a determined young man who some might call headstrong. That has lent to controversy within music business circles, but Brooks has never been afraid of controversy, especially when it comes to his music. His monster recording of "The Thunder Rolls," which deals with the sensitive issue of domestic violence, was accompanied by a music video that was banned from The Nashville Network and Country Music Television. Officials at both companies told Brooks that they would air the superbly produced video if he would let them broadcast a video of him telling battered women how to get help through an 800 number.

Brooks videotaped the spot, then changed his mind about airing it, and the controversial video itself was stillborn as far as TNN and CMT were concerned.

I asked Paul Corbin, director of programming for TNN, to tell me what happened.

The video was brought to Corbin's attention, as well as that of David Hall, vice president and general manager of TNN, and Tom Griscom, vice president of Gaylord Entertainment Company.

"We all looked at it and we all had trouble with it," Corbin said. "While the quality of it was far and above most videos, it showed a husband coming back into a home where there was obviously an abused wife, made up to have bruises on her face, and there was apparently a history of violence. The violence erupted again, he beat her, and then in the presence of an eight-year-old child, she pulls out a gun and kills him. Well, gosh. That's a heck of a way to solve a domestic problem, and in the presence of a child it just really seemed to go too far."

Corbin insisted he would have run the video if Brooks had let the network use his videotaped, anti-violence announcement.

"He just looked into the camera lens," Corbin related, "and he said, 'If you've ever been a victim or you know victims of violence, there's help. You can get help and you can call this phone number.' "

"Why do you think Brooks changed his mind about airing the anti-violence announcement?" I asked.

"Well," Corbin said, "it was never explained why, other than he just didn't want to run it. He had thought about it and just decided not to. There are other schools of thought that say, well it was a good time to exploit and create a little controversy about the video so that there's a lot of attention drawn to the issue, and a lot of publicity and lots of pressure in the public's mind and it's time to take a stand."

TNN was criticized for interfering with Brooks' creative process.

"We happen to feel that we are gatekeepers of the public trust and that we have maintained a certain level of decorum, if you will, with our audience, and we have bragged about the fact that we are a G-rated service."

Corbin pointed out that Brooks' was not the first video to be banned because TNN and CMT officials thought it was offensive. He mentioned to me, off the record, the name of an international star whose video was banned in 1993 because Corbin and his associates felt it featured flagrant sexual activity.

I asked Corbin if he thought Brooks and management felt they would derive more commercial mileage from the banning of the video than they would from its airing, due to publicity.

"I think in retrospect you would think that kind of a decision or that kind of an open discussion may have happened," Corbin said, regarding Brooks and his associates. "I sure think it's likely that it happened."

The violent video was named "Video of the Year" by the Country Music Association, and its producer sarcastically thanked TNN on national television for its success.

It was a cheap and childish shot. It really pisses me off that every time I hear about "The Thunder Rolls," I hear about TNN and CMT banning it. There's never any mention that those networks would have been happy to run it had they been allowed to run Brooks' follow-up announcement. The reluctance of one man might have made for continued violence in the lives of thousands of women.

Bowen made no bones about his delight that the video was banned. He said the banning made for controversy that translated into record sales.

"Unfortunately, Garth took it very personal that they wouldn't play it and hasn't done a video for me since, but he is too young to realize that [the controversy] was an important step in America knowing who he was."

Brooks shocked the entertainment world to a greater degree in the summer of 1992 when he announced that he was considering retiring from show business because its demands kept him away from his family. Later, he said he was considering playing only engagements where he and his family could stay in a town for a few days, instead of moving every night.

I respect Brooks' priorities, and his claim to put family first, and there is no arguing that parents who are at home with their families are usually more effective parents. But I think of all the thousands of American entertainers who preceded Brooks. Many did one-night engagements for fifty or sixty years without complaining about the price it took on their personal lives. Fame carries rewards. It also carries obligations. What if Bob Hope had said he was going to stay home at Christmas with his family? Millions of American servicemen overseas would have been without entertainment at Christmastime.

It is the quality of time at home that matters to parents and their children. Don't the fans who buy the records that subsidize show-business families have expectations? Does Brooks have an obligation to perform for them?

Some people think the announcement about possible retirement is merely a publicity stunt.

A lot of the Nashville show-business veterans, who have rattled around in the back of a bus for decades, thought Brooks' consideration of retirement after only four years in the business made him come off as a wimp. Many of those who are in their advanced years, and whose fame has long since passed, would work the road 365 days a year to have the stardom and success that Brooks enjoys.

Brooks is a positive thinker who once told me that show-business success comes from feeling something in your heart, then thinking it in your mind.

Perhaps that attitude was at work when Brooks played a showcase, a singer's audition for a recording contract, in 1987. It was only one of hundreds of auditions that are held at Nashville's famous Bluebird Cafe, the contemporary version of Tootsie's Orchid Lounge, the haven for "has-beens," "hopefuls," and today's stars.

"I played a showcase and I was like number seven or number eight to go on, and the man that was supposed to go on second never showed up and the producer asked me to go in his place.

Capitol Records was there to see that act, and when I came off stage the Capitol executive, Lynn Shults, asked me if I'd come in and we'd talk."

The result was a recording contract.

Had Ralph Murphy, the songwriter, showed up on schedule to perform, Brooks might never have been heard by the Capitol people—and therefore never heard by the world. Show-business breaks are just that unpredictable, and sometimes, that decisive.

That, essentially, is the story behind the launching of Garth Brooks, although the Bluebird encounter was not the first encounter between Brooks and Shults.

Bob Doyle, who became Brooks' manager, asked if Brooks might come by and audition "live" for Shults and the former Capitol Records Nashville Division President, Jim Fogelsong.

"We were in Fogelsong's office," Shults recalled, "and Garth played about five or six songs on the guitar. My remembrance is that those situations are pretty awkward, because there is a lot of pressure on the prospective artist. The songs were pretty good but didn't really knock either one of us out."

Shults said he and Fogelsong returned to their respective telephone calls and other duties, forgetting Brooks. Shults said he did not go to the Bluebird that fateful night with the idea of hearing Brooks, but merely to listen to Murphy and other writers with the idea of getting tunes for established Capitol artists. He doesn't remember specifically which songs Brooks sang at the Bluebird.

"He performed two songs, just an acoustic guitar and his voice, and in that environment he just absolutely blew me away. My intuition was telling me that this guy is better than anybody that we have on the roster now.

"So I walked over to Bob Doyle and I can't remember if Bob and Garth were both standing there side by side at that moment or not, but I walked over and I said, look, I'm giving you guys an album deal right now on a handshake agreement."

I asked Shults what was so different about Brooks that prompted him to give him a deal on the spot.

"I'll tell you exactly what I think it is," Shults said. "I'm pulling from the history of always being drawn to live performances. There is the magical thing, if you want to describe it that way. It's magical in one way, it's spiritual in another.

Shults said Brooks had the combination.

Few people in the recording industry would dispute that Fogelsong, and more specifically, Lynn Shults, "discovered" Brooks. They brought him to Capitol Records, and consequently the airwaves of the world.

And the day Brooks' second record went to number one, Fogelsong and Shults were fired.

"We got fired because of corporate politics," Shults said. "You know, my vision of it is that Joe Smith, former president of Warner Brothers and Elektra, was brought in to infuse new life into Capitol Records, and in coming into Capitol Records he obviously began making changes and establishing his team."

There was a veritable personnel house cleaning at Capitol Records' Nashville Division.

I asked Shults how Brooks reacted to his firing.

He couldn't answer for the superstar, but added that he was sure it bothered Brooks.

"But Brooks has held that within himself," Shults said. "Like I've held a lot within myself. There is a lot of things that happened during those days and those weeks and months that followed that no one will ever know about because I don't think that Garth is ever going to say, and I'm never going to say.

"We've never had what the world of psychology would call an intimate conversation about it," Shults said.

Brooks was selling boots in a North Nashville shoestore with his wife, Sandy, awaiting his break in Music City U.S.A. He met her when he was a dance hall bouncer in Stillwater, Oklahoma, where Brooks had graduated from Oklahoma State University with a degree in advertising.

He told me that because he was slight of stature, it was his job to break up fights among women customers. He might have been kidding. At any rate, Sandy got into a fracas inside the ladies' room and swung at another girl. Sandy's fist broke through some wall paneling and became stuck. Brooks walked in and freed her hand while hustling the other woman out of the room. Then Brooks threw Sandy out of the bar.

"And she was so cute I asked her to come home with me that night," he said. "She told me to drop dead, so I called her the next day and we started dating."

He had persisted with the diligence he would one day apply to his music.

Shortly after Brooks' meteoric career ascension, he fell prey to the show-business trap of available women. He had earlier committed adultery, and was performing in Missouri and trying to sing "If Tomorrow Never Comes." As Brooks sang, he choked with emotion before thousands of people and asked the band to stop playing. They didn't, so he asked again. Guilt overtook him and he left the arena. As he exited the stage, he heard a solitary voice from somewhere in the hall shout, "Go home to her, Garth."

He did, and claims to have been faithful ever since. Losing his wife, he has said repeatedly, would be psychologically devastating to him.

Brooks has always impressed me as a polite and well-mannered man, but I'm not sure if it's genuine or manufactured. He has wisdom that comes from growing up in a large family, and the knowledge of knowing how to market himself. He told me that he practices daily at least one thing that he learned in his advertising curriculum in college.

He is known for his sincerity. I think it's sincerity with savvy. He's the only person I've ever interviewed who thanked me for doing my homework (interview preparation).

"Garth, I understand you went to Oklahoma State University," I said.

"Yes, I did," he said, "and thank you for knowing that."

"I understand that you majored in marketing and advertising," I said.

"Yes, I did, and thank you for knowing that," he said again.

In forty-two years of interviews, such courtesy has never been exhibited to me before, or since.

Brooks seems to immerse himself in the spirit of his songs more than any singer I've seen in years. He's intense.

"I don't know, what do you call the main character in a song—the antagonist or something like that? [He meant protagonist.] I can get in his body and go away with him, you know, and be him."

"But how about a song that reveals a little bit of Garth Brooks?" I asked.

" 'If Tomorrow Never Comes' is probably the biggest, the closest thing to real life for me. That is, it's very real to my life. In fact, the song was thought up exactly the way the words are now. I was settin' up watching my wife, Sandy, sleeping one night, and it hit me that if tomorrow never comes and she wondered if I loved her I think that would hurt me worse than whatever it was that killed me," he said.

Brooks has the most energetic—and controversial—show in country music history. Actually, he doesn't confine himself to country music but includes smatterings of hard rock 'n' roll, and the influence of Queen and Journey, the rock acts he listened to as a post-adolescent.

His 1991 NBC special showed Brooks running madly around the stage, smashing guitars, throwing water on his band, and swinging from a rope over the hysterical crowd. Country purists had trouble handling the behavior.

The special made network television history because more than 28 million viewers watched. The show garnered NBC's highest rating for a Friday night in two years.

"Are you telling me you have a wild stage show?" I asked Brooks.

"Yeah," he said, "we really do. We have a wild time and a lot of fun."

"Is this because you're an emotional person?" I asked.

"Yeah," he said, "I really am. It's also because I don't think you get ten bucks off your gate ticket because you've got the album, so I think people want something more than the album. I know I do as a listener. I want to go and I want to hear those same hits, but I want to see 'em performed, I want to see 'em done. Entertain me instead of just reproducing the hits."

Brooks claims to be immensely respectful of his singing elders. His idol, he told me, is George Jones. In 1989, he had forgone three opportunities to meet Jones because "he's almost like a God-like figure to me and, and I don't know, to actually bring him down to my level by meeting him and actually shaking his hand, I don't know if I want to do that. I want him to remain forever kind of mysterious."

Brooks had hidden physically from George Jones to avoid meeting him.

Eventually, he not only met but sang on "Rockin' Chair," Jones' biggest record of the 1990s. The song was recorded during the 1991 Fan Fair. He had been invited to sing with Clint Black, Alan Jackson, Vince Gill, Pam Tillis, T. Graham Brown, and others. The session was held up, but it appeared as though Brooks was not going to arrive in time to sing. He called the studio, virtually in tears, to ask that the session be detained long enough for him to perform on the recording, said Mrs. George (Nancy) Jones.

Brooks is in tears a lot.

He told me that when he finally met Jones, he was overcome with emotion, and Jones was embarrassed to the point of walking away.

"The tears just shot out of my eyes," Brooks said. He said that Jones continued to approach him until Brooks regained his composure.

"He'd stay a little longer each time until I could actually talk to him without breaking down."

When Brooks received his first gold album, he sobbed before thousands of applauding fans at Fan Fair, and the footage was aired scores of times as a promotion on The Nashville Network.

When Jones was admitted to the Country Music Hall of Fame in 1992, a composed Jones thanked a national television audience and introduced his wife, standing near the front row. The camera turned on her, but her moment in the spotlight was lost because Brooks, sitting directly behind Nancy but on camera, was crying. Brooks has been accused of being able to turn on the waterworks at will.

On March 29, 1993, the *Nashville Banner* wrote a review of Brooks' appearance with Ms. Walters.

"No More Tears" was the first sentence in the story. "Brooks puddles up a little in his interview with Barbara Walters, but it doesn't get any farther than that," wrote Nancy Sweid.

On Brooks' NBC special, Ms. Smittle, Garth's sister and bass player, said she felt that sensitivity, and that she wished it was common among more men.

I personally feel that Garth Brooks has done for country music what Elvis Presley did for the popularity of rock 'n' roll, what the Beatles did for new approaches to harmony. Country music has never had a more pronounced, ground-breaking pioneer. He has brought his music to millions who otherwise wouldn't have heard country music.

The entire industry is in his debt.

He has made television inroads with programs that were up to now unconcerned with country music. Besides the two-hour, prime-time special, Brooks has had significant time on the "To-night Show," "Saturday Night Live," "Macy's Thanksgiving Day Parade," "Bob Hope Special," "Night of 100 Stars," "The Meaning of Life," "Today," "Good Morning America," "CNN Showbiz Today," "CBS This Morning," "NBC Dateline with Jane Pauley," and the "Barbara Walters Special."

He also sang a pre-recorded version of the National Anthem at the 1992 Super Bowl.

Given Brooks' eagerness to do so many shows, it disturbs me that he hasn't appeared on "Nashville Now" in a long time. He was on the show twice at the beginning of his career when he needed the exposure. On October 25, 1991, Brooks was playing the Grand Ole Opry and I sent word to him that "Nashville Now," that night, was honoring Minnie Pearl's birthday. I asked him to sing "Happy Birthday" to her. He, his wife, Sandy, and the audience sang, then he abruptly left.

My resentment that Brooks no longer does "Nashville Now" might be suspect, as I am host of the show. But that program played a significant part in the launching of Brooks' career, and many Nashville celebrities feel a strong attachment to it, as they do the Grand Ole Opry. Brooks will do television originating from New York City or Los Angeles but boycotts the most popular television show from Nashville.

Big stars, such as Billy Ray Cyrus, Clint Black, and Reba McEntire, whose careers began on the show, return to it.

His absence from the show will have little effect on a career that is so scorching hot. In fact, I'll do something I rarely do, make a prediction.

Seventy-seven million albums were sold out of Nashville, Tennessee, in 1992, by various artists. More gold (sales of 500,000) and platinum (sales of 1,000,000) albums were sold than at any other time in history. Pundits have predicted that the Nashville recording, publishing, and performance industry will gross $9 billion in 1993.

Time will tell.

While there are perhaps thirty acts whose careers are hot right now, none sizzles with the white heat of Brooks'. He is not only the biggest star of the new breed, he was the first.

Here's betting he'll remain in first place long after many others have faded away.

Post Script—On May 10, 1993, I went to the Crazy Horse restaurant and night club in Santa Ana, California, with my producer, Bill Turner, to produce three satellite feedbacks to "Nashville Now." Garth was very gracious to come on the show in an appearance with singer John Anderson. Thanks, Garth! Perhaps I was wrong.

NINETEEN

I knew something was wrong even before Steve, my oldest son, told me. It was New Year's Eve afternoon 1992, a time for festivity, yet his voice was distant and grave.

"Dad," he said, "your dad is dead."

I was in Aspen, Colorado, for our annual family skiing outing. Steve had been with us earlier, but had to depart because of the demands of his Nashville dental practice.

In my first book, *Memories,* I wrote about my father turning into a hopeless alcoholic by the age of twenty-eight. My dad never remembered one Christmas or birthday of mine. He often disappeared, once for seven years, and I grew up accepting that my dad was the town drunk. On January 26, 1967, I received a letter from a relative telling me about the death of my dad's brother, Lester Emery.

"We didn't know where Walter [my dad] was so couldn't send him any word of the death," wrote the author. "Am sending you the piece that came out in the paper and wish you would notify your dad."

I couldn't tell him because I couldn't find him. And as late as a few years ago I thought I had no feelings one way or another about my wayward father.

I was mistaken.

His death, although anticipated, shook me. He was in failing health and eighty-three. I hadn't seen him in years, and found myself, curiously, hurting over a man I didn't know—a man whose only bond with me was a shared last name. I was confused because I didn't know if my pain stemmed from grief, guilt, or both.

I hadn't seen him in a long time, but it had been a long time because he hadn't wanted to see me.

He was a rambler when he was young, a recluse when he was old. When he became too aged and ill to hide elsewhere, he hid within himself. There were times when I visited him he wouldn't look at me. He rarely spoke unless spoken to, and then only to say yes or no when I asked a direct question.

He was even that cold and detached the day his leg was amputated because of a circulatory problem and he faced the possibility of losing other limbs. He lay there, only part of a man, and wanted no sympathy, attention, or anything else from me.

My visits to him were impositions. And while my feelings for him were minimal, they were substantial enough for me not to want to impose.

So why, I asked myself, did I weep at the news of his demise? I told Joy what she already knew, that I was hurting. She told Barbara Mandrell, whose family joined mine on the ski trip.

Barbara told me my grief was understandable, but not justified.

"You did all you could for him," she said, and reminded me of the financial assistance and my foiled attempts to start a relationship.

My first impulse was to return to Tennessee and arrange the funeral and see him buried in the cemetery next to his mother. I began the hopeless task of trying to get out of an immensely popular resort before a national holiday during a blizzard. I discovered I couldn't beg, borrow, or steal an airplane ticket, and had to adhere to my original plans to return to Tennessee on January 2, 1993.

So hours after hearing of my father's death, I went skiing despite my mixture of emotions I didn't understand.

I made, by phone, arrangements for the funeral. One call was to Carl Long, an old family friend and Church of Christ preacher, whom I asked to preach the funeral. When I returned to Tennessee, he and his wife, Joyce, went with Joy and me to pick out a casket. The Lions Club in my hometown of McEwen provided pallbearers, and the members of the Church of Christ volunteered to sing.

My father died broken of spirit, destitute of things. He was buried in a suit I purchased from the funeral home.

I had tried to provide material things for him in his final years. But the staff at the Veterans' Administration Hospital had discouraged it, saying that my dad, given his demented condition, could not adequately watch over his possessions. Anything I bought for him would likely be stolen by other patients.

He suffered alcohol dementia, and while in his seventies got into a fist fight with another elderly patient. I went to see him where he lay in a ward with fifteen old men. Most were recovering alcoholics, and were recovering largely because they could no longer get to a bottle.

Doctors told me that most of the men crawled into themselves and simply didn't want to be bothered, not even with each other. The doctors were right. I felt as if I were in a room filled with zombies. The old men mostly dozed or stared into space. Occasionally, one yawned. That was the most energetic activity I saw.

One of the most distressing things I saw in my father's undoing was the gradual loss of memory. He dearly loved his mother, and once talked to me about her as if she were alive. I think he thought she was, although she died in 1957.

Another time, I took the Emery family Bible to his bedside. The aged King James text was filled with old photographs, presumably of our relatives.

I wanted my dad to identify the people, but he claimed not to know one person in any of the pictures. I never knew if he was telling the truth, or simply being belligerent so I would leave. I had many theories through the years as to why my dad always seemed to want me to leave.

So leave I did.

On January 3, 1993, four days after his death, the *Tennessean* reported: "John Walter Emery, Father of Ralph Emery, Dies at 83."

The mortician dressed my father. I looked at him the next day, moments before his burial, in a suit and tie for the first time in my life.

I once appeared on Dan Miller's talk show on The Nashville Network and he reminded me that I had once criticized my dad for getting drunk on the eve of his mother's funeral. I struggled in vain to get him out of a tavern and he attacked me. I told Miller that perhaps I had been insensitive and failed to realize that alcoholics deal with grief by getting drunk. I'll never know.

My dad was buried, by my design, next to his mother in the McEwen Cemetery. He was always her baby, and she was the last to lose faith in him. Ironically, the day before the burial, former McEwen Mayor Basil Florence was buried. Florence and his wife stood up with my mother and father the night they were married.

Around the grave, against the howling January winds, huddled scores of elderly people, some of whom had not seen my dad since he was a boy. In the fast-paced world of city forgetfulness, we forget how country people forget no one. I was truly touched by the turnout.

Then the grave diggers' hoist began to creak, as the body of John Walter Emery was lowered under the winter-brown grass, the nebulous frost line, and into the bowels of the earth. And as quickly as it began, life with my father, for me, was over.

On Monday, January 4, 1993, hours before my dad was buried, I picked up an edition of the *Tennessean* to read the headline "Memories of Emery Vary Widely." There was also a front-page story about the death in that edition.

The story contained routine biographical information, but it also contained quotations from Skeeter Davis, to whom I was married from 1960 to 1964. The article stated that I had not visited my father recently, but Skeeter had seen him three times since Thanksgiving. The story quoted Skeeter as claiming that my dad wanted to mend his relationship with me.

"I really loved John, he was so sweet," Skeeter was quoted. "John was a person and he did have people who loved him. John did know you. He was sharp, but he started getting sick. He wanted to reconcile with his son."

The story went on to say that Skeeter had wanted to talk to me about seeing my father, but that my dad died before she could.

I don't know which I deem to be lower, Skeeter's remarks or the journalist who quoted her. Is a statement from a woman from whom I'd been divorced for thirty years regarding the death of my father the *Tennessean*'s idea of news?

I feel that Skeeter vindictively used my father's death to get back at me for what I said about her in my first book. I questioned whether she ever loved me. I thought she capitalized upon my broadcasting job to further her career and wondered if she had been a faithful wife.

Her claim that my father was sharp, got sick, and wanted to reconcile made me question her sanity.

I was not the only one in my family who knew about my father's incapacitation. My son, Mike, visited his grandfather, and arrived as he was eating lunch.

"Well, did you enjoy your lunch?" Mike asked my father.

"What lunch?" he replied. "I haven't eaten all day."

And he had no idea who Mike was. Skeeter's brainless remarks did not embarrass me but made me angry.

My father had been on the shelf for seventeen years, so why did she suddenly decide to go see him? I had heard through some folks at the funeral home that Skeeter wanted to bring singers from the Grand Ole Opry to sing at the funeral.

I didn't want that. I wanted a service, not a show. And I, his only child, wanted to plan the proceeding. I didn't want the involvement of an ex-wife to whom I've barely spoken in three decades. Her grief seemed like a gimmick.

One story in the *Tennessean* said that although I was estranged from my father, I was going to handle his funeral arrangements "anyhow."

Anyhow?

The word was clearly inflammatory. Another story expressed confusion as to why I would want to preside over my father's funeral and said I could not be reached for comment.

I wrote a letter to the editor of Nashville's morning newspaper. I thanked the people of McEwen and Humphries County, Tennessee, for their support. I noted that neither my father nor I had lived in McEwen for a long time, but our absence hadn't deterred the outpouring of kindness. I specifically acknowledged the Reverend Carl Long, his wife, the Lions Club, the McEwen Church of Christ, and others "of this wonderful community which I am proud to call my hometown."

Then I offered an explanation, which I softened at the urging of my assistant, Terry Schaefer, and Joy.

"In my recent book, 'Memories,' I stated that my relationship with my father was estranged and that I had no feelings for him. I was wrong. The January 4, 1993, *Tennessean* questioned why I would handle my father's funeral arrangements. My father and mother divorced when I was four years old. After repeated attempts to establish a relationship with him, I gave up. However, in 1975, I took him off the streets for his own safety, as his chronic alcoholism had robbed him of his mental soundness. I have handled his affairs and monitored his medical progress since that time. His death has caused me great pain. Were it not for the kindness of the people of McEwen and Humphries County, it would have been very difficult to get through this very painful time. Sincerely. Ralph Emery."

My mother went with me to dad's funeral. She and my father had been divorced for fifty-five years, and he never remarried. I was curious about what was going through her mind, but I refrained.

I asked that an American flag be draped across his coffin. He had served his country, and I wanted him to receive any dignity in death that could be mustered.

The coffin was closed and prepared for its journey. That was the last time I ever saw my father, but one of many times he didn't talk to me.

It was the only time I truly understood why.

TWENTY

Through the airplane's window I could see mid-winter darkness falling on Washington, D.C., as Joy and I arrived on January 17. As we descended toward Washington National Airport, we strained to see the Lincoln Memorial and the White House, resplendent in nighttime illumination. Our national monuments somehow seem more regal at night. The White House is whiter against ebony.

We wrestled our carry-on luggage up the gateway where a driver bearing a "PIC" sign and my name awaited. He was a volunteer for the Presidential Inaugural Committee.

On the same aircraft with us was the bluegrass great Bill Monroe, who told me President-Elect Bill Clinton's inauguration was the fourth time he had played for an American President. Although I had been to the White House during two previous administrations, this induction was the first time I was to participate in a ceremony of state.

I had been asked by Mrs. Tipper Gore, wife of Vice-President-Elect Al Gore, to be master of ceremonies at one of the four inaugural dinners, specifically, the one that honored her husband.

During the soiree, Gore referred to me as "the voice of Tennessee." I was pleased that he mentioned it, pleased that he remembered, and even more pleased to be a part of history in the making.

I was touched.

The dinner was to be held in the National Pension Building, the name dating back to the War of 1812 when veterans lined up there to collect or apply for their pensions. The first Inaugural Ball was held in this structure in 1885 for Grover Cleveland.

Rehearsal began at 11 A.M. the next day. For three hours, we walked through the ceremony that would precede the arrival of the Commander-in-Chief. Glen Goodwin, the overseer of the dinner, instructed me to pace the performance of the various entertainers, and said everything was contingent on the arrival of the President, scheduled for 7:30 P.M. But he said the President was customarily late because he always stopped to shake hands and chat.

All this reminded me of the stress of doing live television, except that here I did not have the safety net of breaking to a commercial, or chatting with another guest. A few thousand of the nation's best and brightest, who had paid $1,500 per ticket and donated as much as $100,000 to Clinton's campaign, would determine how smoothly I kept the affair going.

The entertainers included chamber members of the Philadelphia Symphony Orchestra, the vocalist Pat Cook (who had sung for Britain's Royal Family), Peter Duchin and his orchestra, Take-Six (an a cappella gospel group), and the Nashville singer and songwriter Gary Morris.

Each act was told that there was a chance of being interrupted in mid-performance, depending on when the President and Vice President arrived.

The rehearsal had to be completed by 2:30 P.M. At this time we all left for our respective hotels so that the Secret Service could "sweep the building." Later Joy and I returned to Pension Hall, accompanied by Rabbi and Mrs. Randall Falk, rabbi emeritus of "The Temple" in Nashville. We were ushered in a back door marked "Talent" and escorted through a metal detector by the Secret Service.

The Secret Service had, in fact, secured the entire building by then, as I learned when I decided to visit the Green Room, where the talent was waiting. I was unhappy with my notes and wanted to revise them with the entertainers to better introduce them.

I sauntered casually toward my destination but was detained about every twenty feet by Secret Service personnel, who wanted me to identify myself and show them my badge.

I introduced Rabbi Falk to the crowd and he gave the invocation. By then it was 8:00 P.M. and the President-Elect still had not arrived. I was directed to announce, "Dinner is served." It was an inappropriate announcement. Dinner was not even close to being served.

I walked over to see how Joy was doing, and ran into the Tennessee Governor, Ned McWherter, who said, "I saw you and the rabbi and thought I was in Nashville."

The President didn't arrive until 8:30 P.M. with a contingent of forty-seven automobiles. Imagine what it must have been like trying to get a motorcade that large through Washington during inaugural week.

He entered the hall at 8:40 P.M.

I returned to my seat near the stage, and the Marine Corps band played the "Star-Spangled Banner" from the balcony.

Goodwin wore a headset tuned to the Secret Service frequency and occasionally gave me updates on Clinton's whereabouts. For instance, "B.C. walks the rope line" as Clinton's final act before stepping on stage.

I surmised who "B.C." was, but had to ask Goodwin about the rope line. He explained it was a thick rope of red velvet along which Clinton would walk, shaking hands with an eager crowd hungry to press the flesh.

Cynthia Morin, hired to stage the event, rushed up to me and asked that I not introduce Mrs. Clinton as Mrs. Clinton but as Hillary Rodham Clinton.

Later, in watching reruns of other inaugural festivities, my executive assistant, Terry Schaefer, noticed that Mrs. Clinton was always introduced as Mrs. Clinton. I imagine a lot of emcees heard about that.

And then they were there, the President-Elect and Mrs. Hillary Rodham Clinton, swept into the hall on air. The band played a deafening and rousing military flourish, and hundreds of people, bejeweled commensurately with their prominence, strained against the velvet rope. The Clintons smiled and shook hands, hardly breaking stride.

It was quite an entrance.

From the floor, I introduced the President-Elect, who in turn said to the audience, "You sure look beautiful." He turned to his wife and said, "You do too." If suaveness has anything to do with re-election, look for Clinton in 1996.

He talked about an event the previous day at the Lincoln Memorial, where 500,000 people had shown up for a nationally televised party featuring the world's leading entertainers.

He made a reference to his famous faux pas when he accepted the Oath of Office for the governorship of Arkansas while holding up his left, rather than right, hand.

"I hope I remember which hand to hold up during the inaugural," he said.

He talked about his bus trip from Monticello, Virginia, home of Thomas Jefferson, Clinton's hero, to Washington, D.C. He said he had thought about the starving children in Somalia while watching the miles of healthy, waving youngsters who lined his route to the nation's capital. He had thought about the national debt, and "all the problems that I was going to be inheriting in a few days."

"I looked out the window," he said, "and there's a little kid holding up a sign. And the sign said, 'It's not just a career, it's an adventure.' "

The audience laughed, the mood was lifted, and at that moment everyone in that room was *ready* for Bill Clinton to inherit the Oval Office.

The President-Elect came off the stage on my side. As he descended the steps, I could tell by his eyes that he recognized me. He stuck out his hand, asked how I was, and to my astonishment, asked, "Do you still have the bus?"

He and Senator Gore had given me a toy bus, a one-of-a-kind replica of the bus they campaigned in the night they visited "Nashville Now" on August 6, 1992. Clinton had since met thousands of people, but nonetheless remembered me and the souvenir. I was flattered.

Both Clinton and former President Bush had appeared on "Nashville Now" during their presidential campaigns. Again, I was flattered, particularly since each candidate asked to be on the program.

Bush was uncharacteristically informal. You'd of thought he was leading, rather than trailing, in popularity polls. He came to the show with his old friend and mine, sausage mogul Jimmy Dean, who had brought the then Vice-President Bush to the show in 1987 just before Bush announced his presidential candidacy.

During the more recent visit, Bush good-naturedly mimicked Dean doing one of his food product commercials. Bush referred to meat that Dean sells on a stick.

"This is fine, just fine!" said the former President, in nasal tones intended to remind of Dean. "Now you all try it, now eat it, it's very good."

Dean broke up.

The former President, who could have spent the entire time reciting campaign rhetoric, instead poked fun at himself and made reference to his five television sets, which he tries to watch simultaneously.

"If I see something I want to watch, I can push a button and flick the other one on or flick it off or put them on mute or tape all five at once—all sitting at my desk," Bush said. "And Barbara gets absolutely livid . . . I think she's very narrow-minded about it, frankly."

I think Bush was encouraged during the part of the program where audience members posed questions to guests. A ten-year-old asked the former chief executive what he intended to do when he retired—in 1996.

"I'm going to spend half the time in Texas and the other half in Maine, I think, and live happily ever after and never sit at the head table again."

Perhaps Bush's relaxed demeanor surfaced because Clinton had been on "Nashville Now" earlier and was extremely informal.

Clinton and his wife yelled the University of Arkansas athletic yell, which is a hog call. Some people asked why I asked Clinton to do the bellicose yell. I had asked Clinton to do it because I knew he was a University of Arkansas alumnus. He even tried to enlist the audience's help, and the few who knew the scream joined in voice. There was the man who would be the next President of the United States hollering "s-o-o-u-u-i-i-e" at the top of his lungs. He was joined in this exercise by Hillary, who also is an alumna of Arkansas. When I went to the commercial break and just before the candidates and their wives left the studio, Al Gore came over to me and said, "Ralph, these are good people."

Clinton was joined by then vice-presidential hopeful Al Gore at the Grand Ole Opry House after leaving my show. *The Tennessean,* Nashville's morning newspaper, said the pair chided the audience, and stopped short of advertising Goo Goo candy bars or Martha White flour, two longtime Opry sponsors.

The Washington audience had come to the inaugural primarily to see the President, almost to the exclusion of the cuisine and the talent. I noticed the audience talking and generally inattentive throughout most of the evening except when Clinton and Gore spoke. Gore arrived at the hall ten minutes early, and that forced me to cut short the performance of Gary Morris. He had done his spellbinding version of "Wind Beneath My Wings," one of the few numbers to actually capture the crowd.

"The Secret Service says Gore is here," Goodwin told me. No one expected the talent to run on time, much less early, and certainly no one expected the Vice President to be early.

"He's not going to ruin my evening by being early," Goodwin joked, and proceeded to whisper commands to his crew into his headset.

I had been told to introduce the Gores as "Vice President-Elect Al Gore and Tipper Gore," and then hand the microphone to Tipper, so that she might reintroduce her husband. I didn't question, I simply complied.

I knew Al Gore when he was a senator from Tennessee and previously when he worked as a newspaper reporter for *The Tennessean*. I had seen him at numerous music business functions through the years.

I have admired his ecology work and was impressed when he

withdrew from a political race four years earlier when his small son sustained major injuries after being hit by an automobile.

He gave a cursory speech with all the obligatory thank-yous, then danced off stage with Tipper as the orchestra broke into a samba.

Their steps signaled the official end of the evening.

Joy and I shared a toast with the other members of the cast and crew. I'm not sure if we were celebrating the program's success, or the fact that it was over. Then we returned to the Washington Hilton.

There is an irony in my involvement with all the merriment for Bill Clinton. I voted for George Bush.

I went to another pre-party the night of my arrival in Washington at Union Station. It began hours after the approximate 500,000 persons had gathered for Clinton's wing-ding on the Mall.

That party was held for James Carville, Clinton's campaign consultant, who, in reality, was the ram-rod of the entire presidential bid, and Paul Begala, another guest of honor.

Ralph Hacker invited me. He's a mover and shaker in Kentucky politics, the voice of the Kentucky Wildcats, and an old friend.

Joy and I had never been to Union Station, so when we entered the main room we had to ask directions to the presidential suite. We arrived to find our badges waiting. Hacker came over to greet Joy and me.

I quickly began to feel at home when I saw Ralph Stanley and his band playing bluegrass music. Seated next to the bandstand was Zel Miller, governor of Georgia and one of the world's great country music fans. Other luminaries were on hand. Joy spotted Ted Koppel, Kim Basinger, Alec Baldwin, Peter Jennings, and Tom Brokaw.

A Dixieland band played at the other end of the room, overflowing with wall-to-wall people. The culinary highlight was authentic Cajun food prepared by a Cajun chef, both flown in from Donaldsonville, Louisiana.

I know that all is fair in love, war, and politics. I know that

Bush is not the first person to lose a presidential election. But as I beheld the mayhem that was Washington, I couldn't help but feel sorry for Bush. By that time, he had begun moving out of the White House.

Four years earlier, he had been the guest of honor. That night, he wasn't even a guest. I think that no matter how brazen one becomes, it must be unthinkably hard to campaign for more than twelve months, hundreds of thousands of miles, countless handshakes, cold coffee and stale sandwiches, and all the rest that goes with the olympian process of becoming elected, only to lose—then be shunned from the victor's party.

Perhaps Washington should change its protocol and make a bigger place for the outgoing President.

George Bush is not a young man. Campaigning was harder on him than it was on his significantly younger opponent. And I knew firsthand how badly he wanted to win that election.

George Bush had been a guest on "Nashville Now" on September 29, 1992. Earlier that day, he telephoned Dean from Air Force One. The President asked Dean to ask me to be nice to him during the prime-time, live interview.

Dean tape-recorded the conversation, then sent a copy of the tape to me.

"I have got a big favor I want of you," Bush said to Dean.

"What do you want, George?" Dean replied.

"I want you to call Ralph Emery, whose show I am going to be on. You remember your old pal? I just thought it would be nice if you would say, 'Now, you be nice to my friend George Bush.' "

"All right," Dean replied. "Well you know he is an intense and loyal fan. He had Clinton and Gore on there, but I think it was just 'cause . . . you know. They were names. And he is firmly and thoroughly and completely ensconced in your corner."

I hope my interviews with both presidential candidates did not show partiality. I was honored to have both men briefly touch my life.

Epilogue

On March 8, 1993, the house lights dimmed and I walked, as I had done thousands of times before, from backstage and through the audience seconds before the theme song rose for "Nashville Now." I had barely gotten beyond the curtain of the set when the audience exploded into applause. For a few seconds, the theme song played by a nine-piece band was inaudible because of the clapping. Some fans even stood.

Ten years earlier when I took the "Nashville Now" microphone for the first time, the only live, prime-time talk show on television had a viewing audience of about 6,000,000 households. Ten years later it had approximately 60,000,000.

The 1993 anniversary show had the highest ratings of any "Nashville Now" program ever aired. "Nashville Now" became a broadcast institution, made me a celebrity, and more than any other program, took country music out of the bars and auditoriums and into people's living rooms, and ultimately, into their hearts.

The Nashville Network is to television what WSM is to radio—the most effective conduit of country music in the world.

I'll always remember our ten-year-milestone show with film clips of previous shows. I hope I'm around to see the twentieth anniversary, whether it's from the host's desk or in front of my own television set.

My co-host that night was Reba McEntire, who began her ascent toward superstardom about the time "Nashville Now" went on the air. A clip of a previous McEntire appearance was shown on our anniversary show, and the studio audience watched on overhead monitors so no one noticed as Reba slid quietly into the chair next to my desk. The studio audience finally realized she was on the stage and about one hundred people leapt from their seats and charged the footlights, restrained only by a solitary security guard. Had he not been there the fans might have run onto the set and shown up on television screens across North America.

"I have grown right along with this show," Reba told the audience. Indeed, when "Nashville Now" first went on the air, Reba had enjoyed success on the country music charts, but was hardly the international superstar she is today.

I was also joined that night by one of my best friends, Barbara Mandrell, whose own network show on NBC ten years earlier was as hot as her glowing career. My third guest was Lee Greenwood, whose song "God Bless the U.S.A." has become the "Star-Spangled Banner" of the twentieth century. The song, featured in two presidential campaigns, premiered on "Nashville Now."

Lorrie Morgan was also a guest that night. She had been a regular visitor on my local morning show, which went off the air after twenty years in November of 1992. On the night of the "Nashville Now" tenth anniversary, Lorrie's song "What Part of No?" was the number-one country song in the nation.

She discussed her seventeen-year struggle in the music business before achieving pronounced stardom and kindly acknowledged the pivotal role "Nashville Now" played in her career.

That show featured footage of celebrities who now are household names but were unfamiliar when they first appeared on "Nashville Now."

Billy Ray Cyrus was shown in his first national exposure in a clip that debuted "Achy Breaky Heart." "The Dance" in another clip was sung by an unknown country artist named Garth Brooks. An unknown singer named Clint Black introduced "Better Man." A mother-daughter duo, The Judds, came forward to the world on the show. The singers Pam Tillis and Trisha Yearwood were first seen nationally on the show. Vince Gill was seen singing his first smash, "When I Call Your Name," one of the most popular country songs of all time.

With the exception of the Grand Ole Opry, no program has done more to establish country music careers than "Nashville Now."

Tennessee Governor Ned McWherter, also on hand for the festivities, said that The Nashville Network brought recognition to our state that we couldn't have got otherwise.

I was pleased when almost everyone who saw the anniversary show said, "I thought 'Nashville Now' had been on longer than that." Somehow, that made the program seem like an old friend.

I've been asked frequently about the secret behind the success of "Nashville Now." There are many reasons, none of which is a secret. One, I think, is the show's appeal to both young and old.

Randy Travis, when he was still Randy Ray, made his national television debut on "Nashville Now" and appealed to America's youth. We aired the flashback shortly before a retrospective on Faron Young, who has been a country star for forty years.

There was Randy, talking about how nervous he was on his first appearance in 1984. There was Faron in 1990, talking about his divorce while wearing a convict's ball and chain. He was in costume for our Halloween show.

"One ball!" he railed, was all he derived from his failed marriage, "just one ball."

Also seen in the flashbacks were Johnny Cash, Tammy Wynette, Conway Twitty, Loretta Lynn, Porter Wagoner, Willie Nelson, George Jones, Ray Stevens, and Dolly Parton.

And there was footage of the legends who have become institutions, such as Minnie Pearl, and the late Roy Acuff, Roger Miller, Dottie West, and Tennessee Ernie Ford.

Not everyone who appeared on "Nashville Now" was a part of the anniversary show, and not everyone who appeared on the show is listed here.

The milestone show exemplified how "Nashville Now" has always considered the non-musical interests of its audience. We aired retrospective footage of George Bush, Bill Clinton, and Al

Gore during their 1992 campaigns for the White House. We showed an interview with baseball manager Tommy Lasorda, whose Los Angeles Dodgers finished last in their league in 1992. Lasorda jokingly said he subsequently called a suicide prevention line, and was put on hold.

Only one live song was played during the anniversary gala, "Footloose." Why the staff band chose a rock selection instead of one of 10,000 country songs that have been performed on "Nashville Now," I don't know. But I was pleased that the band, the musical backbone of the show since its inception, got to play.

The debut of "Nashville Now" was a five-hour spectacular. Performing for five hours on live television seemed longer than the week before Christmas to a child. "Nashville Now" was the very first show ever seen on The Nashville Network and premiered with two stages at two locations in Nashville, one at the Opry House and the other in the Stage Door Lounge at the Opryland Hotel. The show was seen by more subscribers than any cable television network had ever enjoyed on its opening night.

There were remote stages as well, with celebrities beaming country music from across the nation. Rosanne Cash and T. G. Sheppard were at the Savoy Hotel in New York City. Incidentally, Vince Gill later told me he played in Rosanne's band that night. Tanya Tucker and Hoyt Axton were at the Palomino Club in Los Angeles, Tammy Wynette and Don Williams were in Chicago, Bill Monroe and Emmylou Harris were at the "Austin City Limits" studio in Austin, Texas, and Lynn Anderson and George Lindsey were at the After the Gold Rush Club in Denver.

An eighty-piece symphony orchestra backed the Nashville artists, and Larry Gatlin and the Gatlin Brothers sang "Sure Feels Like Love," the first song performed on TNN.

Tanya Tucker sang "I'll Get Over You" and a lot of folks thought it was meant for Glen Campbell, with whom she had recently broken up after a highly publicized romance. Roy Acuff balanced a fiddle on his nose as he had done for years on the Grand Ole Opry, but many national viewers saw it for the first time, and thought his acrobatics were more impressive than his playing.

I was at a loss as to how to close the first show, until Ray Stevens, who had appeared at the Opry House, came over to the hotel studio and sang "It Was a Night," an appropriate finish.

And then we were off.

We held a number of press conferences before the debut. Almost without exception, reporters at each gathering were skeptical and a few were even hostile, discounting the network's potential to survive. We got negative press before a note was ever sounded on the show. I wonder where some of those scribes are today.

I've had indescribable "highs" on "Nashville Now," such as the night the man who raised the flag on the battleship *Arizona* on the morning of December 7, 1941, visited our studio. He was the last man ever to raise it before the Japanese sank it at Pearl Harbor.

Former Marine Corporal Duane Edgar Dewey, a man who received the first Medal of Honor pinned on by President Dwight D. Eisenhower, once visited our studio audience. I even acquired a copy of his presidential commendation, which read, in part, "When an enemy grenade landed close to his position while he and his assistant gunner were receiving medical attention for their wounds during a fierce night attack by numerically superior hostile forces, Corporal Dewey, although suffering intense pain, immediately pulled the corpsman to the ground and, shouting a warning to the other Marines around him, bravely smothered the deadly missile with his body, absorbing the full force of the explosion to save his comrades from possible injury or death."

Meeting that man was, to say the least, a thrill.

I've had maddening moments as well. We used to ask audience members to write on a card something unique about the person with whom they came to the show. Many pranksters used the occasion to fictionalize whoppers about their buddies. So when I got one of these guys in front of the camera to ask him, for example, to yodel as his friend said he could, I found out he didn't yodel at all. The guest and I were made to look ridiculous on national television.

There have also been embarrassing moments. I recall the time the singer David Allen Coe introduced his magic act on "Nashville Now." It was the worst magic act I had ever seen. A blind man could have seen through the tricks, and I had to stand there for ten minutes helping out in an act that was bombing pitiably.

I did my best to bolster him, and that approach has been my policy. No matter who the guest is, I try to draw from him the best he has to offer. I want to make him look good. Sometimes I feel like everybody's straight man, but that's all right. The better the guest looks, the more the audience will watch.

I venture there is no other network show more personally attentive to its guests. We'll grant almost any request. I don't think Grandpa Jones will mind me saying that his hearing loss is so pronounced he wears an aid in each ear. That's not enough, however, for him to hear much in the cavernous studio. So we run a program line, a cord connected directly to our audio board, right into one of his ears. He can hear just fine this way.

I had one overall regret about our anniversary show. In two hours, there wasn't time to show old footage of all the stars who had graced the show. Major entertainers such as Steve Allen, James Garner, Jimmy Stewart, Mickey Rooney, and hundreds of others were not seen in the anthology.

I especially regretted that acts such as the Geezinslaw Brothers, who have kindly flown from Texas once a month to appear on "Nashville Now," were omitted from the program. I would have liked to salute the acts who have supported the show the most. But that was a production decision, and it wasn't mine.

After the show I went home and ate with Joy, as I had done so many times during the decade of nighttime television. On the way home, I realized that I had never questioned whether "Nashville Now" and TNN would last. I simply took the job not looking past my next program. Then country music, and its television network, suddenly monopolized the marketplace. Soon, a brand-new studio, able to hold an audience of 2,100, will be the home of "Nashville Now," according to Val Smith, director of real estate and development for Gaylord Broadcasting Company.

As anniversary night was fast becoming a memory, Joy went to bed and I sat up alone until 2 A.M. and watched a complete, videotaped rerun of the show I had finished just two hours earlier.

As I watched, I bathed in the satisfaction that comes from doing something right, and knowing it.

I could not be more proud of that show, and the men and women who are its cast and crew. We are family who just happen to be unrelated. I felt my spirits soar as the familiar faces of my colleagues came on the screen. I thought of the happiness and hardships that we all know about each other, such as the February 2, 1993, death of Mrs. Jerry (Lynn) Whitehurst, wife of the "Nashville Now" bandleader. We knew she was suffering from terminal brain cancer, and it exacted a terrible toll on Jerry as he watched a once vibrant women deteriorate. The illness was never mentioned on the air except to say, occasionally, that there was an illness in his family, to explain his absences.

When we announced her death, more than 3,000 viewers sent sympathy cards.

And perhaps therein lies the secret of the show's success. It is a family show presented by family for family—the family on the other side of the television screen. "Nashville Now" doesn't merely have viewers, it has followers. Its audience, largely working class, is made up of salt-of-the-earth people who are threads in the fabric of the greatest nation on earth.

People I've never met have offered to do incredible favors for me. They have sent me priceless family heirlooms. They felt I should have them because they felt I was family.

Who could not be warmed by that?

In the wee hours of March 9, 1993, I turned off the television set and eased quietly into bed next to my sleeping wife. I had just finished what some experts say is one of the most stressful things in the world—performing live on television.

But, you know, I pulled the covers to my face and fell easily and blissfully to sleep, as if I were tardy for a dream. Sleep would last for a night.

The dream has been recurring for a decade.

As a member of the uncertain world of show business, I hold no monopoly on dreams. There are no guarantees in show business, or in life itself.

The biggest attraction of the entertainment industry is not the chance for sudden wealth, fame, travel, and all the other perks.

The attraction is that show business is democratic. If the people like you, they vote for you by buying records, tickets, or, in my case, watching my television show and listening to my radio broadcasts.

They've been casting their votes in my behalf for forty-two years. I'll be grateful for eternity.

Show business, and especially the recording industry, is so democratic it personifies the American dream. If you've got what the people want, and are willing to take it to them, you can succeed, no matter how humble your background.

Success in the entertainment industry is a practical exercise in what the architects of the U.S. Constitution had in mind long before music was ever etched into a record.

Show business is an industry where a mailroom worker and fork-lift driver can toil mindlessly in the daytime, rehearse in a garage at night, and wind up recording ten number-one songs in three years, as Alan Jackson did. It is an arena where a would-be contestant can pull up to a record company in a battered pickup, walk in unannounced, and emerge with a recording contract, as Stonewall Jackson did in 1957.

And it is an all-is-fair industry that also shows the dark side of democracy—the side that says no matter how pure your ideas, no matter how solid your talent, the people will decide if you're elected to the office of success.

Many of the best and brightest minds of the twentieth century will never hold public office because they lack that indescribable "something" for which voters vote. Many of the most beloved singers and songwriters in Nashville, admired by their peers, never find greater commensurate glory because the public can't see what their colleagues can.

Yet they press on, these sincere and solitary souls whose heartfelt singing sometimes falls on the public's heartless indifference. Their salvation is show business's democracy, an equalizer that often puts a talented singer in the same circles with one who is successful.

I think specifically of the late O. B. McClinton.

He was a songwriter for Tree International, now Sony-Tree, the world's number-one country song publishing company for twenty consecutive years. His songs were recorded by several other singers, but his own recording career didn't take off.

He was hardly a country music force, as was Charley Pride, another black singer who preceded McClinton into the once all-white circles of commercial country music.

In 1972, after rattling around rhythm-and-blues recording fortresses in Memphis and Muscle Shoals, McClinton moved to Nashville. He dug for the country music gold, but the mother lode would elude him forever. He released "Don't Let the Green Grass Fool You." The song rose to number 37 on *Billboard*'s Top 100. It was a marginal success, but the most McClinton ever had.

In the summer of 1986, while still in relentless pursuit of stardom, he was driving to Nashville after a tour of one-nighters. His stomach hurt so he stopped at a clinic, was administered pain killers, and told to see his Nashville doctor.

This physician gave McClinton stronger medicine and a death diagnosis.

Abdominal cancer was discovered and McClinton was told he had a year to live. It spread to his liver and became inoperable. The calendar would prove the physician to be a pinpoint prophet.

Perhaps country music, often called the white-man's blues, only had room for one major black recording star. McClinton told me that Charley Pride's success had enabled him to step across the line of racial barriers. He was just never able to step too far.

"When they compare me to Charley Pride they don't compare my vocal style," McClinton told me in 1973. "They just compare my complexion."

McClinton, wealthy in talent and spirit, was poor in dollars.

There was no money for twelve months of cancer treatment, and the costs would be staggering.

I saw an opportunity to give back something to the business, and to life itself. I called Buddy Killen, then the president of Tree International, and suggested that he and I give a benefit concert for McClinton. Killen, who owns Nashville's largest restaurant, the Stock-Yard, graciously donated use of its Bull-Pen Lounge, a 300-seat room to which 600 persons would come. For McClinton, the fire marshal looked the other way. Nashville stars and well-wishers, through ticket sales and donations, raised $60,000.

Democracy was in play when Reba McEntire, winner of the Country Music Association's highest award, "Entertainer of the Year," sang for McClinton, who had never been nominated for any CMA award. Democracy was in overdrive when Tom T. Hall, recorder of a dozen number-one songs, held McClinton's hand and sang for a man who'd never reached the Top 30.

Waylon Jennings, Jessi Colter, Ricky Skaggs, Kathy Mattea, Exile, Dobie Gray, Johnny Rodriguez, Ronnie McDowell and Rex Allen, Jr., also donated their time and talent.

Killen, who came to Nashville in 1951, called the show "the best concert we've ever had in town."

Each singer was asked to sing two songs only. The last to go on was McClinton himself, who performed for forty-five minutes.

He entertained country music's foremost musicians, who in turn gave him a thunderous and tear-filled standing ovation. Many of those stars had their names atop the world's biggest marquees. The radiance of those flashing signs paled in comparison to the glow of McClinton's indefatigable determination.

He uplifted those who had come to uplift.

Former Nashville columnist Red O'Donnell had earlier said McClinton's grin was "a smile wide."

McClinton waited out the crowd's applause and at last spoke. He flashed the smile and said, "I know what you're thinking. How can anybody who is dying look so good?"

Another five minutes was lost to the ovation. Some people laughed to keep from crying. Most just cried because they wanted to.

McClinton thanked everyone for coming, including the doctors who had tried in vain to remove the cancer.

He asked his chief physician to stand, and said, "It's a low man that will cut you while you're asleep."

I couldn't help thinking how this singer was giving the most enthralling concert I'd ever heard.

I loved his spirit; I loved the man.

I last saw O. B. a week before he died. I went to his home with a mutual friend, Marty Martel.

His friends financed and the Country Music Foundation approved O. B.'s inclusion in the "Walkway of Stars" at the Country Music Hall of Fame. O. B. was too feeble to attend the ceremony, so Marty and I brought the brass star and letters that spelled his name. These would be set into marble after his death. We thought showing him that he was going to be remembered in the Country Music Hall of Fame would lift his spirits.

He was watching a television news story about homeless people living under a Nashville bridge. He was angered.

"Those people have life!" he railed, "and they're throwing it away!"

He was furious with those so casual about life, for which he was so passionate. If spirit alone could have sustained him, McClinton would have celebrated his centennial.

In the half-dark of his house, I watched the flickering light from the television screen dance on his dissipated face, withered by the unending pressure of incessant pain from the ravaging cancer whose victory was imminent.

I thought of how he had risen from abject, rural Mississippi poverty to travel the world, sing for untold thousands, and was befriended by some of the highest-profiled people of his day.

I started to walk away from McClinton, whom I had seen in the spotlight and whom I would see for the last time sitting on his deathbed. I'd seen bigger stars. I'd never seen a bigger man.

I shook his hand, and looked squarely into his eyes struggling to look back at me. I held a hand that was little more than flesh-covered bones.

"You know how much I love this music and this business," McClinton said to me. I smiled that I did, determined I would not cry before him.

My eyes burned and my hearing somehow intensified. My footsteps sounded like a deafening echo as I forced myself to walk from his side.

And then he called to me.

In a whisper he said, "Ralph—don't let the music die." Those were the last words I heard him speak. He died within the week.

O. B., as long as there are people who love country music as much as you did, country music will always be alive.

Index